VAISNAVISM, SAIVISM
AND MINOR RELIGIOUS SYSTEMS

VAISNAVISM, SAIVISM
AND MINOR RELIGIOUS SYSTEMS

BY

R. G. BHANDARKAR

GYAN

Published by

GYAN

Gyan Publishing House
5, Ansari Road
Daryaganj, New Delhi-110002
Phone: 011-47034999, 9811692060
E-mail: books@gyanbooks.com

Distribution Network
gyanbooks.com
India, USA, Canada, UK, Australia

ISBN: 978-93-6280-152-4 (PB)
First Published, 1913

2nd Impression 2024

Printed at: Gyan Press, Delhi.

VAISNAVISM, SAIVISM AND MINOR RELIGIOUS SYSTEMS
Author: R. G. BHANDARKAR

VAIṢṆAVISM, SAIVISM

AND MINOR RELIGIOUS SYSTEMS

BY

SIR R. G. BHANDARKAR

STRASSBURG

VERLAG VON KARL J. TRÜBNER

1913

GRUNDRISS DER INDO-ARISCHEN PHILOLOGIE UND ALTERTUMSKUNDE
(ENCYCLOPEDIA OF INDO-ARYAN RESEARCH)
BEGRÜNDET VON G. BÜHLER, FORTGESETZT VON F. KIELHORN,
HERAUSGEGEBEN VON H. LÜDERS UND J. WACKERNAGEL.
III. BAND, 6. HEFT.

VAIṢṆAVISM, ŚAIVISM AND MINOR RELIGIOUS SYSTEMS

BY
R. G. BHANDARKAR

Part. I.

VAIṢṆAVISM.

I. Introductory.

§ 1. The old Vedic gods became indissolubly involved in the elaborate and mechanical system of worship that had grown up. Speculations as regards the appropriateness of the rules and modes of worship and their efficacy as regards man's good in this world and the next became prevalent. But all this did not satisfy the religious spirit of the people. Religious speculation of a more natural order came to be established about the close of the Hymn-period and was continued into that of the Upaniṣads. The various problems about God, man and the world engaged the attention of many thinkers and a variety of solutions was arrived at. It is generally believed that the Upaniṣads teach a system of Pantheism; but a close examination will show that they teach not one, but various systems of doctrines as regards the nature of God, man and the world and the relations between them. The religio-philosophic systems of modern times, which are mutually inconsistent, quote texts from the Upaniṣads as an authority for their special doctrines. These references to the old books are correct in the most prominent cases, but when the advocates of the systems force into other texts of an opposite nature a meaning consistent with their own special doctrines, they are manifestly wrong. That the Upaniṣads teach not one but various systems must follow from the fact that they are compilations just as the Ṛgveda-Saṃhitā is. The speculations of the old seers were clothed by them in words, and these were handed down orally and came to form a large floating mass. When the idea of collecting these speculations arose, they were incorporated into books for the use of individual Vedic schools. Hence it is that we find certain verses, passages and whole sections occurring in one Upaniṣad reproduced in another[1].

No doubt, the idea of the immanence of God in the world is very

[1]) See the passage about the superiority of Prāṇa and other bodily elements which occurs in ChU. (V, 1, 1) and in BU. (VI, 1, 1); that about the Pañcāgnividyā occurring in the former (V, 4,1) and the latter (VI, 2, 9); and that about proud Bālāki and Ajātaśatru which occurs in the KBU. (IV) and in BU. (II, 1), and others (TU. II, 8 and BU. IV, 3. 33). As to the recurrence of verses see MU., ŚU. and KU.

prominent in the Upaniṣads. But if that is what constitutes Pantheism, the liberal religious thought of the present day in Europe also must be regarded as Pantheistic. With the immanence of God is associated his transcendence also, as stated in the Vedānta-Sūtra II, 1, 27[1]). In addition to these two doctrines the Upaniṣads teach that God is the protector of all beings, is the lord of all and dwells in the heart of man, that seeing him as he is and everywhere is eternal bliss, that this is to be attained by contemplation and the purification of the soul, and that in the blissful condition the individual soul attains to a perfect similarity with the supreme soul[2]). They also teach the absorption of the individual soul into the supreme as of a river into the ocean and the unconsciousness of the soul when everything but himself fades away from his knowledge. In this respect the doctrine may be regarded as Pantheistic or as setting forth the illusory character of all phenomena. Speculation in the Upaniṣad times was very free and it veered round even to the denial of the soul as a substance[3]).

In the subsequent development of religious thought and worship these Upaniṣad doctrines played an active part. The Henotheism, so fully explained by Max Müller, and its ultimate result, the identification of the various gods, also influenced later thinkers. The conception that the supreme spirit manifests himself in various forms which we find expressed in the Upaniṣads is a development, in the opposite direction, of the idea that one God, for instance Agni, is the same as Varuṇa, Mitra, Indra and Aryaman[4]). If these several gods are one, one god may become several. This led to the conception of Incarnations or Avatāras, which plays such a prominent part in the later religious systems.

But for ordinary people an adorable object with a more distinct personality than that which the theistic portions of the Upaniṣads attributed to God was necessary and the philosophic speculations did not answer practical needs. Thus some of the old Vedic gods and others, which were new, became the objects of worship.

II. The Rise of a New Theistic System.

§ 2. The tide of free speculations culminated in the east into such systems as those of Buddhism and Jainism and, though they denied the existence of God as a creator or did not use the idea for the promotion of righteousness, and the former practically denied the existence of the human soul as a substance, still these systems had the

---

1) See the passage quoted by Śaṃkarācārya in his commentary on the Sūtra.

2) Paramaṃ sāmyam upaiti. See MU. III, 1, 3. The opinion expressed by some eminent scholars that the burden of the Upaniṣad teaching is the illusive character of the world and the reality of one soul only, is manifestly wrong, and I may even say, is indicative of an uncritical judgment. As stated in the text, the Upaniṣads from the very nature of the compilations cannot but be expected to teach not one, but many systems of doctrine.

3) See the passage from BU. III, 2, 13, quoted in my paper "A Peep into the Early History of India", Journ. Bombay Br. Roy. As. Soc. Vol. XX, p. 361.

4) RV. V, 3, 1—2.

needful personal element in the shape of their founders. In the west, however, a theistic system with a god who had come to dwell among men arose. The various religious systems and superstitions that prevailed in the fourth century B. C. are given in the following passage, occurring in the Niddesa, which though of the nature of a commentary is regarded as one of the books of the Pāli Buddhistic Canon[1]: "The deity of the lay followers of the Ājīvakas is the Ājīvakas, of those of the Nighaṇṭhas is the Nighaṇṭhas, of those of the Jaṭilas (ascetics wearing long matted hair) is the Jaṭilas, of those of the Paribbājakas is the Paribbājakas, of those of the Avaruddhakas is the Avaruddhakas, and the deity of those who are devoted to an elephant, a horse, a cow, a dog, a crow, Vāsudeva, Baladeva, Puṇṇabhadda, Maṇibhadda, Aggi, Nāgas, Supaṇṇas, Yakkhas, Asuras, Gandhabbas, Mahārājas, Canda, Suriya, Inda, Brahmā, Deva, Disā is the elephant, the horse, the cow, the dog, the crow, Vāsudeva, Baladeva, Puṇṇabhadda, Maṇibhadda, etc., respectively." Here a Buddhist who cannot but be expected to show scant courtesy to religious systems other than his own, places the worshippers of Vāsudeva and Baladeva on the same level with those of fire, moon, sun and Brahmā, and even elephants, crows, dogs, etc. But the worship of Vāsudeva was destined to become the predominant religion of a large part of India even to the supersession of that of fire, sun, moon and Brahmā and, of course, of the superstitious adoration of the lower animals. And it will be now our duty to trace its rise and progress.

§ 3. In his comment on Pāṇini IV, 3, 98, Patañjali distinctly states that the Vāsudeva contained in the Sūtra is the name of the "worshipful", i. e. of one who is pre-eminently worshipful, i. e. God[2]). The worship of Vāsudeva must be regarded to be as old as Pāṇini.

In an inscription found at Ghosuṇḍi in Rājputāna[3]) which unfortunately is in a mutilated condition, the construction of a wall round the hall of worship of Saṃkarṣaṇa and Vāsudeva is mentioned. From the form of the characters in the inscription it appears to have been engraved at least two hundred years B. C.

In another inscription recently discovered at Besnagar[4]), Heliodora represents himself to have erected a Garuḍadhvaja or a column with the image of Garuḍa at the top in honour of Vāsudeva, the god of gods. Heliodora calls himself a Bhāgavata, was the son of Diya, was a native of Takṣaśilā and is spoken of as an ambassador of the Yavana and as such came on a political mission from Aṃtalikita to Bhāgabhadra who must have ruled over Eastern Mālwa. In this inscription occurs the name Aṃtalikita which in all likelihood is the same as Antialkidas of the Bactro-Greek coins. This name as well as the form of the characters show that it belongs to the earlier part of the second century before the Christian era. At that time Vāsudeva was worshipped as the god of gods and his worshippers

1) This passage has been furnished to me by Mr. Dharmanand Kosambi.
2) See JRAS. 1910, p. 168.
3) Lüders, List of Brāhmī Inscriptions, No. 6.
4) Ibid. No. 669.

were called Bhāgavatas. The Bhāgavata religion prevailed in the northwestern part of India and was adopted even by the Greeks.

In the inscription No. I in the large cave at Nānāghāṭ[1]), the names of Saṃkarṣaṇa and Vāsudeva, in a Dvandva compound, occur along with those of other deities in the opening invocation. This inscription appears from the form of the characters to belong to the first century before the Christian era.

In the passage in the Mahābhāṣya in which Patañjali, to account for the appearance of the name Vāsudeva in P. IV, 3, 98, says that this is not the name of a Kṣatriya, but that of the Worshipful One, the question to be considered is whether Patañjali means this Vāsudeva to be quite unconnected with the Vāsudeva of the Vṛṣṇi race. From the occurrence of the names Vāsudeva and Baladeva close to each other in the passage from the Niddesa referred to above, and that of Saṃkarṣaṇa and Vāsudeva as worshipful or divine persons in a Dvandva compound in two of the three above inscriptions, it appears that the Vāsudeva referred to by Patañjali as the Worshipful One must be the Vāsudeva of the Vṛṣṇi race. But to account for the appearance of the name in the Sūtra, though the required form can be made up in accordance with the next Sūtra (P. IV, 3, 99), Patañjali says that Pāṇini looks at Vāsudeva in his capacity as a divine person and not as a Kṣatriya. One must take it in this sense, since the Ghosuṇḍi inscription noticed above, in which Saṃkarṣaṇa and Vāsudeva are associated as worshipful persons, must be older than Patañjali himself. Besides, Patañjali begins the discussion of the Sūtra by first taking Vāsudeva as the name of a Kṣatriya and raising an objection against it. This objection is answered in one way, Vāsudeva being still regarded as a Kṣatriya, and it is only optionally that he gives another explanation, that that name is not the name of a Kṣatriya, but of a divine person. This optional explanation given in the last resort must, therefore, be understood in the sense given above. And from all the accounts of the Bhāgavata school contained in the whole literature it is clear that the worshipful Vāsudeva belonged to the Vṛṣṇi race.

III. Analysis of the Nārāyaṇīya Section of the Mahābhārata.

§ 4. Having thus established on irrefragable evidence the existence during the three or four centuries before Christ of a religion with Vāsudeva as its central figure and of a school of his followers known by the name of Bhāgavata, I will now proceed to examine the detailed accounts contained in the literature and especially in the Mahābhārata. This was not done before, because the date of the Mahābhārata or any portion of it cannot be ascertained with any approach to certainty. The Nārāyaṇīya section of the Śāntiparvan, to which we shall devote a detailed consideration, is, however, older than Śaṃkarācārya who quotes from it.

[1]) Ibid. No. 1112.

Nārada is represented to have gone to the Badarikāśrama to see Nara and Nārāyaṇa. The latter was engaged in the performance of religious rites. Nārada asked Nārāyaṇa whom he worshipped, while he himself was the Supreme Lord. Nārāyaṇa told him that he worshipped his original Prakṛti (form), the source of all that is and that is to be. Nara and Nārāyaṇa as well as Kṛṣṇa and Hari, sons of Dharma, are represented as the four forms of the Supreme.

Nārada flies into the sky to see that original Prakṛti and alights on a peak of Meru. There he saw white men without senses, not eating anything, sinless, with heads like umbrellas, making a sound like that of thundering clouds and devoted to Bhagavat. Then Yudhiṣṭhira asks Bhīṣma who those people were, and how they came to be what they were. Bhīṣma tells the story of the king Vasu Uparicara, who worshipped God according to the Sātvata Vidhi (form of ritual). He was a glorious king honoured by Indra, devoted to truth and holy. The best of the learned in the Pāñcarātra system were honoured with the first seat at dinner by him. The narrator then proceeds to mention the Citraśikhaṇḍins, who appear to be the original promulgators of this religion. The mountain Meru was the place where they revealed it. They were seven, consisting of Marīci, Atri, Aṅgiras, Pulastya, Pulaha, Kratu, and Vasiṣṭha. The eighth was Svāyaṃbhuva. From these eight emanated this excellent Śāstra. This they promulgated in the presence of the great Bhagavat, who said to the Ṛṣis: "You have composed a hundred thousand excellent Ślokas (stanzas), which contain rules for all the affairs of men and are in harmony with Yajus, Sāman, Ṛc, and Atharvāṅgiras, and lay down precepts about the religion of action as well as that of contemplation or repose. I created Brahman from my peaceful and Rudra from my wrathful nature. This Śāstra will be handed down from person to person until it reaches Bṛhaspati. From Bṛhaspati the king Vasu will obtain it. The king will follow this Śāstra and will become my devotee. After his death this Śāstra will be lost." Telling all this the great god disappeared. Then the Citraśikhaṇḍins spread the religion until it reached Bṛhaspati. Then the old Kalpa having ended and the son of Aṅgiras, the priest of the gods, being born, the gods were happy. The king Vasu Uparicara was his first pupil. He learned this Śāstra from Bṛhaspati. At one time he brought forward an extensive horse-sacrifice, but no animal was killed on the occasion. The oblations were devised in accordance with the words of the Āraṇyakas. The god of gods showed himself to Vasu and accepted his oblation, but was unseen by anybody else. Since the oblation was taken away by Hari without showing himself to Bṛhaspati, the latter got angry and dashed upwards the sacrificial ladle. At that sacrifice, Ekata, Dvita, and Trita, sons of Prajāpati, and sixteen Ṛṣis, many of whom are now known as the authors of literary works, such as Medhātithi, Tittiri, and Tāṇḍya, are represented to have been present. When Bṛhaspati was angry, they all said that the great Hari was not to be seen by any man at random, but by one who was favoured by his grace. Ekata, Dvita and Trita said: "On one occasion we went to the north for the attainment of eternal bliss near the milky ocean and practised austerities for four thousand years and at the end a voice in the air declared: 'Well, how can you see that great Lord? In the milky ocean there is a white island where there are men possessing the lustre of the moon, who are the devotees of the god, possess no senses, do not eat anything and being devoted solely to the god (Ekāntin or monotheistic) are absorbed in him, who is bright like the Sun. Go to that island; there shines my soul'. Accordingly we went to the white island, and, dazzled by the light of that being, were not able to see him. Then the truth flashed upon us that the god cannot be seen by us unless we have gone through austerities. After further austerities for a hundred years we saw the men of the lustre of the moon with their minds fully absorbed in the contemplation of God. The refulgence of each man was like that of the sun on the last day. Then we heard a sound: 'Jitaṃ te Puṇḍarīkākṣa' etc. (Triumphant art thou, Lotus-eyed one). A short time after a voice in the air declared: 'Go you away as you came. That great being is not to be seen by one who is not devoted to him'. Then we returned without being able to see him. How then will you be able to see him?" Having heard this from Ekata, Dvita and Trita, Bṛhaspati finished the sacrifice.

Vasu Uparicara had to live in a hole in the earth on account of the curse of the Ṛṣis, who in a controversy with the gods maintained that no animal should be sacrificed, but only vegetable grain, while the gods contended that a goat should be sacrificed. The question was referred to Vasu who declared in favour of the gods. Vasu was raised from the hole by Nārāyaṇa, whom he had devotedly worshipped, by sending his Garuḍa to lift him up. He was thence taken to the Brahma world.

The story of Nārada's visit to Śvetadvīpa is then continued. He praises the great being by uttering names expressive of his purity and grandeur, and the great being then manifested himself to him, saying that he was not to be seen by one who was not solely devoted to him (Ekāntin) and that, as Nārada was such a one, he showed himself to him. He then proceeds to explain to him the religion of Vāsudeva. Vāsudeva is the supreme soul, the internal soul of all souls. He is the supreme creator. All living beings are represented by Saṃkarṣaṇa, who is a form of Vāsudeva. From Saṃkarṣaṇa sprang Pradyumna, the mind, and from Pradyumna Aniruddha, self-consciousness. "Those who are devoted to me enter into me and are released." The great being calls the four mentioned above his forms (Mūrtis). The production of one form from another is also mentioned; all these forms are, however, styled his forms (Mūrtis). He then proceeds to mention the creation of gods and all other things by himself and their final dissolution into himself. Then are mentioned his incarnations (Avatāras), viz. Varāha, Narasiṃha, the oppressor of Bali, Rāma of the Bhṛgu race and destroyer of the Kṣatriyas, Rāma Dāśarathi, and "he, who will come into existence for the destruction of Kaṃsa at Mathurā and after having killed many demons will finally settle at Dvārakā". In this manner having done all things by his four Mūrtis, he destroyed Dvārakā with the Sātvatas and went to Brahmaloka. After Nārada had heard this from the supreme Nārāyaṇa, he returned to Badarikāśrama.

What follows at the end of chapter 339 and in the next four chapters has little bearing on our subject, except that in one of them the etymological sense of Vāsudeva is given as one who covers the whole world and is the resting-place (adhivāsa) of all beings.

In chapter 344 the path of those who are free from sin is given thus: — The sun is the gate, and after entrance all their material impurities being burnt, they remain as atoms in him; then released from him, they enter into the Aniruddha form and, becoming mind, enter into the Pradyumna form. Leaving that form, they enter into that of Saṃkarṣaṇa, i. e. the form of the individual soul (Jīva). Afterwards being free from the three Guṇas, they enter into the Supreme Soul, who exists everywhere and who is Vāsudeva. In chapter 346 Vaiśampāyana relates to Janamejaya that the Dharma which Nārada got from 'the Lord of the world' Nārāyaṇa himself in all its details and peculiarities, was explained briefly to him (Janamejaya) in the Harigītā. In chapter 348 this Ekāntika Dharma is represented to be the same as that which was communicated to Arjuna at the beginning of the war. At the creation of each Brahmā this Dharma was revealed by Nārāyaṇa, and then at the end of the Brahmā it was lost. In the account of the fourth Brahmā the Dharma revealed is twice called Sātvata. In this manner it goes on up to the present or the seventh Brahmā, in which that Dharma was first communicated to Pitāmaha, and from him it passed in succession to Dakṣa, his grandson, the eldest Āditya, Vivasvat, Manu and Ikṣvāku. Later on it is stated that this original great eternal Dharma, difficult to be known and to be followed, is professed by the Sātvatas.

This Dharma is associated with the non-slaughter of animals (Ahiṃsā), and when properly exercised, the lord Hari is pleased with it. Sometimes one Vyūha or form of the Lord is taught and sometimes two, three or four. Vaiśampāyana winds up by saying that he has thus explained the Ekāntadharma.

§ 5. Here we have two accounts, the second of which is interwoven with the first. The former, however, appears to relate to a more ancient condition of things. The points to be noticed are these: 1. At the sacrifice instituted by Vasu Uparicara no animals were killed. 2. The oblations were devised in accordance with the teachings of the Āraṇyakas which include the Upaniṣads. 3. The chief deity was the God of gods, who is also called Hari. 4. This Hari or God of gods is not to be seen by one who follows the sacrificial mode of worship, such as Bṛhaspati did, nor by persons who practise austerities for thousands of years, as Ekata, Dvita and Trita did, but by one who worships Him with devotion, as Vasu Uparicara did. Here then is an attempt to introduce a religious reform on more conservative principles than Buddhism and Jainism did. The repudiation of the slaughter of animals and the inefficacy of sacrificial worship and austerities are common to this religious reform with Buddhism. But that the supreme lord Hari is to be worshipped with devotion and the words of the Āraṇyakas are not to be rejected, are doctrines which are peculiar to it. Vasu Uparicara's story goes so far only.

In the main account, according to which Nārada visited the white island, we have a reassertion of the doctrine that the Supreme Soul can be seen by one who worships him with devotion. The great Nārāyaṇa manifests himself to him and explains the religion of Vāsudeva and his three other forms (Vyūhas). He also mentions the future incarnations of Vāsudeva, and one of these is that assumed at Mathurā for the destruction of Kaṃsa. The Supreme Nārāyaṇa identifies himself with Vāsudeva in his four forms (Vyūhas). At the end it is stated that the religion is followed by the Sātvatas.

These two accounts seem to represent two stages in the progress of reform. In the earlier one the worship of Vāsudeva and his three other forms is not known. The Supreme God is named Hari, and his worship has not thoroughly emancipated itself from the religion of sacrifices. The reform had no reference to specific historical personages and was promulgated by certain sages who are called Citraśikhaṇḍins and whose names had been handed down by tradition. The later account connects the reform with Vāsudeva and his brother, son and grandson, and the new religion is represented to have been identical with that taught in the Bhagavadgītā. This reformed system is said to have been promulgated by Nārāyaṇa himself. It thus appears that the idea of a religion of devotion arose in earlier times, but it received a definite shape when Vāsudeva revealed the Gītā to Arjuna, and led to the formation of an independent sect when his brother, son and grandson were associated with him as his forms presiding over certain psychological categories or as persons created by him for the purpose. That sect became conterminous with the race of the Sātvatas. We have now to consider who these Sātvatas were.

IV. The Sātvatas and their Religion.

§ 6. In the Ādiparvan Vāsudeva addressing the Vṛṣṇis says that Pārtha does not think them who are Sātvatas to be covetous. Vāsudeva is called Sātvata in Ādip. 218, 12; Kṛtavarman in Ādip. 221, 31; Sātyaki in Droṇap. 97, 36; and Janārdana in Udyogap. 70, 7. At the end of chap. 66 of the Bhīṣmaparvan Bhīṣma says: "This eternal god, mysterious, beneficent and loving should be known as Vāsudeva, and Brāhmaṇas, Kṣatriyas, Vaiśyas and Śūdras worship him by their devoted actions. At the end of the Dvāpara and the beginning of the Kali age, he was sung or expounded by Saṃkarṣaṇa according to the Sātvata rites (Vidhi). At the end of chap. 12 of the third book of the Viṣṇu-Purāṇa it is stated in the account of the genealogy of the Yādavas and the Vṛṣṇis that Satvata was the son of Aṃśa, and all his descendants were after him called Sātvatas. The Bhāgavata represents the Sātvatas as calling the highest Brahman Bhagavat and Vāsudeva (IX, 9, 49) and having a peculiar mode of worshipping him. It mentions the Sātvatas along with the Andhakas and Vṛṣṇis, which were Yādava tribes (I, 14, 25; III, 1, 29), and calls Vāsudeva Sātvatarṣabha (X, 58, 42; XI, 27, 5). In Patañjali under P. IV, 1, 114 Vāsudeva and Bāladeva are given as derivatives from Vṛṣṇi names in the sense of sons of Vāsudeva and Baladeva. Instances given by the Kāśikā of the same are Vāsudeva and Āniruddha. Here Āniruddha means the son of Aniruddha, and therefore Vāsudeva must mean the son of Vāsudeva and not of Vasudeva, as will appear from what follows. In the latter work under P. VI, 2, 34 Sini-Vāsudevāḥ is given as a Dvandva of royal Vṛṣṇi names, each of them being in the plural, and Saṃkarṣaṇa-Vāsudevau as a Dvandva of royal Vṛṣṇi names, each being in the singular, so that Vāsudeva means both the individual of that name and his sons.

From all this and such other passages from Patañjali it will appear that Sātvata was another name of the Vṛṣṇi race of which Vāsudeva, Saṃkarṣaṇa, and Aniruddha were members, and that the Sātvatas had a religion of their own according to which Vāsudeva was worshipped as the Supreme Being, and thus the account given above from the Nārāyaṇīya is amply confirmed.

§ 7. It therefore appears that this religion of devotion to Vāsudeva ascends as high into antiquity as Pāṇini himself. As I have mentioned elsewhere, the Kṣatriyas engaged themselves in active speculations on religious matters about the time of the Upaniṣads[1]) and are mentioned even as the original possessors of the new kowledge. Siddhārtha and Mahāvīra founded in this period of intellectual fermentation new systems of religion in the east or the Magadha country which discarded or passed over in silence the doctrine of the existence even of God and laid down self-abnegation and a course of strict moral conduct as the way to salvation. They belonged to the Śākya and Jñātṛka races of Kṣatriyas, and Buddhism and Jainism might be considered to be the religions of those tribes. The west, however, was not so radical in its speculations, and the race of Sātvatas developed a system of religion which took up the ideas of a Supreme God and devotion to him as the mode of salvation. These Sātvatas and the worship of Vāsudeva-Kṛṣṇa seem clearly to be alluded to by Megasthenes, who was the Macedonian ambassador at the court of Candragupta, the Maurya. Candragupta reigned in the last quarter of the fourth century B. C. The statement of Megasthenes is that Herakles was specially worshipped by the Sourasenoi, an Indian nation, in whose land are two great cities, Methora and Kleisobora, and through it flows the navigable river Jobares. The Sourasenoi were the Śūrasenas, a tribe of Kṣatriyas, who lived in the region in which was situated Mathurā, corresponding to Methora in the above passage, and in which flowed the river Jobares, which has been identified with the Jumna or Yamunā. If the Vāsudeva-Kṛṣṇa worship prevailed in the time of the first Maurya, it must have originated long before the establishment of the Maurya dynasty, and my assertion that it owes its origin to the stream of thought which began with the Upaniṣads and culminated in the east in Buddhism and Jainism, and arose about the time of the latter, is confirmed.

The name expressive of the Supreme Spirit was, however, in the

[1]) Verhandlungen des VII. Internat. Orientalisten-Congresses zu Wien. Ar. Sect., pp. 108-9.

early period Vāsudeva alone. In the passage from the Niddesa and the three inscriptions Vāsudeva is the name that occurs.

In the Bhagavadgītā (VII, 19) it is stated that "He who possesses knowledge gives himself up to me, believing Vāsudeva to be all." Even in the Bhāgavata Mantra of twelve syllables which is usually repeated at the present day and which is mentioned by Hemādri, it is to Vāsudeva that obeisance is made [1]). In Bhīṣmap. chap. 65 Brahmadeva, addressing the Supreme Spirit (Puruṣa Parameśvara), entreats him to become the increaser of the Yadu race and then, referring apparently to a foregone age, he says: "O Vāsudeva, this great secret I have communicated to thee through thy favour as it really is. Having created thyself as the God Saṃkarṣaṇa, thou didst procreate thy son Pradyumna. He created Aniruddha who is Viṣṇu himself, and he created me (Brahmadeva) who am made up of Vāsudeva and created by thee. Dividing thyself in this way, be born as a human being again." In the beginning of chapter 66 of the same Parvan Prajāpati speaks of himself as having asked the supreme lord of all to dwell in the world of men as Vāsudeva (to become incarnate). This Supreme Spirit should, it is said, be known as Vāsudeva, and throughout the chapter that name alone is used in speaking of the eternal God. The substance of these two chapters seems to be that in a former age the Supreme Spirit Vāsudeva created Saṃkarṣaṇa and the rest up to the Brahmā himself, and on the present occasion the latter asked him again to be born in the Yadu race as Vāsudeva, dividing himself into four parts as on the previous occasion. Thus Vāsudeva was the name of the teacher of the religion of devotion, and there appears to be an implication here that he existed with the other three in a previous age. Even as a member of the Vṛṣṇi race the name Vāsudeva occurs in the examples quoted above from the Mahābhāṣya and Kāśikā and no other. In the passages quoted by me in my article on "Allusions to Kṛṣṇa etc." (Ind. Ant. Vol. III, pp. 14 ff.) the name Kṛṣṇa occurs three times, Vāsudeva in three passages and Janārdana in one. But in Kielhorn's edition of the Mahābhāṣya, which is more accurate than the Benares edition which I then used, the reading Kṛṣṇa in two of the three places is supported by one manuscript only and Vāsudeva occurs instead of Kṛṣṇa in one of the two places and the other is entirely omitted, so that Vāsudeva is used four times and Kṛṣṇa only once. In the Bhagavadgītā (X, 37) the Bhagavat says that of the Vṛṣṇis he is Vāsudeva. In the Buddhist Ghatajātaka the two eldest sons of Upasāgara and Devagabbhā are named Vāsudeva and Baladeva. In the prose narrative no other name is given, but the names Kaṇha and Kesava occur in the verses that are interwoven with the prose. The commentator remarks on the first verse that he is there addressed by his Gotra name Kaṇha, for he belonged to the Kaṇhāyana Gotra, thus showing his belief that Vāsudeva was the true proper name of the person. This belief he expresses again in his commentary on a verse occurring in the Mahāummaggajātaka, in which Jambāvātī is mentioned as the beloved queen of Vāsudeva Kaṇha. Here also Vāsudeva is mentioned as

[1]) Vratakhaṇḍa (Bibl. Ind.) p. 225. The Mantra is *Om namo Bhagavate Vāsudevāya.*

belonging to the Kaṇhāyana Gotra, and from the verse itself, in which Vāsudevassa Kaṇhassa occurs, it would appear that Kaṇha was the family name, the sense being Vāsudeva, the Kaṇha, so that the author of the verse itself would seem to regard Vāsudeva as the proper name of the individual, and thus he and the prose narrative agree.

§ 8. Thus then Vāsudeva appears to be a proper name and not a patronymic, and when the Vāsudeva religion or the Bhāgavata school took its rise, that was the name by which the Supreme Deity was known. The conception of Vasudeva as his father must have arisen afterwards, as appears to me from the example Vāsudevaḥ given in the Mahābhāṣya in the sense of "son or descendant of Vāsudeva", and not "of Vasudeva", as must be inferred from the analogous instance of Bāladeva from Baladeva. Baladeva was associated with Vāsudeva and not with Vasudeva. Kṛṣṇa, Janārdana, and Keśava do not appear to be Vṛṣṇi names and were given to Vāsudeva in subsequent times when his worship had widely spread. All these three occur in Patañjali also, but the two latter only once so far as I know. But of these the name Kṛṣṇa is more important than the other two and many others that are used. It appears to be as much a proper name as Vāsudeva, though the latter has a religious signification specially attached to it. How then did this name Kṛṣṇa come to be used? It was the name of one of the Vedic Ṛṣis, the composer of hymn 74 of the eighth Maṇḍala. He speaks of himself as Kṛṣṇa in verses 3 and 4 of the hymn. The author of the Anukramaṇī calls him an Āṅgirasa or descendant of Aṅgiras. In the KB. (XXX, 9) apparently the same Kṛṣṇa Āṅgirasa is alluded to and is represented to have 'seen' the evening libation in its connection with the Brāhmaṇācchaṃsin priest. Kṛṣṇa occurs in a Gaṇa attached to P. IV, 1, 96. In the Gaṇa connected with P. IV, 1, 99 Kṛṣṇa and Raṇa are represented to form the Gotra names Kārṣṇāyana and Rāṇāyana, these mere Brāhmaṇa Gotras falling under the group of Vāsiṣṭhas. The former is the Gotra alluded to by the commentator on the verses in the Jâtakas noticed above. But he apparently does not confine it to the Brāhmaṇa class. Then the name Kṛṣṇa as the son of Devakī occurs in the Chāndogya-Upaniṣad (III, 17). He was the pupil of Ghora, who was an Āṅgirasa. If Kṛṣṇa was also an Āṅgirasa, which is not improbable, it must be inferred that there was a tradition about Kṛṣṇa as a sage from the time of the Ṛgvedic hymns to the time of the Chāndogya-Upaniṣad, and about a Gotra of the name of Kārṣṇāyana, which literally means collection of Kṛṣṇas, of which the original Kṛṣṇa was the founder. This tradition gave rise to the identification of the sage Kṛṣṇa with Vāsudeva, when he was raised to the rank of the supreme deity. Just as the name Janamejaya, the son of Parikṣit, which occurs in the AB., was in subsequent times used as the name of the person to whom the Mahābhārata was narrated and a genealogy was given to him from Arjuna, the Pāṇḍava, so it is possible that Vāsudeva was identified with the sage Kṛṣṇa and a genealogy given to him in the Vṛṣṇi race through Śūra and Vasudeva. Perhaps the best explanation of the fact of Vāsudeva having been called Kṛṣṇa is that given by the commentator of the Gāthās or verses of the Jātakas, supported, as it appears to me, by the author of the Gāthās himself, that Kṛṣṇa was a Gotra name. The Gotra Kārṣṇāyana which corresponds to Kaṇhāyana is not only mentioned as a Brāhmaṇa Gotra belonging to the Vāsiṣṭha group in the Gaṇa alluded to above, but is stated to have belonged to the Pārāśara subdivision of that group in the Matsyapurāṇa (ch. 200)[1]. Though this was a Brāhmaṇa and Pārāśara Gotra, it could be assumed for sacrificial purposes by a Kṣatriya, for according to Āśvalāyana (Śr. S. XII, 15) the Gotra and the ancestors invoked of the Kṣatriyas are those of their priests or chaplains, and the only Ṛṣi ancestors that all the Kṣatriyas have, are Mānava, Aila and Paurūravasa. The names of these do not distinguish one Kṣatriya family from another and, to answer the purposes of such a distinction, the Gotra and ancestors of the priest are assumed. Vāsudeva therefore belonged to the Kārṣṇāyana Gotra, though it was a Brāhmaṇa and Pārāśara Gotra, and as belonging to this Gotra he could be called Kṛṣṇa by name. Having come to be known by that name, all the traditions about the learning and spiritual insight of the old Kṛṣṇa and also of his being the son of Devakī were engrafted on him, and thus, in the Sabhāparvan 38 Bhīṣma says that one of the two reasons for giving the highest honours to Kṛṣṇa was that he possessed the knowledge of the Vedas and dependent treatises (Vedāṅgas), and that he was also a sacrificial priest (Ṛtvij). The Hindu habit of thought of identifying one god with others by regarding the latter either as forms or incarnations of the former and thus evolving monotheism out of polytheism led to the identification of this Vāsudeva with other gods and with the boy Kṛṣṇa of Gokula. These we will notice later on.

§ 9. In the Nārāyaṇīya we have an explanation of the Bhāgavata or Pāñcarātra system. This system also we will notice in its ripened form later. In the meanwhile we will turn our attention to the statement that the Ekāntika-Dharma founded by Vāsudeva has been explained in the Harigītā and on the occasion when the armies of the Kurus and the Pāṇḍavas stood face to face and Arjuna lost heart. The allusion is of course to the Bhagavadgītā.

This passage is noticed in the Bhaktisūtra 83 and its commentary, in which it is stated that Ekāntabhāva (which is the subject of the Nārāyaṇīya), or devotion to one only, is Bhakti alone, since the former is recognised in that passage as identical with the main topic of the Bhagavadgītā. But the Bhagavadgītā contains no allusion to the Vyūhas or forms of the Supreme, Saṃkarṣaṇa and others, while the latter form a characteristic of the Bhāgavata school. The Gītā, however, mentions as the Prakṛtis of Vāsudeva the five elements, the mind, Buddhi or knowledge, and egoism as well as Jīva (VII, 4, 5). The last is identified with Saṃkarṣaṇa in the Bhāgavata system, egoism with Aniruddha, and mind, with which probably Buddhi is associated, with Pradyumna. What appears to be the fact is this: The Bhagavadgītā was composed before the doctrines of the Bhāga-

[1]) Quoted also in Puruṣottama's Pravaramañjarī, Mysore edition.

vata school were reduced to a system, and it was then that the three of the Prakṛtis of the Supreme were personified into Saṃkarṣaṇa, Pradyumna and Aniruddha, who were members of the family of Vāsudeva. In the prevalent worship, however, Saṃkarṣaṇa alone is found associated with Vāsudeva in early times, as is seen from the inscriptions and the passage from the Niddesa noticed in the beginning. Patañjali also notices, under P. II, 2, 34, a verse in which it is stated that certain musical instruments are sounded in a gathering in the temple of Dhanapati, Rāma and Keśava. Here Rāma and Keśava are Balarāma and Vāsudeva-Kṛṣṇa, and it is clear that there were festive gatherings at their temples in Patañjali's time. If the passage in Patañjali under P. VI, 3, 6 "Janārdana with himself as the fourth", i. e. with three companions, may be taken to allude to the three Vyūhas, then it must be understood that the four Vyūhas, Vāsudeva, Saṃkarṣaṇa, Pradyumna and Aniruddha, were known in Patañjali's time. Still it is doubtful, and it may be taken for granted that the two Vyūhas, Vāsudeva and Saṃkarṣaṇa, only were known up to the time of the latest inscription which is to be referred to about the beginning of the first century before the Christian era, so that the system of four Vyūhas was not fully developed up to that time. If this reasoning is correct, it will be seen that the date of the Bhagavadgītā which contains no mention of the Vyūhas, or personified forms, is much earlier than those of the inscriptions, the Niddesa and Patañjali, i. e. it was composed not later than the beginning of the fourth century before the Christian era. How much earlier it is difficult to say. At the time when the Gītā was conceived and composed, the identification of Vāsudeva with Nārāyaṇa had not taken place, nor had his being an incarnation of Viṣṇu come to be acknowledged, as appears from the work itself. When his Virāj or universe-form was shown to Arjuna, as represented in the eleventh chapter, he is twice addressed by the latter as Viṣṇu on account of his dazzling brilliance which rendered everything hot and filled the whole universe. Here Viṣṇu is alluded to as the chief of the Ādityas and not as the supreme being, and Vāsudeva was Viṣṇu in this sense, as mentioned in chapter 10, because the best thing of a group or class is represented to be his Vibhūti or special manifestation.

§ 10. A characteristic of a new system of religion that comes into vogue is that the followers are not satisfied with the idea that the person known as the founder originated the system. They push back the origin by many ages. Siddhārthaka was preceded by many Buddhas, and so was Mahāvīra by many Tīrthaṃkaras. So in the case of the Bhāgavata school we have seen that that system was taught by Nārāyaṇa at the beginning of each Brahman and in the existing Brahman it was first taught to Pitāmaha or Prajāpati and thence it passed to Dakṣa, Vivasvat, Manu and Ikṣvāku. This last order of its revelation is alluded to at the beginning of the fourth chapter of the Gītā which confirms the tradition noticed in the Nārāyaṇīya about the identity of the religion of the Gītā with the Ekāntika religion revealed by Nārāyaṇa. In this respect of pushing back the origin the Bhāgavata system resembles Buddhism and Jainism.

V. Substance of the Bhagavadgītā.

§ 11. We will now pass under review the main contents of the Bhagavadgītā, as from all appearances it is the earliest exposition of the Bhakti system or the Ekāntika Dharma.

Chapter II. Arjuna is reluctant to fight because it involves the destruction of his near and revered relatives and of other men. Bhagavat endeavours to remove the reluctance by speaking of the eternity and indestructibility of the human soul. Here are two stanzas which occur, with a variation in one of the lines, in the Kaṭha-Upaniṣad. Then to fight is spoken of as the duty of a Kṣatriya for whom there is no other good than a just fight. This mode of thinking is characterised as being Sāṃkhya, and the Yoga mode then follows. The condition of mind in the Yoga mode is a determined will. Those who according to the precepts of the Veda perform rites for the fulfilment of various desires can not have a determined steadfast will. For attaining such a will one should think only of the deed to be done and not of the fruits to be derived from it. With a concentrated mind and without any attachment to other objects one should devote oneself to the deed alone. By such devotion to acts with a determined will man finally attains inflexibility of will (becomes sthitaprajña), and all his desires being uprooted, he attains complete serenity of soul or the Brāhmī condition. When he is in this condition at the time of death, he obtains quiescence in Brahman. This comes to the same doctrine as that stated in the Kaṭha and Bṛhadāraṇyaka-Upaniṣads, that when all desires in the heart are uprooted, the mortal becomes immortal and attains to Brahman [1]). The discipline, however, prescribed for the attainment of this end is not simply moral, but religious also, since it is stated that after having controlled the senses which render the mind restless, a man should devote himself to Bhagavat.

§ 12. Chapter III. There are two paths, that of devotion to knowledge for the Sāṃkhyas and that of devotion to Karman or action for the Yogins. Every one is born for a life of activity, but the deeds done do not tie him down to the world, if he does them for worship (Yajña) and not for his private purposes. No Karman is necessary for one whose enjoyments consist in himself, who is satisfied with himself and contented in himself. But for other people action is necessary, and it must be done without any selfish desire. Janaka and others obtained perfection by devoting themselves to actions alone, i. e. by the pursuit of an active life. But the action should be dedicated to the Supreme, and one should not seek any fruit for himself. But such a frame of mind is not attainable by ordinary men, who are under the influence of their physical nature and sensual passions. Then a question is asked what it is that prompts man to sin. The reply is that it is desire and anger which are all-powerful and envelop a man's spiritual existence. Desire acts through the senses, but intelligence is

[1]) *Yadā sarve pramucyante kāmā yesya hṛdi śritāḥ*, KU. VI, 14 and also BU. IV, 4, 7.

superior to the senses, and superior to this latter is the will (Buddhi), and the soul is superior to Buddhi. Knowing oneself to be higher than Buddhi, one should curb oneself by efforts and kill desire which acts through the series, viz. senses, intellect, will. Here the superiority of one faculty over another is an idea borrowed from the Kaṭha-Upaniṣad. In connection with the teaching that action should be done disinterestedly, Bhagavat makes the closest possible approach to the Sāṃkhya doctrine that the soul being deluded by egoism (Ahaṃkāra) regards himself as the agent of the actions done by the qualities of nature (Prakṛti), and that, misled by the qualities of nature, he forms an attachment to qualities and actions.

§ 13. Chapter IV. The chapter begins with Bhagavat's mention of his communication of this system to Vivasvat in the first instance, as alluded to above. Incidentally the question of his existence at the time of Vivasvat comes up, and he then explains his being born again and again and assuming incarnations for the destruction of the wicked by means of his Prakṛti. They who know the incarnations and the celestial deeds of Bhagavat, are released from the body and are not born again. By means of knowledge men, being purified and their passions destroyed and being devoted to him and resorting to him and resting on him, attained to the condition of Bhagavat. Bhagavat resorts to men in the manner in which they resort to him; men everywhere follow his path.

The idea of action without attachment is further developed. Then metaphorical Yajñas are mentioned, such as the sacrifice of the senses into the fire of restraint, of the objects of the senses into the senses, of the operation of the senses and of the vital breaths into the fire of Yoga, which is the control of the self. All these Yajñas cannot be accomplished without acts. Of these the Yajña of knowledge is the best; for by its means one sees all things in one self and in God (Supreme Spirit). This highest knowledge brings about freedom from all sin, and destroys the polluting effect of action. The realisation of the Yoga sets aside the significance of the actions. This highest knowledge puts an end to all doubt and one becomes a spirit — a spirit totally free. When acts are done in this condition, they do not defile a person. Here the tendency to rationalise Yajñas or sacrifices, which set in in the Upaniṣad period, is seen in a developed form, since the restraint of the senses, the attainment of knowledge, and such other practices are characterised as Yajñas or sacrifices.

Another point that deserves notice is the statement that Bhagavat deals with men in the manner in which they deal with him, that is, the spirit with which God is approached by men is reciprocated by God. This is followed by the affirmation that men everywhere, whatever the differences of their views, follow the path of Bhagavat. Here lies in germ the principle that all religions have a basis of truth in them.

§ 14. Chapter V. Sāṃkhya and Yoga are brought into connection with Saṃnyāsa and Karmayoga. They are not independent of each other. Following either thoroughly, one obtains the fruit of both. The place which is obtained by Sāṃkhyas is obtained also by Yogas. For Jñānayajña or sacrifice of knowledge enabling a man to see all things in himself and in God, and this knowledge bringing about freedom from sin, the same condition is attained to which an active life or pursuit of actions (Karmayoga) brings about, when the actions are done disinterestedly or without aiming at the fruit, with an eye directed towards Brahman only, the true essence of things. Though this is so, still Saṃnyāsa is difficult to be realised without Yoga. With Yoga one attains to it soon. A Yogin does not think that he does something when he sees, hears, eats, sleeps, etc. This is so when these acts are done without any attachment, the aim being the realisation of Brahman. The Yogins perform deeds by their body, mind, will, or simply by their senses, without any attachment for the sake of spiritual purification. By means of Yoga, Jñāna is obtained, and in this condition man looks at all things alike. When a man looks at all things with the same regard, what he aims at is the Brahman and in it he rests. This leads to the consideration of the final peace in Brahman and the method of attaining it. This peace in Brahman resembles the condition of an Arhat in Buddhism, but the Bhagavadgītā does not end there and adds that in this condition of deliverance a person comes to know the Supreme Soul as one to whom all kinds of worship and austere practices are directed as the lord of all worlds and the friend of all beings; and it is this knowledge that leads to peace.

§15. Chapter VI. He who does not attach himself to the result of his actions and does what he ought to do, is Saṃnyāsin as well as Yogin. Karman or action is necessary to become a sage (Muni). When he has attained the dignity of a sage, the essence of it is peace. Then follows a description of the state of a man who has attained Yoga. Practice of Yoga, or contemplation, is then described. When a man goes through the Yoga practices, he attains serenity in Bhagavat, i. e. becomes absorbed in him in peace. All the functions of the mind are suspended in the condition of Yoga. Seeing himself by himself he rests in himself. Then follows an explanation of the process of abstraction and concentration. A Yogin sees himself in all things and all things in himself, looks at all things in the same light. The Supreme Spirit is not lost to him who sees him everywhere and sees everything in him, the Supreme Spirit. He who looks upon the Bhagavat as one, though he exists in all things, exists in him, though he moves about everywhere. He who regards all as himself (and looks upon them in the same light) in matters of happiness and misery is the best Yogin. Then Arjuna remarks on the difficulty of this Yoga. "The mind", he says, "is restless". But Bhagavat replies that it can be controlled by practice as well as by reflection on the vanity of things (Vairāgya). At the end Bhagavat teaches that he is the greatest Yogin, who, having faith in him, adores him with his whole soul centred in him.

The Yoga described in this chapter is found in some of the Upaniṣads, especially in the Śvetāśvatara. The affirmation "sees himself in himself and everywhere else" occurs in the Bṛhadāraṇyaka (IV, 4, 23). The author winds up the chapter with a verse which is in every sense theistic, as he does the fifth chapter, in order, it would appear, that the description of the mental discipline contained in the last chapter and of Yoga in this might not lead to non-theistic conclusions. Care is taken to bring the whole into connection with the Supreme Soul.

§ 16. Chapter VII. In the last six chapters has been explained the whole process of Karmayoga from beginning to act regardless of the fruit, to the attainment of the condition of Yogin, who acting solely with a view to the acquisition of the Brāhma condition, is free from passions, looks upon all things alike; and it is added at the end that he is the best of the Yogins, who adores Bhagavat with faith and with a devoted heart. This is added to show that the processes up to the attainment of the Yoga condition are difficult to be practised by men with such passions as we possess and the way to be free from them is to surrender oneself to God, and therefore in this chapter Bhagavat goes on to explain the nature of created beings and of his relation to them. He begins by saying that God's Prakṛti is eightfold: the five elements, mind, will (Buddhi), and egoism. Jīva is another Prakṛti, which supports the world. From these are produced all objects or beings. Bhagavat is the source and the last resting place of the world. There is nothing further than him. All these things are strung together in him as gems in a string. That which is the characteristic excellence of a thing is Bhagavat himself. All the three qualities and the conditions resulting from them proceed from him. Bhagavat is not in them and they are not in him. Bhagavat is beyond all these three conditions. The world, deluded by the conditions resulting from the three qualities, does not know Bhagavat, the Supreme Spirit, who is beyond them all. This Māyā of Bhagavat consisting of these qualities is very difficult to be got over, and this Māyā they get rid of, who take refuge in him. Wicked men do not resort to Bhagavat, their understanding being clouded by Māyā and resorting to Āsura or demoniacal condition. The devotees of Bhagavat are of four kinds. Of these the Jñānin, or the enlightened, is the best. The Jñānin sticks to Bhagavat as his best refuge. The enlightened man surrenders himself to him, regarding Vāsudeva as everything. Other people are attached to other deities and undertake different vows. Their faith in their deities is generated by Bhagavat and strengthened by him. They worship those deities with that faith and attain fruit. That fruit is yielded by Bhagavat himself. But it is perishable. Not knowing Bhagavat's true nature, which is unchangeable and excellent, ignorant people regard him as something indiscrete at first and afterwards made discrete. He is not intelligible to all beings, being enveloped in Yogamāyā (mystic power). He knows the past, the present and the future, and nobody knows him. By likes and dislikes all beings are deluded and those only, who are released from the infatuation of likes and dislikes, with their sins being destroyed by the practice of virtue, adore the Supreme. Those who know Bhagavat to be Adhiyajña (presiding over worship) and Adhibhūta (presiding over beings), come to know him when they depart this life.

For the idea of all existing things being strung together in the Supreme we may compare MU. II, 2, 5 and BU. III, 8, 3—4; 6—7. Ordinary people are represented as resorting to other deities, led by several desires. The Bhagavat confirms their faith in their deities, and the fruits that they receive from those deities are also given by him. But the fruits that they get from them are perishable. Here appears the same idea as that noticed in chap. IV and to be noticed in chap. IX, viz. that the worshippers of other gods are really Bhagavat's worshippers, and that there is a principle of unity in all religions.

§ 17. Chapter VIII. Arjuna begins by putting questions about the three subjects mentioned in the last verse of the last chapter and about Brahman and Adhyātma. Bhagavat then explains these. About perceiving him at the time of death he says: "He who leaves his body while remembering me at the time of death, attains to the same condition as mine." Finally he states that he who departs this life while meditating on the all-knowing, eternal ruler, who is smaller than the smallest thing, who is the protector of all, whose form is unthinkable, whose brilliance is like that of the sun, and who is beyond all darkness, with devotion, his whole soul gathered between the brows with the power of concentration, reaches that Supreme Being, who is higher than the highest. He then mentions the attainment of the Unchangeable, with the mind concentrated, and the reaching of the final goal after leaving the body by means of a Yoga process and by the utterance of the syllable 'Om' and the remembrance of Bhagavat all the while. Bhagavat is easily attainable by one who meditates on him with a singleness of mind and is devoted to him. Every being is subject to transmigration, but is free from it when he reaches Bhagavat. During the night of Brahman all these things are resolved into the indiscrete (Avyakta), and, when the day dawns, they spring out again from it. There is another substance, different from that Avyakta and itself indiscrete (Avyakta), which is not destroyed when all others are destroyed. This substance which is indiscrete, is unchangeable and that is the highest resting place, which being attained to, there is no return. That is Bhagavat's highest abode. That supreme soul, in whom all these beings are and who has spread out all this, is to be attained by single-minded devotion. Then he proceeds to mention the two paths. Those who die while the sun is in his northern course (Uttarāyaṇa), go to Brahman, and those who die while he is in his southern course (Dakṣiṇāyana) go to the orb of the moon, from which the soul returns.

It is worthy of observation that after mentioning that the man who meditates on the Supreme at the time of death reaches him, he mentions the attainment of the Akṣara, which is the highest goal, by resorting to a Yoga process. This seems to be like looking back on the Yoga practices for the attainment of the Akṣara (Brahman) mentioned in the Upaniṣads such as the Muṇḍaka (II, 2, 3) and the Śvetāśvatara (I, 14). In the first passage, the syllable 'Om' is compared to a bow, the soul to the arrow, and Brahman to the target which is to be hit. In the second a person is instructed to use his own body as the nether wooden piece and the Praṇava as the upper one and, practising meditations, which is like rubbing of the wooden pieces against each other, to discover the God hidden like Agni in the pieces of wood. Here the Akṣara Brahman of the Muṇḍaka is transformed into Deva

(God) in the Śvetāśvatara-Upaniṣad, and the Bhagavadgītā also prescribes the meditating on Bhagavat while the syllable 'Om' is being uttered. Here, therefore, we see the effort to invest the unchangeable and indiscrete Brahman with a strong distinct personality. Later on in the chapter another Avyakta is mentioned, besides that into which all things are resolved at the dissolution of the universe. This Avyakta is eternal and indestructible and is called Akṣara and the highest goal. Here, however, this Akṣara is at once rendered theistic by being spoken of as the highest abode or condition of Bhagavat.

§ 18. Chapter IX. In this chapter Bhagavat proceeds to explain the direct and indirect knowledge which constitute the royal lore and the royal secret. It is to be directly perceived. It is holy and easy to be practised. The Bhagavat spread out all this universe. All things are in him and he is not in them, and still the objects are not in him. Wonderful is his lordly power. He is the sustainer of all beings and is not in them. His self brings all things into existence. As the air which exists in the sky is everywhere, so all beings are in him. At the dissolution of the world all beings are dissolved into his Prakṛti, and at the beginning of a new Kalpa they are discharged forth again. All these acts do not contaminate him, as he does them without any desire. With himself as the director, the Prakṛti brings forth the moveable and immoveable things. Foolish men disregard him who has assumed a human form, not knowing his true nature, viz. that he is the lord and the great ruler of all; but great souls, assuming a godly nature, knowing him to be the origin of all beings, adore him with single-mindedness. Some people worship him by Jñānayajña, i. e. a rationalised sacrifice, taking him as one or several or as having his face in all directions. He is a subsidiary as well as the main sacrifice. He is Svadhā, herbs, Mantra, ghee. He is Agni and he is also oblation. He is father, mother, nourisher and grandfather of the world. He is Ṛc, Sāman, etc. He is the way, sustainer, lord, witness, shelter and friend, etc. The knowers of the three Vedas, the drinkers of Soma, worshipping him by means of sacrifice, desire habitation in heaven, where they enjoy many pleasures. After their merit has been exhausted, they come back to the mortal world again. Those who thus follow the ritual of the three Vedas come and go. He looks after the welfare of those who think of him and meditate on him with single-mindedness and adore him. Those who worship other deities must be considered as worshipping him, but they do so not according to prescribed rules. He is the receiver and lord of all kinds of Yajñas or worship, but those people do not know him as he really is, and therefore they fail. Those who worship other deities attain to them, and his worshippers attain to him. All the oblations thrown into the fire, all that is eaten and given and the austerities practised should be dedicated to him. In this way these actions do not serve as a bondage, and one becomes a real Saṃnyāsin and goes to him. He who adores Bhagavat with single-mindedness becomes holy, even if he be wicked. He becomes immediately holy and obtains peace. Even women, Vaiśyas and Śūdras, when they resort to him, attain to the highest place. The seeker of the good should direct his mind towards him, should be his devotee, should worship him, should bow to him, and acting in this way and being thus fully devoted to him, he will reach him.

Here the performance of sacrificial rites is, in the manner which has become usual, mentioned as efficacious for the acquisition of a place in heaven. From this place persons return when their merit is exhausted, but there is no return when a man devotes himself to Bhagavat with all his heart. God is further personalised and brought home to man by being declared as his father, mother, nourisher, grandfather, friend, refuge, etc. The attitude to other gods is of toleration. The worship offered to them is really offered to Bhagavat, but the worshippers do not know Bhagavat as he truly is and therefore go wrong.

§ 19. Chapter X. The gods and Ṛṣis do not know the origin of Bhagavat. He was before them all. He who knows Bhagavat to be the unborn and unbeginning lord of all worlds, is free from all sins. All the mental conditions, knowledge, absence of ignorance, forgiveness, truth, self-control, serenity, pain and pleasure, etc. are from him. The seven ancient Maharṣis and four Manus sprang from him whose descendants are all these men. Good men adore Bhagavat with pure faith, knowing him to be the origin of all and that everything is set in motion by him. They, with their minds directed towards him, with their souls centred in him, enlighten each other, speak about him, and thus they are satisfied and are happy. Out of sympathy for them he dispels the darkness of ignorance by the light of knowledge, being himself in his true condition.

When they adore him thus constantly full of love, he grants them that condition of mind by means of which they reach him. Then questioned by Arjuna as to the Vibhūtis or excellent forms of each species or group which pervade the world, Bhagavat proceeds to mention them. He is the soul that dwells in the heart of men and is the origin, the middle and the end of all beings. He is Viṣṇu of the Ādityas, the sun of all shining things, Kapila of the Siddhas, Prahlāda of all Daityas, Rāma of wielders of weapons, philosophy (Adhyātma) of all lores, Dvandva of compounds, Kīrti (fame) of all females, Vāsudeva of Vṛṣṇis, and Dhanaṃjaya of Pāṇḍavas. That object which has excellence and splendour should be known as arising from his lustre.

There is to be observed here one special characteristic of the Bhakti school, and that is that all the devotees meet together, enlighten each other as to the nature of God and contribute by discourses on him to each other's elevation and gratification. This is almost a characteristic mark of Bhaktas as distinguished from the Yogins, who have to go through their exercises singly and in solitude.

§ 20. Chapter XI. The Virāj form of God, i.e. all beings looked at simultaneously as constituting one whole, as also his destructive form, in which all enter into his mouth and are absorbed, is described in this chapter. Arjuna praises him that he does not see the end, the beginning, the middle of him, that he is the guardian of eternal righteousness and entreats him to give up this frightful form and assume the more usual and the more agreeable human form. In verse 30 Arjuna addresses him as Viṣṇu, saying that his dazzling brilliance makes everything hot and his lustre has filled the whole universe.

The idea of looking at the universe as a form of god is as old as the Puruṣasūkta (RV. X, 90). God's having eyes everywhere, face everywhere, arms everywhere and feet everywhere is expressed in RV. X, 81, 3. This verse is repeated in Śvetāśvatara-Upaniṣad III, 3.

§ 21. Chapter XII. This chapter starts with a question as to the difference between the contemplation on the original indiscrete cause which is unchangeable (Akṣara) and the worship of him (Vāsudeva), and the reply is, they are the best devotees, who, fixing their minds upon him, meditate on him with a concentrated attention and faith. Those who, with their senses restrained, meditate on the indiscrete, unchangeable, undefinable, as existing everywhere and unthinkable, also reach him, but the trouble to them is greater. Bhagavat delivers from the ocean of death those who, dedicating all their actions to him and meditating on him, worship him; and he teaches Arjuna to fix his mind on him and concentrate his will on him and, if he can not fix his mind firmly upon him, then to endeavour to obtain him by continual remembrance of him. If this last is not feasible, he should perform deeds for his sake, and doing this he would obtain success. If, however, he is not able to do this with his mind fixed on him, he should abandon desire for the fruit of all his actions. Then follows an enumeration of the virtues of those who are devotees of God and are specially dear to him, such as not hating any being, being the friend of all, being humble, being indifferent to praise or censure, etc.

In this chapter the meditation on the Akṣara or unchangeable indiscrete cause is again mentioned as opposed to the worship of Bhagavat as a personal God. In similar passages in the previous chapters the personalisation is effected at once by inserting a clause applicable only to a personal God. But here the meditation on Avyakta is spoken of as successful, but is condemned as being very difficult to be practised, and the theistic aim of the work is kept in view.

§ 22. Chapter XIII. This body is the Kṣetra, and he who knows this body as his own, is Kṣetrajña. The Bhagavat is also Kṣetrajña in all the Kṣetras. This subject about the Kṣetra and Kṣetrajña has been variously treated by the Ṛṣis in verses of various metres and determined by the words of the Brahmasūtra unfolding reasons. Kṣetra consists of the twenty-four elements mentioned in the Sāṃkhya system and desire, hatred, pleasure and pain, and body, life and courage, which are Ātmaguṇas according to the Vaiśeṣikas. Bhagavat then proceeds to enumerate the virtues, such as humility, sincerity, etc., which constitute, it is said, Jñāna or knowledge, but which are to be taken as means to knowledge. Then are alluded to knowledge, or true philosophy, and its reverse. He then mentions the Jñeya, or thing to be known, and it is Parabrahman, which has no beginning nor end, which is neither existent nor non-existent, and which has hands and feet everywhere and which has eyes, head and face everywhere, which has ears everywhere, and which pervades all. And thus the description of godhead proceeds in the words of the Upaniṣads. Prakṛti and Puruṣa are unbeginning. All changes and qualities are produced from Prakṛti. Prakṛti is the cause in bringing about effect, and Puruṣa is the cause in the enjoyment and sufferance of happiness and misery. The Puruṣa, being connected with Prakṛti, enjoys or endures the properties or effects of the Prakṛti; and the cause is his being connected with the Guṇas or qualities. Besides all these various principles, there is in this body Puruṣa, the Supreme Soul, who is the witness of everything, who is the sustainer, enjoyer and the great lord. By meditation some see the self by self, others see it by Sāṃkhyayoga and Karmayoga. Any moving or unmoving thing that comes into existence is produced by the union of Kṣetra and Kṣetrajña. He, who sees the Supreme Lord equally in all things, who is not destroyed when other things are destroyed, sees truly. Seeing God equally in all things, a man does no injury to himself and attains to the highest goal. He truly sees, who sees all acts as done by Prakṛti and Puruṣa as not the actor. When he regards all separate beings as existing in one place and sees development proceeding thence, he becomes Brahman. The Supreme Spirit, though dwelling in the body, does not do anything and is not contaminated, because he is unbeginning and is devoid of qualities and unchangeable. The spirit is not contaminated, just as space or ether existing everywhere is not. Just as the sun illuminates the whole world, so does the Kṣetrajña illuminate the Kṣetra.

The Karmayoga leading up to the condition of a Yogin, who looks at all things with the same regard and makes no distinction between them and himself, has been described in the first six chapters. In the next six the Bhaktiyoga, or loving adoration of God, is the subject treated of; and the final effect of it is the formation of the fully righteous character which distinguishes a Bhakta who is dear to Bhagavat. With chapter XIII begins the consideration of subsidiary subjects. In this Bhagavat speaks of the Kṣetra and Kṣetrajña, or the soul and its dwelling place, and of another soul, that is, himself also dwelling in the Kṣetra. In connection with this subject he refers to the poetic works of the previous Ṛṣis and to the words of the Brahmasūtra. What these works are it is difficult to say; but what follows is, first, the mention of the twenty-four principles generally associated with the Sāṃkhya system, as well as seven others, all of which constitute the Kṣetra; secondly, the enumeration of the virtues that qualify one to the attainment of knowledge; thirdly, the statement about knowledge (Jñāna), or that which is true philosophy, and also Ajñāna, which is the reverse; and fourthly, the description of the Jñeya or the thing to be known, which is Parabrahman or the Supreme Soul. This last contains the attributes given in the Upaniṣads, and a verse and a half are verbally quoted from the ŚU. There are also other statements in the concluding verses which resemble KU. V, 11 and ŚU. V, 4. Then there is a statement about the nature of the Prakṛti and Puruṣa quite in keeping with the Sāṃkhya system; but the existence of the highest spirit in the body along with the animal soul is mentioned. Thus is the atheism of the Sāṃkhya system studiously avoided, whenever there is a reference to its doctrines. Then follow reflections on God and the seeing of the Supreme Soul everywhere. The works, therefore, upon which this chapter is based are some of the Upaniṣads and some treatises setting forth the constitution of the world and the principles of morality. These treatises may have been the discourses first independent and afterwards included in the Śāntiparvan and other parts of the Mahābhārata, or they may have been others of which we have no trace; but there is no mention here of the Sāṃkhya system by name nor a special reference to it as elaborated in later times by Īśvarakṛṣṇa. The idea of the twenty-four principles is ancient and seems to have been appropriated afterwards by the founders of the philosophic systems, as it suited their purpose. But no chronological conclusions can be deduced from the mention of those twenty-four principles. The doctrine that all action proceeds from the Prakṛti and the soul is inactive and simply enjoys or suffers, which is a true Sāṃkhya doctrine, but is calculated to absolve a man from moral responsibility, is also mentioned; but it appears to come incidentally along with the twenty-four principles.

§ 23. Chapter XIV. The great Brahman is the womb (Yoni) for Bhagavat into which he throws seed. Of all the wombs that produce bodily forms, Brahman is the greatest. Bhagavat then proceeds to detail the nature of the three Guṇas, their products and their results in the future world. These Guṇas prove as bondage, and when they are got over, then the man is free from the bondage and becomes immortal. The distinguishing characteristic of one who is free from these three Guṇas is a quiet undisturbed serene mood, in which happiness and misery are alike, and gold, clod of earth and stone are alike, in which agreeable and disagreeable things are alike, and praise and censure are also alike, etc. He who invariably resorts to Bhagavat by Bhaktiyoga becomes free from these three Guṇas and attains to the condition of Brahman. Bhagavat is the support of the immortal and unchanging Brahman and of eternal righteousness (duty) and of unending happiness.

Here then is a distinct affirmation of the soul's attainment of freedom from passions by means of continuous devotion to Bhagavat or God. The word Brahmayoni occurs in MU. III, 1, 3 and is to be interpreted, in the light of the opening statement in the above, as one whose Yoni is Brahman.

§ 24. Chapter XV. Bhagavat proceeds to the comparison of Saṃsāra, or the whole extent of things, to the pippal-tree. This tree is to be cut by the weapon of indifference or non-attachment; and then should be sought that place from which there is no return. One should surrender himself to the original Puruṣa. Those reach that unchanging position or place, who are free from pride, ignorance, desires, and the pair of happiness and misery. That is the highest abode of Bhagavat, which is not illuminated by the sun, the moon or the fire. When a soul departs from a body, it takes away the Indriyas, of which Manas is the sixth, and brings them in when it assumes another body. The soul itself is a part of Bhagavat and is eternal. This soul, placing itself in these six Indriyas, resorts to all objects of sense. The brilliance existing in the sun, which illumines the whole world, and which exists in the moon as well as in fire, is to be known as that of Bhagavat. By becoming Soma Bhagavat raises all herbs. By becoming fire he contributes to digestion. He dwells in the heart of all. From him proceeds consciousness of one's condition, knowledge, and the rejection of what is not true. Bhagavat alone is to be known by means of all the Vedas and as the author of Vedāntas and the knower of the Veda. There are two souls in the world, one that changes, and the other that is unchangeable. Besides these, there is another who is the highest and is called Paramātman, and who as the unchangeable lord supports all the three worlds after entering into them. Bhagavat is known to be that Highest Soul in the ordinary world and also in the Vedas.

There is one new point brought out in this chapter. And that is that the animal soul goes out of the body along with the six senses and enters new ones in that condition. The comparison of the composite universe to the pippal-tree occurs in KU. (VI, 1), MaiU. (VI, 4), and the non-illumination of the highest abode of Bhagavat is mentioned in a verse in KU. (V, 15), MU. (II, 2, 10) and ŚU. (VI, 14). The doctrine of the existence of the third highest Puruṣa should also be noted as a characteristic of this theistic work. The triad, Kṣara, Akṣara or Ātman (individual soul), and the ruling one God, is mentioned in ŚU. (I, 10), which work is a precursor of the Bhagavadgītā.

§ 25. Chapter XVI. Bhagavat now proceeds to enumerate the virtues which constitute the divine endowments (Daivī Saṃpad), and the vices that constitute demoniacal possessions. From divine endowments results final deliverance, and from the demoniacal possessions follows destruction. There are two classes of created beings: one is divine and the other demoniacal. In persons of the latter class there is no purity nor correct conduct nor truth. They regard the world as unreal, without substratum or support, without God, disconnected and, what more, springing from lust. Holding this view these wicked and dull persons with their ferocious deeds bring about the destruction of the world. Full of insatiable lust and possessed of vanity, pride, and arrogance, they act in an unholy manner, sticking to their own false conceits. They accumulate wealth by foul means for enjoyment, and boasting of their possessions, their power, their parentage, they treat others with contempt and eventually go to the infernal regions. If they worship at all, they simply utter the name and assume a false garb. They are full of egotism and hate Bhagavat, as abiding in their own bodies and those of others. These wicked men he consigns to the race of the demons. Desire, anger and covetousness are the three doors to hell. These three, therefore, should be abandoned. He who avoids these three doors, reaches the highest goal. He who abandons sacred precepts and acts according to his own will, does not obtain success, happiness or the highest goal. The sacred precepts must, therefore, be followed whenever a man has to do anything or avoid anything.

Here two classes of men, good and bad, are mentioned. Among the latter are included not only worldly men who do not care for God or morality, but the followers of philosophical or religious systems different from that of Bhagavat seem also to be included. They set aside the sacred Śāstra or precepts, denied God, as Buddhists and Jainas did, and regarded the world as unsubstantial or unreal, as the former did.

§ 26. Chapter XVII. Arjuna asks: "What is the frame of mind of those who set aside the sacred precepts and still worship with faith? Is it characterised by the quality of goodness, activity or ignorance?" Bhagavat answers: "Faith is of three kinds, characterised by goodness, activity, and darkness or ignorance. The faith of a man depends upon the quality of his heart. A man is what faith makes of him. As is his faith, so is the man". The good worship gods, the active, Yakṣas, and Rakṣases or evil spirits, and the ignorant, ghosts and spectres. Men of a demoniacal frame of mind perform terrible austerities full of ostentation and egotism, and cause attenuation of the elements composing the body and of the Bhagavat who dwells in it. He then mentions three kinds of food, modes of worship, austerities and gifts, in keeping with the three qualities. For instance, in the case of worship or sacrifice, that is in keeping with the quality of goodness, which is performed without any regard for the fruit and in accordance with the sacred ritual. That springs from the quality of activity, which is done for the attainment of fruit and out of ostentation; and that which is done without regard for the sacred precepts and without Dakṣiṇā or rewards to the priest and without any faith, proceeds from the quality of ignorance. As to charitable gifts, those spring from the quality of goodness, which are made because it is a duty to give to one from whom no return is expected; while that which is made with an interested motive and with a desire for return, springs from the quality of activity. And in this manner all the four subjects are treated. At the end the doing of good acts by the repetition of the syllables "Om, tat, sat" is mentioned. In this chapter the truth that man's religious faith and the character of the God that he worships, depend upon his own character, whether good or bad, is clearly recognised.

Not only the nature of the God worshipped, but also the diet, the mode of worship, charity or gifts, and the practice of austerity differ according as a man's nature is influenced by one or other of the three qualities, goodness, activity and ignorance.

§ 27. Chapter XVIII. This chapter begins with a question by Arjuna as to the principles of renunciation and abandonment. Bhagavat replies that renunciation is the giving up of works springing from desires, and abandonment is the abandonment of fruits of actions. Some say that all Karman should be abandoned; others say that worship, charity and austerity should not be given up. The decision is that these last should not be abandoned, as they bring about purity of the soul. The actions should be done without being attached to them or desiring for the fruits. That duty that must be done, should not be abandoned. Giving up that duty is an ignorant deed. When action is avoided because it is wearisome, its abandonment springs from the quality of passion. When the essential action is done because it should be done without any desire for fruit or attachment, that abandonment springs from goodness. It is not possible for a living being to abandon all actions. He who abandons only the fruit, is really one who has abandoned actions. According to the Sāmkhya doctrine, there are five different causes: the resting place, agent, instrument, varied movements and fate. In this manner it goes on. Some acts or states of mind are represented to vary according to the three qualities, such as knowledge, the deed done and the doer, Buddhi or will, firmness and happiness, and the duties of the different castes.

The man who worships him from whom all beings have sprung and who has spread out all this by doing the duties assigned to him, for which the three qualities have fitted him, attains final success. He then proceeds to mention all those virtues and other states of mind, such as self-control, freedom from passions, which conduce to the realisation of the Brahma-condition. When this condition is realised, a man is free from sorrow and desire and, being equally disposed towards all beings, he develops in himself the highest love for Bhagavat, and knowing Bhagavat fully and truly, enters into the Bhagavat. One should do all acts, intent only upon God, and then one obtains the eternal place by the favour of God. A man should fix his mind upon Bhagavat alone, dedicating all his actions to him, and then he gets over all evils by the grace of Bhagavat. Then Bhagavat winds up the whole by teaching Arjuna to surrender himself with all his heart to God (the Ruler), who abides in the hearts of all things and moves them, as if forming parts of a wheel; and then he says, by his favour Arjuna would obtain perfect peace and an eternal resting-place. He is further instructed to dedicate his whole mind to Bhagavat, to become his devotee, to worship him, to bow to him, and in this way he (Arjuna) would reach him. This is styled the deepest secret. Then Arjuna is told to set aside all other methods of salvation and surrender himself to Bhagavat alone, and Bhagavat would then free him from all his sins. And thus the chapter ends.

This is the Ekāntika Dharma or monotheistic religion which, as the Nārāyaṇīya tells us, was communicated to Arjuna. The method of salvation here revealed is to lead a life of action, but the fruit of the action one should not be intent on. The action should be done disinterestedly, that is, a man should be selfless in doing it. The action should be dedicated to Brahman, that is, it should be done because the universal order requires it to be done. This is tantamount to saying that one should do one's duty because it is a duty. When a more personal interpretation is given to it, the doctrine comes to this, that one should act with the sole object of carrying out God's will. The frame of mind that is generated by consistently acting in this manner, is freedom from passion, a sense of the omnipresence of God and an equal regard for all things. This leads to the realisation of the highest love of God and, knowing Bhagavat thoroughly, by this means a man is absorbed in him.

But to do one's duty consistently and selflessly is a matter difficult, since all beings are subject to the influence of the three qualities or, in our modern phraseology, of passions and appetencies. These can be got over by surrendering oneself to God.

VI. The Sources of the Religion of the Bhagavadgītā.

§ 28. This constant insistence on actions being done without any regard for the fruit, that is, disinterestedly or selflessly, forms a peculiarity of the Bhagavadgītā. But the idea is not new. In the Īśopaniṣad it is stated in the second verse that a man should desire to live a hundred years doing actions resolutely, and in that way and no other, will action not contaminate him. And the non-contamination as the result of an elevated state of mind is spoken of in ChU. IV, 14, 3; BU. IV, 4, 23; and MaiU. VI, 20.

The attributes of the Supreme Being the Gītā draws from the Upaniṣads, as has been already shown in the remarks on the different chapters. While the personality of God is fully acknowledged in certain parts of the Upaniṣads, mere Brahman, the personality of which is not so distinct, is also spoken of in some places. When the Bhagavadgītā takes in these passages, it takes care to distinctly personalise the Akṣara or Brahman, as we have shown. The source from which the Gītā derives its doctrines about the conquest of the self and the attainment of a condition of peace and serenity, is the general atmosphere of religious and moral sentiment that came to prevail from the beginning of the earliest Upaniṣad speculations to the formation of definite religious systems, orthodox and heterodox. Consequently, though the Gītā speaks of the Brahma-Nirvāṇa, it ought not to be supposed that it borrows this doctrine of final peace and serenity from Buddhism. The source resorted to by these systems was common to all.

Besides the Upaniṣads and the religious and moral atmosphere prevalent at that time, the Gītā avails itself of the philosophy that had come into existence in early times. This is the philosophy of the Sāṃkhya and the Yoga. Though the twenty-four principles of the former system, together with the Puruṣa or soul as the twenty-fifth, as known in later times, and the doctrine of the activity of the Prakṛti only and the non-activity of Puruṣa are alluded to in the Bhagavadgītā, still it adds another soul called the Uttama Puruṣa or the Supreme Soul, which is not found in the later Sāṃkhya, thus giving a theistic character to the philosophy. In their account of the creation the Purāṇas follow this philosophy, and the later Vaiṣṇava and Śaiva systems adopt it in a more or less qualified manner. But the word Sāṃkhya does not seem to be used in the Bhagavadgītā to indicate the later non-theistic system. In the second chapter and in the fifth, Sāmkhya indicates a philosophy based upon knowledge, and Yoga, one based on action. Again the five causes that are alluded to in the last chapter as mentioned in the Sāṃkhya system do not appear to be known to the later Sāṃkhyas. The speculative philosophy, therefore, that existed about the time of the Śvetāśvatara-Upaniṣad and the Bhagavadgītā, was known by the name of Sāṃkhya, and out of it grew the non-theistic system of later times. The Yoga, the philosophy of action, too did prevail, but it culminated, as indicated before, into a concentration of mind, the ordinary operations being suspended, on the Brahman, Akṣara, or the Supreme Soul.

§ 29. Thus the Bhagavadgītā is the result of the development of the religious and philosophic speculation that prevailed before the rise of Buddhism. But the origin of the idea of Bhakti, or love of God, which is the characteristic of the work, has formed the subject of a great deal of speculation in modern times, and to this point we will now turn. In the Upaniṣads, Upāsanā, or fervent meditation of a number of things, such as Manas (mind), the sun, the Puruṣa in the sun or the moon, food, vital breath, etc., regarded as Brahman, i. e. thinking of them as Brahman, is prescribed. Such a fervent meditation cannot but magnify the thing and give it a glorious form, so as to excite admiration and even love. Again what is called the Internal Ātman (soul) is said in the Bṛhadāraṇyaka to be dearer than a son, wealth and everything else (I, 4, 8). Here the word Ātman may possibly be taken to mean one's own soul. In the same Upaniṣad there is another passage which runs thus: "This is that Great Unborn, who is of the form of thought among vital airs, who dwells in the cavity of the heart, who is controller of all, ruler of all, the lord of all. By doing good or evil deeds he does not become better or worse. He is the ruler of all beings, he is the causeway or dike that separates things from one another and prevents them being confused together (he is the preserver of order). The Brāhmaṇas desire to know him by the words of the Vedas, by worship, charity and austerity. Knowing him, one becomes a sage. The recluses, desiring him as the place to live in, renounce the world. On this account the wise men of old did not desire progeny, saying to themselves: 'What shall we do with progeny, when we have got this Being, this world to live in?'; and thus they gave up desire for sons, wealth and the world, and lived the life of mendicants" (IV, 4, 22). Now, if those wise men of old gave up all the pleasures of the world to contemplate and dwell with the Supreme Being, so eloquently described, must it not be considered that they were actuated by love for him, though the word Bhakti does not occur here? And at the bottom of all those rapturous sayings about the peace attained by seeing the Supreme Soul in the world and the heart of man, there must be a feeling akin to love. And during the period when the Ṛgveda poetry was composed, love for God or gods was often an abiding sentiment in the heart of the poet, as is evident from the words: "Dyaus is my father" (RV. I, 164, 33); "Aditi (the boundless) is father, mother, and son" (RV. I, 89, 10); and from such prayers as "O father Dyaus, avert all evils", "Be accessible to us and gracious as a father to the son", etc. Though the later sacrificial ritual destroyed the spirit of these verses and converted them into simple verbal formulae, still, the feeling that was in the heart at the time when they were composed, must have continued, though it found no expression for a time and exhibited itself again mixed with wonder and admiration in the times of the Upaniṣads. It certainly was not absent during this last period. The text about the two birds, the friends and companions of each other, by which are meant the Supreme and individual souls exists in the Ṛksaṃhitā (I, 164, 20) and is repeated in the Muṇḍaka-Upaniṣad (VII, 1, 1).

In the last (MU. III, 2, 3) and in the KU. (II, 23) there is a verse to the effect that this Supreme Soul is not to be attained by lectures (from a teacher), nor by intelligence, nor by much learning; he is to be attained by him whom the Supreme Soul favours; to him he discloses his form. Again we have the doctrine that the supremely wise Being, the life of all, leads a man to do good deeds, whom he desires to elevate (KBU. III, 8); and another, that God dwelling in the heart of all beings controls them, which latter forms the subject of a celebrated passage in the BU. III, 7. From this it is clear that the doctrine that the individual soul is dependent on the Supreme and that the latter alone works out his salvation, was acknowledged in Upaniṣad times.

§ 30. In this manner all the points that constitute the Ekāntika religion of the Bhagavadgītā are to be found in the older religious literature. The word Bhakti, however, in the sense of love is not to be found except in a verse in ŚU. But that word is not always used in the sense of love even by Rāmānuja. In his system Bhakti means constant meditation and corresponds to the Upāsanā of the Upaniṣads. The word etymologically signifies resorting to and then loving the thing resorted to. It is used in this sense by Pāṇini in Sūtra IV, 3, 95; but the word, as explained by the commentators, has a passive sense and means a thing resorted to, liked or loved; and general and special terminations are prescribed, which, when affixed to a noun, indicate one by whom the thing expressed by the noun is liked or loved. In this sense the word Bhakti is used by Yāska also, when he speaks of certain things as Agnibhaktīni, Indrabhaktīni, i. e. things which resort to, or relate themselves to, Agni, etc. Thus the idea of love was associated with the word in early times, though it then signified l o v e d instead of l o v e. Properly speaking, by the rules of Pāṇini himself, it ought to signify the latter, as the suffix *ti* indicates Bhāva or condition. Howsoever the word may have come into use in later times, the thing expressed by it, viz. love for the Ātman or the Supreme Soul, was an idea implied and often expressed by the word *priya* or *preyas* in the Upaniṣad period.

§ 31. The state of things which must have led to the evolution of the religion of the Gītā seems to me to be this. About the time when the systems of religion we have been considering arose, there was a tendency amongst the people which often worked itself out, as is evident from the Pāli Birth-Stories, to give up worldly life and betake themselves to a residence in forests or mountains. Even Buddhism, Jainism and other like systems considered an ascetic life to be a sine qua non of religious elevation. There is reason to believe that Śramaṇas existed before the rise of Buddhism. The religious systems that had sprung up were mostly atheistic. The Indian mind had become prone to indulge in mere moral discourses and thoughts of moral exaltation, unassociated with a theistic faith, as appears clear from Buddhism and other systems and also from dry moral dissertations of which the Mahābhārata is full. Such a system as that of the Bhagavadgītā was, therefore, necessary to counteract these tendencies. Theistic ideas were so scattered in the Upaniṣads, that it was necessary for practical purposes to work them up into a system of redemption capable of being grasped easily. These appear to be the conditions under which the Gītā came into existence. I am not inclined to dissolve Vāsudeva and Arjuna into solar myths; but Vāsudeva could not have been living when the Bhagavadgītā was composed as a discourse delivered by him, any more than Buddha was living when his discourses were reduced to the form of books. It is worthy of remark that both of them are called Bhagavats when speaking. Vāsudeva must already have been deified before the Bhagavadgītā was written.

As regards the attitude of the Bhagavat to the older belief, it is evident that it is conservative and he came to fulfil the law and not supersede it. It must already have been seen that he looks at the sacrificial religion from almost the same point of view as the Upaniṣads. The cherishing of desires which the sacrificial rites encouraged is considered harmful, and the fruit attained by means of them is perishable. It was because this Ekāntika religion was so conservative, that it gradually made its way into Hindu society in general, though it did not succeed in uprooting the religion of sacrifices. Still it always retained its character as a religion for women and for all castes, Śūdras included, and in its later development it was associated with such Vedic rites as then remained when it was professed by the Brāhmaṇas, but not so associated when its followers were of lower castes, among whom it continued to exercise great influence. The Bhagavat's attitude towards the worshippers of other gods has already been explained. It was strictly liberal. All worship, to whomsoever it was directed, reaches him ultimately, but the devotees of other gods do not know Bhagavat as he truly is and thus go wrong. This attitude must have had something to do with the influence of the Vāsudeva-Kṛṣṇa cult over the lower classes.

VII. Identification of Vāsudeva with Nārāyaṇa.

§ 32. The word Nārāyaṇa is similar to Nāḍāyana, which last is formed by P. IV, 1, 99 and means the Gotra Nāḍāyana. The termination is significative and means in this case the resting place or the place to which Nāḍa or a collection of Naḍas go. So Nārāyaṇa means the resting place or goal of Nāra or a collection of Naras [1]. In the Nārāyaṇīya (XII, 341) Keśava or Hari says to Arjuna that he is known as the resting place or goal of men (narāṇām). The word Nṛ or Nara is also used to denote gods as manly persons, especially in the Vedas, so that Nārāyaṇa may be construed as the resting place or goal of gods. There is a tradition which connects Nārāyaṇa with the primeval waters. Manu (1, 10) and also Hari in the above passage say that the waters were called Nārās because they were the sons of Nara and, since they were the first resting place of Brahmā in the first case and of Hari in the second, the two were called Nārāyaṇas. The Purāṇas, such as the Vāyu and the Viṣṇu, agree with Manu. Again there is a tradition that Brahmadeva sprang from the lotus in the

[1]) See Medhātithi's commentary on Manu 1,10.

navel of Nārāyaṇa or Viṣṇu (MBh. III, 12, 34 and XII, 349, 18). In the Vāyu-Purāṇa Nārāyaṇa is represented as prior to Avyakta or matter in an undeveloped form, and from Avyakta sprang the mundane egg, and from the latter arose Brahmadeva. All these traditions in various forms seem to go back to RV. X, 82, 5 and 6, which may be thus translated: "Prior to the sky, prior to this earth, prior to the living gods, what is that embryo which the waters held first and in which all the gods existed? The waters held that same embryo in which all the gods exist or find themselves; on the navel of the unborn stood something in which all beings stood". In this we have first the waters mentioned; on those waters stood the embryo, which corresponds to the Brahmā of the later tradition, who created everything; and the unborn corresponds to Nārāyaṇa from whose navel he sprang. In this embryo all the gods, it is said, found themselves. This corresponds to the Naras, men or gods, whose goal or resting place was Nārāyaṇa, so that this confirms the identity between Brahmā and Nārāyaṇa mentioned by Manu and some of the Purāṇas. Nārāyaṇa, therefore, who, by the other authorities cited above, is considered prior to Brahmadeva and to the Svayaṃbhū of Manu, is another person and has a cosmic character and is not a historical or mythological individual. This idea of Nārāyaṇa was developed in the period of the later Brāhmaṇas and Āraṇyakas. In the Śatapatha-Brāhmaṇa (XII, 3, 4) Puruṣa Nārāyaṇa is represented to have sent forth from the place of sacrifice Vasus, Rudras and Ādityas by means of the morning, midday and evening libations respectively, he alone remaining in the place. Prajāpati tells him to sacrifice again, and the substance of the whole is that Nārāyaṇa placed himself in all the worlds, in all the gods, in all the Vedas and in all the vital airs, and they were placed in him. This shadows forth the rising of Nārāyaṇa to the dignity of the Supreme Soul, who pervades all and in whom all things exist and who in the beginning sent forth all the gods, being himself their receptacle or resting place as indicated in RV. X, 82, 6. In another place (XIII, 6, 1) Puruṣa Nārāyaṇa is mentioned as having conceived the idea of a Pañcarātra Sattra (continued sacrifices for five days) as the means of obtaining superiority over all beings and becoming all beings. He performed the sacrifices and attained to that dignity. Here also Nārāyaṇa's becoming the Supreme Ruler and becoming all are spoken of. Nārāyaṇa is represented as the author of the Puruṣasūkta (RV. X, 90). This appears to be as much a fanciful representation, as that of Viśvakarman and others as authors of other hymns. As in these last cases, it has a connection with the deity to which the hymn refers, so that Nārāyaṇa is another name of the Puruṣa, and these two names are associated together, as we have seen, in the above citations from the Śatapatha-Brāhmaṇa. In the Taittirīya-Āraṇyaka (X, 11) Nārāyaṇa is described with all the attributes of the Supreme Soul, which are usually found mentioned in the Upaniṣads. In the Mahābhārata and Purāṇas, he figures as the supreme god, especially in connection with the creation; mythologically he is represented as lying on the body of a huge serpent in the ocean of milk, the original conception of his connection with the primeval waters being still kept to.

Nārāyaṇa thus became an object of worship. In the Ghosuṇḍi inscription noticed before, there is what appears to be a dedication of an enclosure to Nārāyaṇa (Nārāyaṇa-Vāṭikā).

§ 33. The heaven of this Nārāyaṇa was the Śvetadvīpa or white island. In the Kathāsaritsāgara (54, 19; 21; 23) Naravāhanadatta is represented to have been carried to the white island by Devasiddhi and to Hari reposing on the body of the serpent Śeṣa and attended by Nārada and other devotees. In another place in the same work (115, 101—3) certain gods are spoken of as having gone to Śvetadvīpa and seen Hari in a house made of great gems lying on the serpent bed with Lakṣmī sitting at his feet. In the Harivaṃśa (14 384) it is stated that Yogins and Kāpilasāṃkhyas who desire Mokṣa or final deliverance, go to the white island or Śvetadvīpa, by reciting the prayer and praise composed by Balin. Evidently, therefore, Śvetadvīpa or white island is the heaven in which Nārāyaṇa, spoken of sometimes as Hari, dwells. It corresponds to the Vaikuṇṭha of Viṣṇu, the Kailāsa of Śiva, and the Goloka of Gopālakṛṣṇa; and to that heaven of Nārāyaṇa it was that Nārada went and saw him and learned from him the monotheistic religion of Vāsudeva. There is, therefore, no need to suppose that that white island was a Christian country peopled by white races.

§ 34. Nārāyaṇa, being thus evolved as the Supreme Being in the later Brāhmaṇic period, was, of course, prior to Vāsudeva, and in the epic times when the worship of the latter arose, Vāsudeva was identified with Nārāyaṇa. In the Vanaparvan (chaps. 188, 189) there is a description of the condition of things at the time of dissolution of the universe, in which it is stated that there was water everywhere and there was a boy lying on a couch on a branch of a Nyagrodha tree. He opened his mouth and took in Mārkaṇḍeya, who roamed in the inside and saw the whole universe and was struck with wonder. Then the boy vomited or threw him out, when he saw again the waters alone. Mārkaṇḍeya then asked the boy who he was; then he said: "Formerly I gave to waters the name of Nārāḥ, and those were my resting place (Ayana), and therefore I am Nārāyaṇa", and thus he goes on to describe his greatness. Finally Mārkaṇḍeya, who tells the whole story, says to Yudhiṣṭhira that Janārdana, his relative, is this same Nārāyaṇa. The burden of the whole of the Nārāyaṇīya section seems to be this identity between Nārāyaṇa and Vāsudeva. Besides this Nārāyaṇa, the creator of all, there was a tradition about another who was always associated with Nara. This companionship seems to be traceable to the Upaniṣad idea of two birds dwelling in a tree, friends and associates of each other. That one of those, who is called the lord and the onlooker, is in the present tradition Nārāyaṇa and the other, who is engaged in eating the fruit of the tree, Nara. The old idea was transferred to the new conception of Nārāyaṇa as the resting place or abode of all men. In the opening chapter of the Nārāyaṇīya it is stated that Nārāyaṇa, the eternal soul of the universe, with four forms became the son of Dharma. The four forms or four sons were Nara, Nārāyaṇa, Hari and Kṛṣṇa. The first two of these devoted themselves to the practice of austerities in the Badarikāśrama. The same story is given in the Vāmana-Purāṇa (chap. 6). These four are represented as the sons of Dharma and had Ahiṃsā (non-killing) as their mother. This story seems to be significant. About the time when the new systems of religion arose, the ideas that were undergoing fermentation were Dharma or righteousness and Ahiṃsā or non-slaughter as against the old ceremonial of sacrificial rites and the killing of animals in accordance with it. These four names, therefore, were names connected with the introduction of a new system of religion, not heterodox, which concerned itself with righteousness and non-slaughter of animals. That is what appears to be meant by Dharma being called the father of these four and Ahiṃsā their mother. Nara and Nārāyaṇa are sometimes called Ṛṣis, and that is probably to be traced to the conception of Nārāyaṇa as the Ṛṣi or composer of the Puruṣasūkta. These gods must have been very famous at the time when the Mahābhārata was composed, since in the opening stanza of the different books obeisance is made to these two gods. In the Vanaparvan (12, 46; 47) Janārdana is represented to have said to Arjuna: "Oh invincible one, thou art Nara and I am Hari Nārāyaṇa and we, the sages Nara-Nārāyaṇa, have come to this world at the proper time; thou art not different from me, oh Pārtha, and I am not different from thee; it is not possible to know any difference between us." In chap. 30 (verse 1) of the same Parvan the god of gods (Śiva) says to Arjuna: "In a former birth (body) thou wast Nara and with Nārāyaṇa for thy companion performedst austerities for many thousands of years in Badarī". In the Udyogaparvan (49, 19) it is said: "The two heroes, Vāsudeva and Arjuna, who are great warriors, are the old gods Nara and Nārāyaṇa. This is the tradition." In this manner there are a good many examples of the identification of Arjuna and Vāsudeva with Nara and Nārāyaṇa. And thus the old tradition about the two Ṛṣis who were warriors at the same time was brought into connection with the two interlocutors of the Bhagavadgītā.

VIII. Identification of Vāsudeva with Viṣṇu.

§ 35. Viṣṇu is a Vedic deity. There are but few hymns addressed to him in RV.; but his personality is by no means unimportant. The long strides which he takes, and the three steps by which he measures the universe, are always described with an enthusiastic spirit. His first two steps can be discerned and approached by men, but the third no one can dare transgress, and it is beyond the flight of birds (RV. I. 155, 5). The wise see the highest place of Viṣṇu (paramam padam), as it were an eye fixed in the heaven (RV. I. 22, 20). In the highest place of Viṣṇu there is a well of honey, and there the gods rejoice (RV. I, 154, 5). Viṣṇu appears as the comrade and helper of Indra.

Viṣṇu, however, in spite of his comparatively subordinate position in RV. began to rise in importance in the time of the Brāhmaṇas, while during the epic and Purāṇic period he rose to the rank of the supreme spirit. The moment which seems to have been in operation during this process of elevation, was reverence for the third step or the mysterious highest abode of Viṣṇu beyond the ken of all. In the Brāhmaṇic period we have the mention of Agni as the lowest of the gods and Viṣṇu as the highest (AB. 1, 1). Then we have a story in Śatapatha-Brāhmaṇa and Taittirīya-Āraṇyaka of a sacrificial session held by the gods for the attainment of splendour, glory and food. They proposed to themselves that he amongst them, who by his deeds reached the end of the sacrifice before the others, should attain the highest place among them all. Viṣṇu reached the end before the others, and he thus became the highest of the gods; and therefore they say that Viṣṇu is the highest of the gods (ŚB. XIV, 1, 1). When this was written, Viṣṇu had already attained to the supreme dignity, and the story is invented to account for it. There is again in the same Brāhmaṇa (1, 2, 5) the story of Viṣṇu the dwarf. When the gods and Asuras were contending for a place for sacrifice, the latter agreed that they would allow as much land for the former as was equal to the size of the dwarf. Viṣṇu was then made to lie down, but gradually he grew so large as to encompass the whole earth, and so the gods got the whole earth. Here a miraculous power has been attributed to Viṣṇu, though he is not necessarily the Supreme Spirit. In the Maitri-Upaniṣad (VI, 13) food is called the form of Bhagavad-Viṣṇu, which sustains the universe. In the Kaṭha-Upaniṣad (III, 9) the progress of the human soul is compared to a journey, and the end of the path which he traverses is called the highest place of Viṣṇu (paramam padam). This is the final goal and the abode of eternal bliss, and the use of the word in this sense lends support to the view that the elevation of Viṣṇu to the dignity of the Supreme Being was due to the fact that the expression was capable of being used to denote this sense. Some time after, Viṣṇu became even a household god. In the ceremony of the seven steps contained in the marriage ritual the bridegroom has to say to the bride, when she puts forth a step: "May Viṣṇu lead you or be with you." This formula occurs in the Gṛhyasūtras of Āpastamba, Hiraṇyakeśin and Pāraskara, but not in that of Āśvalāyana. In epic times Viṣṇu grew to be in every respect the Supreme Spirit; and Vāsudeva is identified with Viṣṇu. In chapters 65 and 66 of the Bhīṣmaparvan noticed before, the Supreme Spirit is addressed as Nārāyaṇa and Viṣṇu and is identified with Vāsudeva.

In the Anugītā portion of the Āśvamedhikaparvan (chaps. 53—55) Kṛṣṇa, while returning to Dvārakā, meets on the way a sage of the name of Uttaṅka of the Bhṛgu race. The sage asks Kṛṣṇa whether he had established peace between the contending kinsmen, Pāṇḍus and Kurus, and established affectionate relations between them. Kṛṣṇa replies that the Kurus had been destroyed and the Pāṇḍus were in possession of the supreme sovereignty. The sage got angry and said that he would pronounce a curse against Kṛṣṇa, but if he explained to him the philosophy of the soul (Adhyātma), he would desist. Kṛṣṇa then does explain this philosophy at the request of Uttaṅka and shows him his universal form (Virāṭ svarūpam). The Svarūpa is the same as, or similar to, that shown to Arjuna according to the Bhagavadgītā, but it is here called the Vaiṣṇava form (rūpa), which name does not occur in the other passage. Thus then between the period of the Bhagavadgītā and that of the Anugītā the identity of Vāsudeva-Kṛṣṇa with Viṣṇu had become an established fact. In the Śāntiparvan (chap. 43) Yudhiṣṭhira addressing Kṛṣṇa sings a hymn of praise, in which Kṛṣṇa is identified with Viṣṇu. In the epic times, Viṣṇu is regarded as the Supreme Spirit, but the names of Nārāyaṇa and Vāsudeva-Kṛṣṇa apparently occur more frequently or are more prominent.

§ 36. Still many parts of the Mahābhārata represent a condition of things in which the divinity of Vāsudeva-Kṛṣṇa was not generally acknowledged. In the above passage from the Anugītā, the sage Uttaṅka is about to pronounce a curse on Kṛṣṇa, as if he was an ordinary individual, and desists only when his universal form is shown to him. Similarly in many passages noticed by Dr. Muir (O. S. T. IV, pp. 205ff.) Kṛṣṇa's divinity is denied; and Saṃjaya and Bhīṣma make strenuous efforts to establish it. What appears to be the fact is that the religion of Vāsudeva, in which divine honours were paid to him, was professed by the Sātvatas, as observed in several of the passages noticed above, and its gradual extension to other tribes and people of the country is shadowed forth in these portions of the great epic. In the Purāṇic times, however, the cult of Vāsudeva ceased to be militant, and three streams of religious thought, namely the one flowing from Viṣṇu, the Vedic god at its source, another from Nārāyaṇa, the cosmic and philosophic god, and the third from Vāsudeva, the historical god, mingled together decisively and thus formed the later Vaiṣṇavism. There is, however, a fourth stream, which in modern times in some of the systems of Vaiṣṇavism has acquired an almost exclusive predominance, and to this we shall now direct our attention.

IX. Identification of Vāsudeva-Kṛṣṇa with the Cowherd God (Gopāla-Kṛṣṇa).

§ 37. There is no allusion to the cowherd Kṛṣṇa in the authorities we have hitherto quoted. The inscriptions, the work of Patañjali and even the Nārāyaṇīya itself indicate no knowledge of the existence of such a god. In the last the Avatāra of Vāsudeva is mentioned as having been assumed for the destruction of Kaṃsa, but of none of the demons whom the cowherd Kṛṣṇa killed in the cow-settlement (Gokula). The contrast between this and the statements in the Harivaṃśa (vv. 5876—5878), Vâyu-Purāṇa, chap. 98, vv. 100—102, and Bhāgavata-Purāṇa, II, 7, of Kṛṣṇa's Avatāra having been assumed for destroying all the demons that appeared in the cow-settlement as well as of Kaṃsa is significant. When these works were written, the legend about the cowherd Kṛṣṇa must have already become current and his identification with Vāsudeva-Kṛṣṇa been effected. And the story of the Vṛṣṇi prince Vāsudeva having been brought up in a cow-settlement is incongruous with his later career as depicted in the Mahābhārata. Nor does any part of it require the presupposition of such a boyhood as has been ascribed to him.

In the Sabhāparvan (chap. 41), however, Śiśupāla in traducing Kṛṣṇa alludes to his valorous deeds, such as the killing of Pūtanā and others, which were done in the cow-settlement, and speaks of Bhīṣma's having praised them. But the praise bestowed on Kṛṣṇa by Bhīṣma (chap. 38) does not contain a mention of these deeds. This passage therefore is interpolated [1]).

The name Govinda does occur in the Bhagavadgītā and other parts of Mahābhārata. It is an ancient name, beeing derived by a Vārtika on P. III, 1, 138. If this name was given to Kṛṣṇa, because of his having had to do with cows, while a boy in Gokula, and his previous history in the cow-settlement was known, when the genuine portions of the Mahābhārata were composed, we should have found an etymology of the name expressive of that connection. But, on the contrary, in the Ādiparvan it is stated that Govinda is so called, because in the form of a boar he found the earth (Go) in the waters, which he agitated (chap. 21, 12); and in the Śāntiparvan (chap. 342, 70) Vāsudeva says: "I am called Govinda by the gods, because formerly I found the earth which was lost and lodged in a den". The origin of the name may be traced to this legend, but more probably Govinda is a later form of Govid, which in the Ṛgveda is used as an epithet of Indra in the sense of 'the finder of the cows'. This epithet, as another, Keśiniṣūdana, which is also applicable to Indra, must have been transferred to Vāsudeva-Kṛṣṇa, when he came to be looked upon as the chief god.

From all this it appears that the story of Kṛṣṇa's boyhood in the Gokula was unknown till about the beginning of the Christian Era. The Harivaṃśa, which is the chief authority for it, contains the word *dīnāra*, corresponding to the Latin word *denarius*, and consequently must have been written about the third century of the Christian era. Some time before that the stories of Kṛṣṇa's boyhood must have been current. The nature of the tribe of cowherds among whom Kṛṣṇa lived, is to be gathered from the words of the boy-god addressed to his foster-father Nanda, in order to dissuade him from celebrating a festival to Indra, and induce him to worship the mountain Govardhana instead. "We are cowherds", he says, "wandering in forests, main-

1) The Southern recension of the Mahābhārata contains many interpolations. In the Nārāyaṇīya chap. 338 of the Northern recension corresponds to chap. 344 of the Southern. We have six verses in the latter which are not contained in the former. They speak of animals made of flour being killed instead of real live animals. This is a later doctrine, which is strongly advocated by the Mādhva Vaiṣṇavas, but denied with as much pertinacity by Smārtas. In the present case in the Sabhāparvan, chap. 22, vv. 27—36 about Kṛṣṇa's doings in Gokula are in S. and not in N. Chap. 23 in S. about Kṛṣṇa's birth and removal to Gokula is not in N. Chap. 24, S. vv. 4—5 about Jarāsaṃdha's declining to fight with Kṛṣṇa, because he was a Gopa, are not found in chap. 23, N., which corresponds to that chapter. Chaps. 33 and 34 in S. are not in N. The first is about Sahadeva's expedition to the Pāṇḍya country and the second about Ghaṭotkaca's being sent to Laṅkā and Vibhīṣaṇa's paying tribute out of respect for Kṛṣṇa. At the end of chap. 39 in S., corresponding to chap. 36 in N., there is an interpolated passage, in which the worship done to Kṛṣṇa is derided as having been done to a Gopa or cowherd. This is not found in N. Chaps. 42—61 in S. are not found in N. They contain a mention of the Avatāras of Viṣṇu and his exploits in Gokula. Chap. 64 in S. corresponds to chap. 41 in N. Thus attempts have always been made to bring by means of interpolations the stories told in the Mahābhārata to the form which they subsequently assume. The passage dealt with in the text is a clear interpolation.

taining ourselves on cows, which are our wealth; cows are our deities, and mountains and forests" (H. 3808). The cowherds lived in a Ghoṣa or temporary encampment, which was capable of being easily removed from place to place, as when they left Vraja and encamped in Vṛndāvana (H. 3532). Ghoṣa is defined as Ābhīrapallī, which is generally understood as the enclosure of cowherds. But the original signification of the word Ābhīra is not a cowherd. It is the name of a race, whose original occupation was the tending of cows; and consequently the name became in later times equivalent to a 'cowherd'. For these reasons the cowherds among whom the boy-god Kṛṣṇa lived, belong to a nomadic tribe of the name of Ābhīras. These Ābhīras occupied the tract of country from Madhuvana near Mathurā to Anūpa and Ānarta, the regions about Dvārakā (H. 5161—5163). The Ābhīras are mentioned in the Mahābhārata (Mausalaparvan, chap. 7) as having attacked Arjuna, who was carrying the women of the Vṛṣṇis from Dvārakā to Kurukṣetra after the extinction of the male members of the Vṛṣṇi race. They are described as robbers and Mlecchas and lived near Pañcanada, which is probably Panjāb. The Viṣṇu-Purāṇa locates them near the Aparāntas (Konkan) and Saurāṣṭras, and Varāhamihira assigns them nearly the same position. Though they are mentioned as a southern people (Bṛ. S. 14, 12) and as living in the southwest (Bṛ. S. 14, 18), the Ābhīras must have migrated in large hordes into the country. They were at first mere nomads and afterwards settled in the country from about the eastern confines of the Panjāb to the vicinity of Mathurā and in the south up to Surāṣṭra or Kāṭhiāvāḍ, i. e., they must have occupied the whole of Rājputāna and a tract to the northeast of it. After they were settled, they took to various occupations, one of which was of course the old one, namely the tending of cows. The descendants of the old Ābhīras are called Āhirs at the present day, and we have now Āhirs following the occupation of carpenters, goldsmiths, cowherds and even priesthood. At one time they founded a kingdom in the northern part of the Marāṭha country, and an inscription of the ninth year of the Ābhīra king Īśvarasena, the son of Ābhīra Śivadatta, is found at Nāsik [1]). From the form of the characters the inscription probably belongs to the end of the third century. The Purāṇas mention a dynasty of Ābhīras composed of ten princes [2]). Another inscription of an earlier date is found at Gundā [3]) in Kāṭhiāvāḍ, in which the charities of Rudrabhūti, a general, who is called an Ābhīra, are mentioned. The inscription belongs to the reign of a Kṣatrapa king of the name of Rudrasiṃha, who held power in Śaka 102 corresponding to 180 A. D. If then about the end of the second century and in the third the Ābhīras enjoyed high political position, they must have migrated into the country in the first century. They probably brought with them the worship of the boy-god and the story of his humble birth, his reputed father's knowledge that he was not his son, and the massacre of the innocents. The two last correspond to Nanda's knowing that he was

---

[1]) Lüders, List of Brāhmī Inscriptions, Nr. 1137.
[2]) See Vāyu-Purāṇa, vol II. chap. 37, page 453, Bibl. Ind.
[3]) Lüders, List of Brāhmī Inscriptions, Nr. 963.

not the father of Kṛṣṇa and Kaṃsa's killing all children. The stories of Kṛṣṇa's boyhood, such as that of killing Dhenuka, a demon in the form of a wild ass, were brought by Ābhīras [1]), and others were developed after they came to India. It is possible that they brought with them the name Christ also, and this name probably led to the identification of the boy-god with Vāsudeva-Kṛṣṇa. The Goanese and the Bengalis often pronounce the name Kṛṣṇa as Kuṣṭo or Kriṣṭo, and so the Christ of the Ābhīras was recognised as the Sanskrit Kṛṣṇa. The dalliance of Kṛṣṇa with cowherdesses, which introduced an element inconsistent with the advance of morality into the Vāsudeva religion, was also an after-growth, consequent upon the freer intercourse between the wandering Ābhīras and their more civilised Āryan neighbours. Morality cannot be expected to be high or strict among races in the condition of the Ābhīras at the time; and their gay neighbours took advantage of its looseness. Besides, the Ābhīra women must have been fair and handsome as those of the Āhir-Gavaliyas or cowherds of the present day are.

§ 38. The story in the Buddhistic Ghatajātaka represents Vāsudeva and his brothers to be the sons of Kaṃsa's sister Devagabbhā and Upasāgara. They were made over to a man of the name of Andhakaveṇhu and to his wife Nandagopā who was the attendant of Devagabbhā. In this version there is a reminiscence of Devakī in the name Devagabbhā; and Nanda and Yaśodā or Gopā of Gokula are compounded together to form the name of the maid-servant who brought up Devagabbhā's sons as her sons. And in Andhakaveṇhu the names of the two kindred Yādava tribes, Andhaka and Vṛṣṇi, are compounded together, and the compound becomes the name of the husband of the maid-servant. Now as Andhaka and Vṛṣṇi were according to the highest authorities two distinct names and were the names of the two tribes, this story contains a confused reminiscence of the true legend and was of a later growth. All the Jātakas were not written at one and the same time. While some belong to a pre-Christian period, others must be assigned to post-Christian times, and the Ghatajātaka appears to me to belong to the latter class. The compound Nandagopā, therefore, though it contains a clear reminiscene of the fosterparents of the boy-god Kṛṣṇa, cannot be considered to point to a pre-Christian period for the identification of Vāsudeva-Kṛṣṇa with Gopāla-Kṛṣṇa.

X. The Pāñcarātra or Bhāgavata System.

§ 39. We have thus gone over the last element which goes to form the Vaiṣṇavism of later times. That element, however, does not form a prominent part, or forms no part at all, of the systems which are based upon the old Pāñcarātra doctrines. As we have seen, the Ekāntika Dharma or monotheistic religion was that which was promulgated by the Bhagavadgītā; but the Pāñcarātra system, consisting, as it did, of the worship of Vāsudeva and his several forms, shows no organic connection with that work, though Bhakti or devotion is common to

[1]) Journ. Roy. As. Soc. for 1907, p. 981.

both. That system must have developed in about the third century B. C., as we have already seen from the inscriptions and passages in books referred to before. Their being free from the Gopāla-Kṛṣṇa element is thus intelligible, and the later Vaiṣṇava systems, such as that of Rāmānuja and Madhva, which more or less recognise the old Bhāgavata doctrines or ideas, have entirely neglected that element. In other systems, however, it is recognised and in a general way in popular Vaiṣṇavism. The authorities on which the Bhāgavata system was based are the Pañcarātra-Samhitās; and Rāmānuja in his comments on the Brahmasūtras, II, 2, 39—42, quotes from some of these. The first quotation is from the Pauṣkara-Saṃhitā, which is intended to show that, when Brāhmaṇas worship the fourfold soul with the traditional names, it should be considered authoritative. The second is from the Sātvata-Saṃhitā, which is to the effect that this great Śāstra contains the secret of Brahman and imparts discrimination to Brāhmaṇas who worship the true Brahman bearing the name of Vāsudeva. There are two from the Parama-Saṃhitā. One of these gives the nature of Prakṛti, which is unsentient, of use to another than "itself", eternal, always changeable, composed of three qualities, and is the sphere within which the action of agents is done. The other represents somebody, probably Śāṇḍilya himself, as saying that he has studied all the Vedas with the dependent treatises and Vākovākya, but not having found the way to supreme bliss clearly stated in them. One of these Saṃhitās, bearing the name of Sātvata, has been printed and is available. It begins by saying that Nārada saw Paraśurāma on the Malaya Mountain and was told by him to visit the Ṛṣis, who were in search of the place of Hari, and to instruct them in the Sātvata method of worship (Kriyāmārga). Nārada does this and explains to them the secret traditional methods (Rahasyāmnāya). Nārāyaṇa is spoken of here as the supreme spirit. The secret methods were formerly explained by the bearer of the discus (Vāsudeva), when asked by Saṃkarṣaṇa. Saṃkarṣaṇa spoke to Viṣṇu at the beginning of the Tretā age, asking why his countenance had become red. The answer is: "Because the people will be afflicted with passion in this age". Being asked how they will be delivered from passion, Saṃkarṣaṇa is told that they will be delivered by adoring the eternal and highest Brahman in three ways. The Supreme Spirit, who has hands and feet and eyes everywhere and is endowed with six Guṇas or qualities, is Para or the Highest. It is one and the support of all. Besides this there is a triad, each member of which is distinguished from the others by a distinction in knowledge and other qualities. These three should be known as Vyūhas, or forms, who confer the desired fruit with ease. Balarāma then asks about the mode of service. Bhagavat then explains it as follows:— "When the pure Brahman, which is the aim and end of the creation, exists in the heart of qualified Brāhmaṇas, who worship Vāsudeva, the highest Śāstra, which is a great Upaniṣad of Brahman, springs forth from it for the redemption of the world and confers discrimination; it contains divine methods and has for its fruit final deliverance [1]). I will then

[1]) Two lines out of this are contained in the quotations from Rāmānuja given above.

explain that to you which is of various kinds. This Śāstra, along with Rahasya, is fruitful to those who have gone through Yoga with its eight parts and whose soul is devoted to mental sacrifice. The Yogins, who are Brāhmaṇas guided by the Vedas and who have given up the mixed worship, are competent for the worship of the single one, dwelling in the heart. The three orders, Kṣatriya and others, and those who are *prapanna* or have resorted to self-surrender are competent for the worship of the four Vyūhas accompanied by Mantras, and also unaccompanied by them, so far as regards the series of ceremonies concerning the four Vyūhas as well as the actions and the collection of Mantras concerning the Vibhavas [1]. All these persons should be free from attachment and absorbed in the performance of their duties and be devotees of the supreme lord by their deeds, words and mind. In this manner, the four (orders) become competent, when they are initiated (for service) with Mantras. Hear now the process concerning the single form". Then follows the statement of the mystic arrangement of letters and formulae and the meditations. This work throughout contains the mystic modes of worship by means of Mantras variously arranged. The allusion at the end of chap. 66 of the Bhīṣmaparvan to Saṃkarṣaṇa's having sung or expounded Vāsudeva according to the Sātvata rites (Vidhi) refers in all probability to such rites as are detailed in this Sātvata-Saṃhitā.

Śaṃkarācārya, in his notice of the Bhāgavata school under Br. S. II, 2, 42, gives five methods of worshipping the supreme lord, Bhagavat Vāsudeva, in his fourfold form, which, along with the explanations given by the commentators, are as follows: — (1) Abhigamana or going to the temple of the deity with the speech, the body and the mind centred on him; (2) Upādāna or collecting the materials of worship; (3) Ijyā or worship; (4) Svādhyāya or the muttering of the usual Mantra; (5) Yoga or meditation. By worshipping him in these ways for a hundred years, all sin is destroyed and the devotee reaches Bhagavat.

§ 40. The book called Nāradapañcarātra, published by the Asiatic Society of Bengal, contains the Saṃhitā called Jñānāmṛtasāra. The glories of the boy Kṛṣṇa are sung in this work. Nārada desiring to know Kṛṣṇa's greatness and the methods of his worship is recommended to go to Śaṃkara, or Śiva, and seek instruction from him. Nārada repairs to Kailāsa and enters the palace of Śaṃkara, which has seven gates. At these gates there are pictures and sculptures relating to the scenes of Kṛṣṇa's childhood and his various deeds in the cow-settlement, such as Vṛndāvana, Yamunā, Kṛṣṇa's sitting on the Kadamba tree with the garments of the cowherdesses and their return from bath in the Yamunā river in a naked-condition, the destruction of the serpent Kāliya, the holding up of the Govardhana mountain on the palm of his hand, the journey to Mathurā and the lamentations of the Gopīs and his foster parents, etc. Sculptures representing some of these events were discovered on a pillar excavated at Mandor near Jodhpur about two years ago [2]. The age of the pillar has been

[1] Vibhavas are the incarnations of the Supreme Spirit.
[2] Archæological Survey of India, Annual Report 1905—1906, p. 135 ff.

considered not earlier than the fourth century A. D. The idea of imagining such sculptures on the gates of Śiva's palace could have occurred to a writer only when the practice of adorning gates and pillars with such sculptures had become general. The Jñanāmṛtasāra, therefore, could not have been earlier than the fourth century and appears to me to be considerably later, as will be presently shown. Goloka or the world of cows is the heaven in which Kṛṣṇa dwells and which is reached by those who adore him, and several Mantras are given in this book, the reciters of which are rewarded with a place in that heaven. The servitude of Hari through devotion is the highest Mukti or absolution according to this work. There are six modes of adoring Hari, viz. (1) remembrance of him, (2) utterance (of his name and glory), (3) salutation, (4) resorting to his feet, (5) constant worship of him with devotion, and (6) surrender of the whole soul to him. The Bhāgavata-Purāṇa adds three more, viz. hearing (his praise), servitude, and companionship (Sakhyam). These last two are preliminary to the surrendering of the whole soul. In this book Rādhā is mentioned as the highest of the women whom Kṛṣṇa loved, and she is represented to have been formed by the original lord becoming two, one of which was Rādhā (II, 3, 24 ff.). The exaltation of this woman is thus one of the main objects of this Saṃhitā.

The Saṃhitā we have been considering, seems thus to be entirely devoted to the advancement of the cult of the Kṛṣṇa of the cow-settlement or Gokula and of his beloved mistress Rādhā, now raised to the dignity of his eternal consort. The Vyūhas which form a peculiarity of the Pāñcarātra school, are not mentioned in it. The creed afterwards promulgated by Vallabhācārya is exactly similar to that set forth in this book. This Saṃhitā, therefore, must have been written a short time before Vallabha, that is, about the beginning of the sixteenth century. The Rāmānujīyas consider this Saṃhitā to be apocryphal.

XI. The Avatāras of Viṣṇu or Nārāyaṇa.

§ 41. An Avatāra or incarnation of a god differs from mere identification of two gods in this, that in the former case the god that is considered an incarnation acts like a human being, or even a brute, at the same time that he has the miraculous powers of a god. The transition, however, from the idea of identification to that of incarnation is easy. The person in the flesh is identified with the god who is a mere spirit, so that the habit of thought which in Vedic times led to the identification of some of the Vedic deities with Agni, has been at work even in this conception of the Avatāras. The Avatāras of Nārāyaṇa or Viṣṇu are variously given by the various authorities. In the passage in the Nārāyaṇīya translated above, six only are given, viz. the boar, the man-lion, the dwarf, Rāma of the Bhṛgu race, Rāma Dāśarathi, and that assumed for the destruction of Kaṃsa (Vāsudeva-Kṛṣṇa). This passage is followed after a short interval by another in which the incarnations are given as ten, the additions being Haṃsa (swan), Kūrma (tortoise), and Matsya (fish) in the beginning and Kalkin at the end. The one preceding Kalkin is called Sātvata, i. e. Vāsudeva-Kṛṣṇa. This passage, following so closely on the first, appears to be interpolated when the number of Avatāras became fixed at ten. The Harivaṃśa mentions the six given in the first of these two passages. The Vāyu-Purāṇa gives the incarnations in two passages (chap. 97, vv. 72 ff. and chap. 98, vv. 63 ff.), in the first of which there are twelve, but some of them appear rather to be incarnations of Śiva and Indra. In the second the number ten, which about that time must have come into usage, is made up by adding to the six mentioned above the four: Dattātreya, one unnamed called the fifth, Vedavyāsa, and Kalkin. In the Varāha-Purāṇa we have the ten incarnations which came to be accepted later, containing the Fish, Tortoise, Buddha, and Kalkin, in addition to the six mentioned above. The Agni-Purāṇa gives the same ten. The Bhāgavata-Purāṇa enumerates the incarnations in three different passages. In the first, contained in chapter 3 of Book I, twenty-two are mentioned. In the passage in chapter 7 of Book II we have twenty-three, and in chapter 4 of Book XI sixteen are given. It deserves notice that among the Avatāras mentioned in this Purāṇa are Sanatkumāra; the divine sage (Nārada), who expounded the Sātvata system; Kapila, who explained to Āsuri the Sāṃkhya system, which determines the collection of principles; Dattātreya, who is represented to have taught Ānvīkṣikī to Alarka and Prahrāda and the attainment of excellence by means of Yoga to Yadu and Haihaya; Ṛṣabha, son of Nābhi and Merudevī, who abandoned attachment to all things, acquired serenity and, looking at all things alike and possessing Yoga power, acted as if he were a non-living creature; and lastly Dhanvantari, the teacher of the science of medicine. Rsabha, from the parentage given here and other indications, appears clearly to be the same as the first Tīrthaṃkara of the Jainas. He was probably raised to the dignity of an incarnation as the Buddha of the Buddhists was. There is hardly a wide-spread cult of any of these incarnations except Dattātreya, who is adored and worshipped by a large number of people to this day, and Rāma of whom more will have to be said hereafter. Kṛṣṇa, of course, though included in the Avatāras stands on independent grounds, and his worship over the widest area is due, not to his having been considered an Avatāra, but to his being the peculiar object of adoration to the followers of a new religion or religious reform, as I have ventured to call it, which first took its rise among the Sātvatas.

XII. Later Traces of the Bhāgavata School and General Vaiṣṇavism.

§ 42. We will now resume the chronological thread we have traced from Megasthenes to the latest inscription, that at Nānāghāṭ, which is to be referred to the first century B. C. For about four centuries after this there are no epigraphical or sculptural traces of any Brāhmaṇic religious system; and they reappear about the time when the Guptas rose to power in the first quarter of the fourth century. The Gupta princes, Candragupta II, Kumāragupta, and Skandagupta, are styled Paramabhāgavatas on their coins. They were thus worshippers of Bhagavat or Vāsudeva. Their dates range from 400 to 464 A. D.

On a panel at Udayagiri, there is a figure of a four-armed god, who is probably Viṣṇu. The inscription below bears the date 82 G. E., i.e. 400 A. D.[1])

There is a pillar at Bhitarī in the Ghāzīpur District of the U.P., on which there is an inscription which records the installation of an image of Śārṅgin and the grant of a village for its worship by Skandagupta, whose dates range between 454 and 464 A.D.[2]) Śārṅgin must have been Vāsudeva-Kṛṣṇa, Skandagupta himself being a Bhāgavata.

A temple of Viṣṇu was erected in 456 A. D. by Cakrapālita, son of Parṇadatta, appointed viceroy of Surāṣṭra or Kāṭhiāvāḍ by Skandagupta. The inscription which records this opens with an invocation of Viṣṇu in the Vāmana or the dwarf incarnation[3]).

In an inscription at Eraṇ in the Sāgar district, C. P., belonging to the reign of Budhagupta and bearing the date 165 G. E., corresponding to 483 A. D., Mātṛviṣṇu and his younger brother Dhanyaviṣṇu are represented to have erected a Dhvajastambha or flag-staff in honour of the god Janārdana. Mātṛviṣṇu is called a great devotee of Bhagavat *(atyanta-Bhagavad-bhakta)*[4]). The god Janārdana must therefore be Vāsudeva-Kṛṣṇa.

A copperplate inscription of A. D. 495, found near the village of Khoh in Bāghelkhaṇḍ, records the grant of a village, by a chief named Jayanātha, to Bhagavat for repairs to the temple of that god and for the performance of ordinary ceremonies[5]).

An inscription on an iron pillar near the Kutub Minār at Delhi speaks of that pillar as a flag-staff to Viṣṇu erected by a great king named Candra, who enjoyed universal sovereignty and was a great devotee of Viṣṇu. The inscription is not dated, but if the king Candra referred to here was Candragupta II, it belongs to the latter part of the fourth century or the beginning of the fifth[6]).

In his Meghadūta (v. 15) Kālidāsa compares the cloud adorned with a piece of a rain-bow, with Viṣṇu in the shape of the cow-herd adorned with a shining peacock feather. Here there is an identification of Gopāla-Kṛṣṇa with Viṣṇu; and, if the Vikramāditya who was the patron of Kālidāsa was Candragupta II of the Gupta dynasty, this must be considered to be a record belonging to the early part of the fifth century.

We have already alluded to the sculptures on a pillar excavated at Mandor near Jodhpur. These sculptures represent the overturning of a cart by the baby Kṛṣṇa, the holding of the Govardhana Mountain

[1]) Corp. Inscr. Ind. Vol. III, p. 21 ff.
[2]) Ibid. p. 52 ff.
[3]) Ibid. p. 56 ff.
[4]) Ibid. p. 88 ff.
[5]) Ibid. p. 121 ff.
[6]) Ibid. p. 139 ff.

by Kṛṣṇa on the palm of his hand, and such other events. I refer them tentatively to the fifth century.

In Śaka 500, Maṅgalīśa, a prince belonging to the early Calukya dynasty of the Deccan, got a cave scooped out, in which a temple to Viṣṇu was constructed, and an image of Viṣṇu was installed in it. The provision for the performance of Nārāyaṇabali (offerings to Nārāyaṇa) was made by assigning the revenues of a village for the purpose [1]). In this cave-temple there are figures of Viṣṇu or Nārāyaṇa lying on the body of a serpent, with Lakṣmī rubbing his feet, and of the Boar and Narasiṃha incarnations, and of Harihara in which the peculiar marks of Hari, or Viṣṇu, and of Hara, or Śiva, are combined [2]).

In mentioning the priests who are qualified to install and consecrate the images of certain gods, Varāhamihira says that this function in the case of Viṣṇu should be assigned to Bhāgavatas [3]). Bhāgavatas were thus recognised in his time as the peculiar worshippers of Viṣṇu. Varāhamihira died in Śaka 509. i. e. 587 A. D. [4]).

Amarasiṃha, the author of the well-known Kośa or thesaurus, was a Buddhist. After giving the words expressive of gods generally, when he comes to the names of particular gods, he begins by giving those of Buddha and proceeds next to give the names Viṣṇu, Nārāyaṇa, etc., of which we have thirty-nine. After finishing these he says that Vasudeva was his father. This means that the thirty-nine names previously given are the names of Vāsudeva. If we examine these, we shall find that before Amara's time Vāsudeva had already been identified with Viṣṇu and Nārāyaṇa. Except the name Dāmodara, there is no other connecting Vāsudeva with Gokula, and the etymology of Dāmodara which connects him with that cow-settlement is doubtful. While Kaṃsārāti, or the enemy of Kaṃsa, does occur, we have no such name as Pūtanāri, the enemy of Pūtanā, or any other derived from the names of the many demons he slew while he was a boy. There are also no names of incarnations except the doubtful one, Balidhvaṃsin, which, however, has been interpreted by one commentator as the destroyer of ignorance by means of Bali or oblations. There are, of course, several names derived from those of other demons, such as Madhuripu and Kaiṭabhajit, but these are not the enemies destroyed by Viṣṇu in his incarnations as they are usually mentioned. After giving the name of the father of Vāsudeva-Kṛṣṇa, Amara proceeds to mention those of Saṃkarṣaṇa, or Baladeva, and afterwards of Pradyumna and Aniruddha. Thereafter he mentions those of Lakṣmī, the wife of Nārāyaṇa or Viṣṇu, then those of the weapons of the god and his ornaments, and ends with the names of Garuḍa, the vehicle of Viṣṇu. After finishing these he proceeds to the other great god of the Hindus, Śambhu or Śiva. Here Amara appears clearly to have in view the four forms, or Vyūhas, of Vāsudeva recognised by the Bhāgavatas, so that in his time the prevalent form of Vaiṣṇavism was that embraced by the

[1]) Ind. Ant. Vol III. p. 305; Vol. VI. p. 363.
[2]) Fergusson and Burgess, Cave Temples, p. 407.
[3]) Bṛ. S. 60, 19.
[4]) Bhau Daji, Lit. Remains, p. 240.

Bhāgavatas. Amara's exact age is doubtful, but, if he was a Buddhist, he must have belonged to the Mahāyāna sect, the sacred language of which was Sanskrit. This system was in full swing in the fourth, fifth and sixth centuries [1]). Amarasiṃha, therefore, must have flourished in this last century, or, if we believe in the traditional verse which asserts his contemporaneousness with Kālidāsa and in Candragupta II as Vikramāditya, the famous patron of learning, he must have flourished in the early part of the fifth century. The identity of Vāsudeva-Kṛṣṇa with Gopāla-Kṛṣṇa is very rarely alluded to, while that with Viṣṇu and Nārāyaṇa is clearly set forth.

About the middle of the seventh century Bāṇa in his Harṣacarita represents a sage of the name of Divākaramitra, who, originally a Brāhmaṇa, became a Buddhist, as being surrounded in the Vindhya mountains, where he had his abode, by followers of a number of sects, two of which were the Bhāgavatas and Pāñcarātras.

In the Daśāvatāra temple at Ellora there is a figure of Viṣṇu on the body of a serpent with Lakṣmī rubbing his feet and Brahmā seated on a lotus coming out of his navel. There are also images of the Narasiṃha, Vāmana and Varāha incarnations, as well as of Kṛṣṇa holding the Govardhana Mountain over the flocks of the cow-settlement. This temple was constructed about the middle of the eighth century in the time of Dantidurga of the Rāṣṭrakūṭa race. There are similar figures of Avatāras in the Kailāsa temple scooped out in the latter part of the eighth century, in the time of Kṛṣṇa I, uncle of Dantidurga. Among these is also the scene of the destruction of Kāliya by Kṛṣṇa.

There is an inscription in a cave at Pabhōsa, about 32 miles south-west of Allahabad, which probably had a human figure above and runs thus: "The maker of the images of Śrī-Kṛṣṇa and the milk-maids". The date is uncertain, but the inscription is referred to the seventh or eighth century by Bühler [2]).

At Sirpur in the Raipur district, C. P., over the front of a shrine-door there is a sculpture of Viṣṇu or Nārāyaṇa reclining on the folds of the serpent Śeṣa, and from his navel springs a lotus on which is seated Brahmā. Down the two outer sides of the shrine-door are some of the incarnations of Viṣṇu, one of which is that of Rāma and another of Buddha, whose image is in the usual meditative attitude. The temple belongs probably to the eighth century [3]).

At Osia, 32 miles north of Jodhpur, there is an old temple adjoining to the house of the local Jahagirdar. On two pilasters, projecting from the shrine into the Sabhāmaṇḍapa, are two images of deities both seated on Garuḍa. Both have four hands, but one of them holds a conch-shell, the discus, the mace and the lotus, and the other bears a plough-share and a mace in his two hands, the other two being empty. The last has his head canopied by a five-hooded serpent.

---

1) Vide my 'Peep into the Early History of India', Journ. Bo. Br. Roy. As. Soc., Vol. XX. p. 395.

2) Ep. Ind. Vol. II. p. 482.

3) Annual Progress Report of Archæological Survey, Western Circle, for 1903—04, p. 21.

They are apparently Vāsudeva and Saṃkarṣaṇa. The temple cannot be later then the ninth century [1]).

In a work called Dharmaparīkṣā Amitagati, the author, who was a Digambara Jaina, says that there were according to the legendary lore current among the Jainas sixty-three eminent men: the twelve supreme sovereigns, the twenty-four Arhats (Jinas), and nine Rāmas, nine Keśavas, and the nine enemies of these nine. The last of the Viṣṇus (Keśavas) was the son of Vasudeva, and his Brāhmaṇa devotees call him the pure, the supreme being. They say: "He who meditates upon the god Viṣṇu, who is all-pervading, a whole without parts, indestructible and unchangeable, who frees a man from old age and death, is free from misery". He is traditionally known to have ten forms or incarnations. These ten forms are the same as mentioned in the Varāha and Agni-Purāṇas (see above), and which are now generally accepted. Thus Buddha had come to be recognised as an incarnation of Viṣṇu before the date of the Dharmaparīkṣā, which is Vikrama 1070, corresponding to 1014 A. D. If the approximate date assigned to the temple at Sirpur is correct, Buddha must have been admitted into the Brāhmaṇic pantheon before the eighth century. Amitagati also speaks of the mighty Viṣṇu having become a cowherd in Nanda's Gokula and of the all-knowing, all-pervading protector of the world (Rāma) as being oppressed by the fire of separation from Sītā like a mortal lover.

Hence, we have evidence of the existence of the cult of Viṣṇu, principally in accordance with the mode professed by the Bhāgavatas from the fourth to the eleventh century. The doctrine of the incarnations had also become an article of ordinary faith, and the founder of Buddhism and the first Tīrthaṃkara of the Jainas also came later to be recognised as incarnations of Viṣṇu.

XIII. The Cult of Rāma.

§ 43. The architectural remains passed under review contain only figures of the incarnations of Viṣṇu and are not to be taken as proving the existence of the cult of any of these incarnations. But at the present day the cult of Rāma exists over a pretty wide area. In the temples and other religious structures hitherto noticed, there is none dedicated to his worship nor any flag-staff like those erected in honour of Janārdana or Vāsudeva-Kṛṣṇa. Rāma, however, was considered as an incarnation of Viṣṇu even in very early times. There are passages in the Rāmāyaṇa pointing to this, but there is good reason to believe that they are spurious or interpolated. But the passage in the Nārāyaṇīya, which we have frequently referred to, contains his name, and so do all the Purāṇas that have been noticed. These in themselves are not sufficient to enable us to determine approximately the period in which he came to be regarded as an incarnation. But in the tenth chapter of the Raghuvaṃśa the story of the birth of Rāma is preceded by the usual appeal to Viṣṇu or Nārāyaṇa lying on the body of the

[1]) See the forthcoming Annual Report of the Arch. Surv. of India.

great serpent, with Lakṣmī rubbing his feet, in the milky ocean and his promise to be born as a son of Daśaratha for the destruction of Rāvaṇa. Amitagati also speaks in 1014 A. D., as we have seen, of Rāma's being regarded as the all-knowing, all-pervading protector of the world. The Vāyu-Purāṇa, which is the earliest work of that class, must have been written about the fifth century; so that the belief in Rāma's being an incarnation of Viṣṇu existed in all probability in the early centuries of the Christian Era. But there is no mention of his name in such a work as that of Patañjali, nor is there any old inscription in which it occurs. Amarasiṃha, too, has no place for him in his scheme of Brāhmaṇic gods. These circumstances, as well as those mentioned above, show that, though he was regarded as an Avatāra, there was no cult in his honour. Still, as depicted by Vālmīki, Rāma was a high-souled hero and poets, including those nameless ones who wrote Purāṇas in the names of old Ṛṣis, particularly Bhavabhūti, still more highly exalted his character. Rāma, therefore, won a place in the heart of the Indian people, and that must have soon led to the foundation of the cult. But when this took place it is difficult to say. Madhva or Ānandatīrtha, the founder of a sect to be noticed hereafter, is represented to have brought the image of Digvijaya Rāma from Badarikāśrama and sent Naraharitīrtha to Jagannātha about the year 1264 A. D. [1]) to bring what was called the original idols of Rāma and Sītā. The cult of Rāma, therefore, must have come into existence about the eleventh century. There exist manuals giving the modes of worship by means of Mantras or formulae and magic circles, like those prescribed in the Sātvata-Saṃhitā for the worship of Vāsudeva. The ceremony in connection with his birth on the 9th of the bright half of Caitra is given in his Vratakhaṇḍa [2]) by Hemādri, who flourished in the thirteenth century. That writer, as well as Vṛddha-Hārīta [3]), gives the modes of worshipping him as an incarnation along with others on certain occasions, so that it appears that his worship as an incarnation has been of a longer duration than that based on terms of equality with Vāsudeva-Kṛṣṇa. Twenty-four images, differing from each other in the order in which the four objects, viz. the conch-shell, discus, mace and lotus, are placed in the four hands of the principal god Vāsudeva or Viṣṇu, are mentioned by both those authors, and the twenty-four names [4]) corresponding to these twenty-four images, Keśava, Nārāyaṇa, Govinda, etc., which include those of the four Vyūhas, are repeated by us at the beginning of every ceremony that we perform at the present day; that is, obeisance is made to the twenty-four forms of the god by usimg the word *namaḥ* (salutations) after the dative of each of the names, and the sense is

---

[1]) See below.

[2]) P. 941 (Bibl. Ind.)

[3]) Vratakhaṇḍa pp. 1034 ff.; Vṛddha-Hārīta-Smṛti (Ānandāśrama Sanskr. Ser.), chap. X. v. 145.

[4]) (1) Keśava, (2) Nārāyaṇa, (3) Mādhava, (4) Govinda, (5) Viṣṇu, (6) Madhusūdana, (7) Trivikrama, (8) Vāmana, (9) Śrīdhara, (10) Hṛṣīkeśa, (11) Padmanābha, (12) Dāmodara, (13) Saṃkarṣaṇa, (14) Vāsudeva, (15) Pradyumna, (16) Aniruddha, (17) Puruṣottama, (18) Adhokṣaja, (19) Narasiṃha, (20) Acyuta, (21) Janārdana, (22) Upendra, (23) Hari, (24) Śrīkṛṣṇa.

'Salutations to Keśava, Nārāyaṇa, etc.'. The name of Rāma, however, is not included in them, while two other Avatāras, Narasiṃha and Vāmana, are mentioned. Every Śrāddha ceremony is wound up by the expression "May Janārdana-Vāsudeva, who is a form of the ancestors, or the father, grandfather and great grandfather, be satisfied by this act". All this shows that Vāsudevism has penetrated into every one of our ordinary ceremonies, which include a repetition even of Vedic Mantras, while this is not at all the case with the cult of Rāma, which is, therefore, of a modern growth. There is a work, entitled the Adhyātma-Rāmāyaṇa, which Ekanātha [1]), a Mahārāṣṭra saint, who flourished in the sixteenth century, calls a modern treatise, composed of excerpts from older writings and having no pretence to be considered as emanating from the old Ṛṣis. The object of this work throughout has been to set forth the divinity of Rāma. The first book of it comprises what is called Rāmahṛdaya, which was narrated to Hanūmat by Sītā, who says that as the original Prakṛti, she does every thing and did all the deeds mentioned in the Rāmāyaṇa, while Rāma as the only existing soul is inactive, unchangeable and blessed, and is a mere witness of her deeds. After she has concluded, Rāma explains the threefold nature of the knowing spirit, viz. (1) the original, (2) that conditioned by Buddhi or finite intelligence, and (3) the appearances, the last two of which are fictitious. The fifth canto of the last book is styled Rāmagītā, which is meant to correspond to the Bhagavadgītā of Vāsudeva and which is narrated by Rāma to Lakṣmaṇa, who takes the place of Arjuna. The doctrine is thoroughly adualistic as that of the previous portion. The world and the individual soul are illusory, and one spirit alone exists. There is another book called Rāmagītā published in Madras, which represents itself to be contained in a larger work called Sattvapārāyaṇa and is composed of eighteen chapters like the genuine Bhagavadgītā. It is narrated to Hanūmat by Rāma. In the beginning it professes itself to be based on the one hundred and eight Upaniṣads, some of which are manifestly very recent. This work, therefore, must be a very modern compilation. Thus the works designed to give importance to Rāma as a religious teacher are of recent origin.

XIV. Vāsudevism or Vaiṣṇavism in the South.

§ 44. We have seen that Saṃkarṣaṇa and Vāsudeva had come to be worshipped as gods in the Marāṭha country by about the first century B. C. The cult must have spread further south up to the Tamil country, but there is no evidence to show at what time it was introduced there. The Bhāgavata-Purāṇa (Book XI, chap. 5, vv. 38—40) says, in the usual prophetic style, that in the Kali age there will be found men here and there devoted to Nārāyaṇa, but in large numbers in the Draviḍa country, where flow the rivers Tāmraparṇī, Kāverī and others, and that those who drink the water of these rivers will mostly be pure-hearted devotees of Vāsudeva. When the

[1]) See his Bhāvārtha-Rāmāyaṇa, Āraṇyakāṇḍa.

Purāṇa goes out of its beaten track to make such a statement as this, the fame of the devotees of Vāsudeva, who had flourished in the Tamil country, must have spread over other parts of India when the Purāṇa was compiled. The Purāṇa was regarded as sacred in the thirteenth century, when Ānandatīrtha, who flourished between about 1199 and 1278 A. D., places it on the same level as the Mahābhārata and devotes a treatise to the determination of its drift, as to that of the latter. About the same time Bopadeva prepared an abstract of it at the request of the councillor Hemādri. The Bhāgavata, therefore, must have been composed at least two centuries before Ānandatīrtha to account for the reputation of the sacred character which it acquired in his time. It cannot be very much older, for its style often looks modern and in copying from the older Purāṇas it falls into mistakes, such as the one pointed out by me in another place [1]). The Draviḍa devotees, therefore, noticed in the Bhāgavata, must have mostly flourished before the eleventh century. These devotees, who are known by the name of Āḷvārs, are generally reckoned as twelve in number and are divided into three classes by S. Krishnaswami Aiyangar [2]) in accordance with the received chronology which he follows to determine their sequence, though in itself it assigns a preposterously high antiquity to them. Their names, Tamil and Sanskrit, are as follows: —

Class	Tamil name	Sanskrit name
Ancient	Poygai Āḷvār	Saroyogin
	Bhūtattār	Bhūtayogin
	Pēy Āḷvār	Mahadyogin or Bhrāntayogin
	Tirumaḷiśai Āḷvār	Bhaktisāra
Later	Namm Āḷvār	Śaṭhakopa
		Madhurakavi
		Kulaśekhara
	Periy Āḷvār	Viṣṇucitta
	Aṇḍāḷ	Godā
Last	Toṇḍaraḍippoḍi	Bhaktāṅghrireṇu
	Tiruppāṇ Āḷvār	Yogivāhana
	Tirumangai Āḷvār	Parakāla

The date of the first, ordinarily given, is B. C. 4203 and of the last, B. C. 2706, and the others range between these two. Not only are these dates fanciful, but even the sequence shown above is unreliable. Krishnaswami places the last in the earlier half of the eighth century A. D. and all the preceding ones impliedly before that date. But there is distinct evidence to show that Kulaśekhara flourished much later. He was a king of Travancore, and one of the works composed by him styled Mukundamālā contains a verse from the Bhāgavata-

1) Early History of the Dekkan (Second Edition), pp. 32—33.

2) Ind. Ant. Vol. XXXV, p. 228.

Purāṇa (XI, 2, 36)[1]. Again in an inscription on a tablet, existing in a temple at Narēgal in the Dharwar district, translated by Dr. Fleet[2], it is stated that Permāḍi of the Sinda dynasty vanquished Kulaśekharāṅka, besieged Chaṭṭa, pursued Jayakeśin, and seized upon the royal power of Poysala and invested Dhorasamudra, the capital of the Poysala dynasty. In another inscription[3] this Permāḍi is represented to be a vassal of Jagadekamalla II, whose dates range between A. D. 1138 and 1150. While the former was in power as Mahāmaṇḍaleśvara in the seventh year of Jagadekamalla, i. e. in A. D. 1144, a certain grant was made by a body of sellers of betel leaves and nuts. The Kulaśekharāṅka, mentioned as being vanquished by this Permāḍi, must be a prince reigning on the western coast as the others, Jayakeśin, the Kadamba prince of Goa, the Hoysala king, and so forth, were. Putting this statement and the quotation from the Bhāgavata-Purāṇa together, it appears highly probable that the Āḷvār Kulaśekhara lived in the first half of the twelfth century. The sequence, therefore, given above cannot be implicitly believed in. Still it may be admitted that the earliest Āḷvārs flourished about the time of the revival of Brāhmaṇism and Hinduism in the north, which extended up to the Marāṭha country, as we have shown from inscriptions and antiquarian remains, and must have extended still farther to the south. The earliest Āḷvārs may be placed before, about the fifth or sixth century, but there is nothing to show that Vaiṣṇavism had not penetrated to the Tamil country earlier, i. e. about the first century. But an impetus, such as the rise of the Āḷvārs indicates, could in all probability come only from the energy of the revival.

The hostile relations into which the Āḷvārs and the Śaiva saints, Nāyanmārs, came with the Buddhists and Jainas, lend support to the view we have advocated.

The Āḷvārs composed, mostly in Tamil, what are called Prabandhas or songs in praise of the deity full of piety and devotion and containing also religious truths. They are considered as very sacred and spoken of as the Vaiṣṇava Veda. The reverence paid to the Āḷvārs is very great, and their images are placed by the side of the god representing Viṣṇu or Nārāyaṇa in some form and worshipped. It may be noted here that Kulaśekhara Āḷvār's favourite deity was Rāma, the son of Daśaratha.

XV. Rāmānuja.

§ 45. There were two classes of teachers among the Vaiṣṇavas of the south, viz. the Āḷvārs and the Ācāryas. The former devoted themselves to the culture of the feeling of love and devotion for Viṣṇu or Nārāyaṇa and composed songs, while the object of the latter was to carry on disputations and controversies and seek to establish their own theories and creeds. The first class we have already noticed briefly.

1) *Kāyena vācā manasendriyair vā*, etc.
2) Jour. Bo. Br. R. As. Soc., Vol. XI. p. 244.
3) Ibid. p. 251.

The first of the second class appears to have been Nāthamuni. His successor was Yāmunācārya or Yāmunamuni. Rāmānuja succeeded Yāmunamuni, one of whose last directions to his successor was to compose a commentary on Bādarāyaṇa's Brahmasūtra. The necessity for such a work was felt by the leaders of the Vaiṣṇava faith, since they found it not possible to maintain the doctrine of Bhakti or love in the face of the theory of Advaita or monism of spirit set up by Śaṃkarācārya as based upon the Brahmasūtras and the Upaniṣads. During the period of the revival of Brāhmaṇism and Hinduism there was such a fermentation of thought as that which existed when Buddhism, Jainism and other heterodox systems on the one hand, and Vāsudevism on the other, arose. The present fermentation, however, did not rest on independent thought, but was based upon the sacred works that had been handed down from the earlier times. The Pāli Buddhism made way for the Sanskrit Mahāyānism, and against this last controversies were carried on by the school of Nyāya founded by Gautama and by the Mīmāṃsakas, especially by Śabarasvāmin and Kumārilabhaṭṭa. But the Mīmāṃsakas attacked not only the Buddhists, but the Aupaniṣadas, or a school of thought based upon the Upaniṣads. They maintained the efficacy of the sacrificial religion alone and denied it to the faith and practices of the latter school. The efforts of this school were therefore directed towards the maintenance of their position that their system alone can lead to supreme bliss. The person who appeared prominently on the scene on this occasion was Gauḍapādācārya and some time after him the pupil of his pupil, Śaṃkarācārya. The theory that this latter set up, was that there exists one spirit alone and the feelings of individuality and other attributes of the animal spirit and the variety of the inanimate world owe their origin to a principle of illusion and are consequently unreal. This doctrine left no room for the exercise of love and piety in the world of reality, though its followers allow it in the ordinary illusive condition of the human souls, and therefore it laid the axe at the root of Vaiṣṇavism. The great wish of the southern leaders of the latter faith was the overthrow of this doctrine of illusion, or Māyā, on the same Aupaniṣada grounds on which it was set up. And this wish of his predecessor was carried out by Rāmānuja, and henceforward every Vaiṣṇava system and even, in one or two cases, Śaiva systems had to tack on Aupaniṣada or Vedāntic theories to their own doctrines.

§ 46. Rāmānuja was born in Śaka 938 corresponding to 1016 or 1017 A. D. In his youth he lived at Kāñcīpura or Conjeevaram and was a pupil of Yādavaprakāśa, who was an Advaita philosopher and therefore professed spiritual monism. Rāmānuja, whose inclinations were towards Vaiṣṇavism, was dissatisfied with the teachings of his master, and the ultimate result was his separation from him. He applied himself to the study of the Prabandhas of the Āḷvārs and drank in their spirit. When he became a successor of Yāmunācārya, he lived at Śrīraṅgam, near Trichinopoly, and did his life's work there. He is said to have gone on a pilgrimage to the noted holy places of upper India. In the latter years of his age he was subjected to persecution by the Chola prince of his time, who wanted him to renounce Vaiṣṇavism for Śaivism, in consequence of which he took refuge in 1096 A. D. in the dominions of the Hoysala Yādava princes, who reigned in Mysore and whose capital was Dvārasamudra, the modern Haḷēbīḍ. There he converted Viṭṭhala Deva, popularly called Biṭṭi Deva, Biṭṭi being, in all likelihood, the corruption of Viṭṭhala or Viṭṭhi. This took place in 1098 A. D. Viṭṭhala Deva was not the reigning prince, but administered some of the frontier provinces in the name of his brother Ballāla, who was on the throne [1]). Viṭṭhala Deva or Biṭṭi Deva was called Viṣṇuvardhana after his conversion to Vaiṣṇavism. This is the ordinary account. But what appears true is that his name was originally Viṣṇu, which was corrupted into Biṭṭu or Biṭṭi in the Kanarese, the vernacular of the district, so that his original name Biṭṭi Deva is the same as Viṣṇu Deva which he is represented to have assumed after his conversion. He reigned from 1104 to 1141 A. D. [2]) Rāmānuja composed the following works: — Vedāntasāra, Vedārthasaṃgraha, Vedāntadīpa, and commentaries, or Bhāṣyas, on the Brahmasūtras and the Bhagavadgītā [3]).

§ 47. The Vedāntic theory, or the theory based upon the Brahmasūtras and the Upaniṣads, which Rāmānuja set up to provide scope for the feeling of Bhakti, or love for God, and the spirit of worship, was that there are three eternal principles, the individual or animal soul (Cit), the insensate world (Acit), and the Supreme Soul (Īśvara). There are Upaniṣad texts to support this, and one of them is that in the ŚU. (I, 12) to the effect that all Brahman, regarded as composed of the enjoyer or sufferer, the objects from which enjoyment or suffering springs, and the controller or mover, is threefold. But the Brahmasūtras lay it down on the authority of the Upaniṣads that Brahman is the material as well as the efficient cause of the world. To make this possible in his system, Rāmānuja resorts to the passage in BU. of the Mādhyaṃdina school, beginning from III, 7, 3, in which the Supreme Soul is stated to be the internal controller (Antaryāmin) of the individual soul as well as of the external world. The form that he gives to his theory is that the individual soul and the insensate world are the attributes of the Supreme Soul. They constitute his body, as stated in the Upaniṣad also, and thus they with the controlling inward Supreme Soul constitute one entity called Brahman, just as the body and the indwelling soul constitute the human being. Before creation the body of the Supreme Soul exists in a subtile form and, when creation takes place, it develops in the form of the existing universe; thus Brahman is the material cause of the external world. It is also the efficient cause, when, as the internal controlling soul, it wills to create. The subtile form of the insensate world is the Prakṛti, a term first invented by the original author of the Sāṃkhya doctrine. It develops under the guidance of the indwelling Supreme Spirit until the mundane egg is produced. The successive stages of Mahat, Ahaṃ-

[1]) See Krishnaswami Iyengar's paper in No. 8 of the magazine Viśiṣṭādvaitin for most of these facts.

[2]) Imperial Gazetteer, Vol. XVIII, p. 173.

[3]) See Krishnaswami's paper alluded to above.

kāra, etc., are like those of the Sāṃkhya system, which has been adopted by the Purāṇas also in the account of the creation. And the creation after the production of the mundane egg is also made by Īśvara as the internal controller of Brahmadeva, Dakṣa, etc.

Īśvara or God is free from all faults or defects. He is eternal, pervades all living and non-living things, is the internal controller of all, is pure joy or blessedness, is possessed of the auspicious qualities of knowledge, power, etc., is the creator, protector and destroyer of the world, and is resorted to by those who are afflicted, who wish to gain knowledge, who seek to attain a certain end, and who are already enlightened [1]). He confers the fourfold fruit of existence [2]). He is possessed of a wonderful celestial body of unsurpassable beauty and has for his consorts Lakṣmī [3]), Bhū (the earth), and Līlā (sport). This Īśvara appears in five different modes: —

I. Para or the highest, in which mode Nārāyaṇa, called also Parabrahman and Para-Vāsudeva, lives in a city called Vaikuṇṭha, which is guarded by certain persons and which has doorkeepers; seated in a pavilion of gems on a couch in the form of the serpent Śeṣa placed on a throne having the eight legs, Dharma and others; attended by Śrī, Bhū and Līlā; holding the celestial weapons, conch-shell, discus, and others; adorned with celestial ornaments, such as a tiara and others; possessed of numberless auspicious attributes, knowledge, power, and others; and his presence being enjoyed by the eternal spirits, such as Ananta, Garuḍa, Viṣvaksena, and others, and by delivered souls.

II. Vyūha, in which the Para himself has assumed four forms, Vāsudeva, Saṃkarṣaṇa, Pradyumna and Aniruddha for convenience of worship and for purposes, such as creation, etc. Of these Vāsudeva is possessed of the six qualities; Saṃkarṣaṇa has two, viz. omniscience and sustaining power; Pradyumna, two, viz. controlling power and unchangeableness; and Aniruddha, creative power and all-overcoming prowess [4]).

III. Vibhava, which mode consists of the ten Avatāras, fish, tortoise, etc.

IV. Antaryāmin, in which mode he dwells in the heart and is to be seen by Yogins and accompanies the individual souls even when they go to heaven or hell.

V. Idols or images set up in houses, villages, towns, etc., made up of a material chosen by the worshipper, in which he dwells with a body not made up of matter [5]).

Other authorities leave out Vāsudeva from the Vyūhas and have the other three only. The Arthapañcaka has another form of the Antaryāmin, in which form he dwells in everything and rules over all, is

---

1) These are the four, Ārta, Jijñāsu, etc., mentioned in BhG. (7, 16).

2) Artha, or worldly prosperity, Kāma, or the objects of desire, Dharma, or religious merit, and Mokṣa, or final deliverance, are the four objects of existence.

3) From the Tattvatraya of Lokācārya.

4) These are translations of the word Jñāna, Bala, Aiśvarya, Vīrya, Śakti, and Tejas, according to the definitions in the Yatīndramatadīpikā.

5) Yatīndramatadīpikā 9.

bodiless, all-pervading and store of all good attributes, and is called Viṣṇu, Nārāyaṇa, Vāsudeva [1]), etc.

Self-consciousness, knowledge, union as a soul with a body, agency, are attributes common to the supreme and individual souls [2]). The latter is self-illumined, joyous, eternal, atomic, imperceptible to the senses, unthinkable, devoid of parts, unchangeable, the substratum of knowledge, subject to God's control, depending on God's existence for his own existence, and an attribute of God [3]). This description of the individual soul differs a great deal from that of Śaṃkarācārya, who attributes no agency or substantiality to it; and the dependence on God in a variety of ways cannot, of course, be thought of under the doctrine of spiritual monism. The soul's being an atom is also denied by Śaṃkara's school and various others. The souls are many and are divided into: (1) Baddha or tied down to the circle of existences from Brahmadeva to the vilest worm, as well as the vegetable souls; (2) Mukta or finally delivered; and (3) Nitya or eternal. Of the first class, those that are rational, that is, not brutes or vegetables, are of two sorts: (1) desirous of enjoyment; (2) desirous of final deliverance. Of those that are desirous of enjoyment, some devote themselves tho the acquisition of wealth and the satisfaction of carnal desires, and others, who seek to attain the happiness of heaven, perform all rites and sacrifices, make pilgrimages to holy places and give in charity. Some of these devote themselves to Bhagavat and others to other deities. Some of those who desire final deliverance seek the consciousness of their pure soul only (Kevalin), and others eternal bliss. Of these latter, some are Bhaktas, who seek to attain God by resorting to Bhakti with all its details, having first of all studied the Vedas and acquainted themselves with the Vedānta and the philosophy of rites (Karman). The three upper orders alone can practise Bhakti, but not the Śūdras. Others are Prapannas, who are those who take refuge in God, feeling themselves poor and helpless. Of Prapannas, some seek the first three objects of life, while the rest, finding no happiness in these, renouncing everything worldly, desire eternal bliss (Mokṣa) alone and, seeking the advice of a preceptor and acquiring from him the impulse to action, fling themselves on the will of God, not having the power of going through the Bhakti process and being helpless. This Prapatti or surrender to God can be practised by all orders, including Śūdras [4]).

What are necessary for the efficacy of the method of Bhakti, are Karmayoga or the performance of actions, and Jñānayoga or the acquisition of knowledge. Karmayoga is the performance of all acts, rites and ceremonies without regard for the fruit resulting from them. These are the worship of the deity, practice of austerity, pilgrimage to holy places, giving in charity and sacrifices. This Karmayoga purifies the soul and leads to Jñānayoga, or acquisition of knowledge.

---

1) See my Report on the Search for Sanskrit Manuscripts during 1883—84, p. 69.
2) Yat. 8.
3) Tattvatraya.
4) Yat. 8.

This knowledge consists in seeing oneself as distinct from Prakṛti, or matter, and as an attribute of God himself (Śeṣa). This Jñānayoga leads to Bhakti. Bhaktiyoga, or the method of Bhakti, consists in continuous meditation accompanied by the practice of the eight Yoga processes, Yama, Niyama, etc. This is to be attained by (1) the purification of the body by the use of unpolluted and unprohibited food, (2) chastity, (3) constant practice, (4) the performance of five great rites and ceremonies according to one's means, (5) virtues such as truth, uprightness, compassion, charity, non-destruction of life, (6) hopefulness or absence of despondency, and (7) absence of elatedness. Bhakti, as promoted by these seven means, assumes the form of actually seeing (God) and produces the final mental perception. Prapatti consists in the resolution to yield, the avoidance of opposition [1]), a faith that God will protect, acceptance of him as saviour or praying him to save, and sense of helplessness resulting in throwing one's whole soul on him [2]). Prapatti thus comes to self-surrender [3]).

The Arthapañcaka mentions a fifth way called Ācāryābhimānayoga, which is for one who is unable to follow any of the others and consists in surrendering oneself to an Ācārya or preceptor and being guided by him in everything. The preceptor goes through all that is necessary to effect his pupil's deliverance as a mother takes medicine herself to cure an infant.

Sixteen modes of worship are to be practised by the devotees of Viṣṇu, as stated in a passage quoted from the Padma-Purāṇa by a recent writer of the Rāmānuja school. Eight of these are the same as those included in the nine modes of Bhakti enumerated in a previous section as mentioned in the Bhāgavata-Purāṇa, Sakhya, or friendship or companionship, being omitted. The other eight are: (1) imprinting the marks of the conch-shell and the discus and other weapons of Hari on the body; (2) the making of a vertical mark on the forehead; (3) repeating of Mantras on the occasion; (4) drinking the water used in washing the feet of Hari; (5) the eating of the offerings of cooked food made to him; (6) doing service to his devotees; (7) the observance of fast on the 11th of the bright and dark halves of each lunar month; (8) laying Tulasī leaves on the idol of Hari.

A text from the Hārītasmṛti is also quoted giving nine modes of worship (Bhakti), three of which are common to it with the Bhāgavata-Purāṇa. The other six are the same as the eight in the above, the first two being combined and the third being omitted. The vertical mark on the forehead mentioned above consists of two lines made with white earth and a connecting cross line at the bottom with, in the middle, a yellow line made with turmeric powder or a red line composed of the same material reddened by mixing it with lime.

---

1) The two expressions thus translated have also been otherwise explained as bearing good-will to all and the absence of ill-will.

2) There is another reading here which should be translated as throwing oneself upon him and a feeling of helplessness. Thus there are six constituents of Prapatti. These are: (1) ānukūlyasya saṃkalpaḥ (2) prātikūlyasya varjanam, (3) rakṣiṣyatīti viśvāso (4) gōptṛtvavaraṇaṃ tathā, (5) ātmanikṣepa- (6) kārpaṇye ṣaḍvidhā śaraṇāgatiḥ.

3) Yat. 7.

§ 48. In Northern India there are not many followers of Rāmānuja; in Southern India there is a very large number. There are two schools among them, known by the names of Vaḍakalai, or northern learning, and Tenkalai, or southern learning. The essential difference between them is brought out by the different illustrations [1]) that they give of the connection between God's grace and man's effort in bringing about final deliverance. The illustration used by the former, or the northern, is that of a female monkey and her cub. The cub has to hold fast its mother on the abdomen to be conveyed to a safe place. The southerns use the illustration of the cat and its kittens. The female cat catches hold of the kitten, without any effort on its part, and takes it to a place of safety. In the first case the doctrine is that the process of deliverance must begin with an act of a person seeking it. In the other case the process begins with God himself. In keeping with this distinction is the idea of Prapatti or self-surrender held by the two sects. The first maintains that Prapatti is one of the ways resorted to by the devotee and begins with him. The southern school holds that it is not one of the ways, but it is a frame of mind which characterises all those who seek absolution and reject all other ways in favour of this. Those who resort to other ways have not arrived at the right mood which leads to God. When a soul is in this frame of mind, God himself takes entire possession of him, while by the other ways man, as it were, makes approaches towards him. The Vaḍakalai lays down that Prapatti is for those who cannot follow other ways, such as Karmayoga, Jñānayoga and Bhaktiyoga, while the Tenkalai holds that it is necessary for all, whether able or not, to follow the other ways. The first school says that one should give himself up to God when one finds other ways, which have been resorted to, to be fruitless. The second holds that self-abandonment to God should precede the trial of other ways. Self-assertiveness is the characteristic of the first, but it is forbidden by the second and self-abandonment is enjoined. The northerners say that the six ways of Prapatti or self-surrender given above are preliminaries to the Prapatti which results from them. The southerners say that Prapatti must take place first and then the six follow as results. The northern school teaches that a person belonging to an inferior caste should be treated well only so far as conversation by words is concerned. The southerners say that they should be admitted to an equal treatment in all respects and no distinction be made. The syllable Om should be omitted from the eight-syllabled Mantra, according to the Vaḍakalai, when taught to others than Brāhmaṇas; the Tenkalai does not make this distinction and provides for the teaching of the whole Mantra in the same form to all [2]).

§ 49. It will be seen from the short summary here given that Rāmānuja derives his metaphysical doctrines from texts in the Upaniṣads and from the Brahmasūtras, while his theory of the production

[1]) The following remarks are based on Viśiṣṭādvaitin, Vol. 1, No. 8, pp. 200ff., and Mr. Govindācārya's article, JRAS. 1910, pp. 1103ff.

[2]) This mantra is "Om Namo Nārāyaṇāya".

of the external world is that adopted by the Purāṇas and based on the twenty-four elements of the Sāṃkhya system. His Vaiṣṇavism is the Vāsudevism of the old Pāñcarātra system combined with the Nārāyaṇa and Viṣṇu elements. The last name does not occur often in the literature of his school. The most prominent name is Nārāyaṇa, though Vāsudeva takes his proper place when the Supreme Soul and the Vyūhas are spoken of. The name of Gopālakṛṣṇa is conspicuous by its absence, and Rāmānuja's system is free from that repulsive form which Vaiṣṇavism assumes when Rādhā and other cowherdesses are introduced. Rāma too does not appear to be a favourite deity. Rāmānuja's doctrines as to the way of reaching the Supreme Soul are the same as, or amplified forms of, those in the Bhagavadgītā. But in this system Bhakti is reduced to the form of a continuous meditation on the Supreme Soul. It thus corresponds to the Upāsanās, or meditations, described by Bādarāyaṇa, and does not mean a boundless love for God, as the word is commonly understood, though the meditation that is enjoined implies tacitly a feeling of love. The tendency of Rāmānuja's system seems to be to give an exclusive Brahmaṇic form to the traditional method of Bhakti, or devotion to God, and this is distinctly seen in the doctrines of the Vaḍakalai, while the Tenkalai, or southern learning, is more liberal and so shapes the doctrines of the system as to make them applicable to Śūdras also. But we shall find the Śūdras asserting themselves when we come to the disciples of Rāmānanda and to the Marāṭha saints and teachers, Nāmdev and Tukārām.

The fifth Upāya, or way to God, given in the Arthapañcaka, of surrendering oneself completely to a teacher or preceptor, doing nothing oneself and the preceptor doing all that is necessary for one's redemption, seems suspicious. It has a striking resemblance to the Christian doctrine of Christ suffering or, in the words of our author, going through the processes necessary for redemption, the believer doing nothing but putting complete faith in his saviour. If the prevalence of Christianity in and before the time of Rāmānuja in the country about Madras is a proved fact, this doctrine as well as some of the finer points in the theory of Prapatti may be traced to the influence of Christianity. Rāmānuja's system is known by the name of Śrīsampradāya or the tradition springing from Śrī.

XVI. Madhva or Ānandatīrtha.

§ 50. The great object of the Vaiṣṇava teachers of the eleventh century and upwards was to confute the theory of Māyā, or the unreality of the world, and establish the doctrine of Bhakti, or love and faith, on a secure basis. Rāmānuja effected this by the system which he promulgated and which we have already noticed. But in order to reconcile his doctrine with the theory set forth in the Brahmasūtras on the basis of the Upaniṣads, that God is the material as well as the efficient cause of the world, he propounded the doctrine of God's being a composite person, having for his body the individual souls and the inanimate world. Even this Madhva considered objectionable as having a tendency to depreciate the independent majesty of God, and therefore he denies his being the material cause of the world. All the Sūtras of Bādarāyaṇa which set forth that doctrine, have been interpreted by him in an entirely different way. Probably he would have set aside the Brahmasūtras altogether, but he could not do so, since the work had acquired an uncontested authoritativeness as regards religious truth before his time. He had therefore to show that his system did not go against the Brahmasūtras and therefore accepted them and interpreted them in almost a fantastic manner. Texts from the Upaniṣads, too, which do not agree with his doctrines, he treats similarly. In opposition to the pure monism of Śaṃkara and the qualified monism of Rāmānuja, Ānandatīrtha sets forth five eternal distinctions or individualities, viz. the distinction between (1) God and the individual spirit, (2) God and the inanimate world, (3) the individual spirit and the inanimate world, (4) one individual spirit and another, (5) one inanimate object and another. According to the Madhvavijaya, or the history of the triumphs of Madhva, by Nārāyaṇa, the son of Trivikrama, there was in the town of Rajatapīṭha a family known by the name of Madhyageha. Madhva's father was called Madhyagehabhaṭṭa [1]; the name given to Madhva after his birth was Vāsudeva. After Vāsudeva had received the usual education of a Brāhmaṇa, he was initiated as an anchorite by Acyutaprekṣācārya who thus became his Guru. After his initiation he went to Badarikāśrama in the Himālaya and brought back the idols of Digvijaya Rāma and Vedavyāsa. He was raised to the seat of high priest in the presence of kings. Ānandatīrtha went from country to country, putting down the advocates of the doctrine of Māyā and others, and established the Vaiṣṇava creed. He had for his pupils Padmanābhatīrtha, Naraharitīrtha, Mādhavatīrtha, and Akṣobhyatīrtha. Naraharitīrtha was sent to Jagannātha in Orissa to bring the original idols of Rāma and Sītā. Ānandatīrtha's other names were Pūrṇaprajña and Madhyamandāra, or wish-giving tree of the family of Madhya.

The date of his death given in the list preserved in several of the Maṭhas, or establishments of the sect, is Śaka 1119, and as he lived for seventy-nine years, the date of his birth has been given as Śaka 1040. But these statements are open to serious doubts. There is an inscription in the Kūrmeśvara temple at Śrīkūrmam in the Chicacole Tāluka of the Ganjām District in which Naraharitīrtha is represented to have constructed a temple and placed in it an idol of Yogānandanarasiṃha in the year Śaka 1203 [2]. The first person therein mentioned is Puruṣottamatīrtha, who is the same as Acyutaprekṣa [3], then his pupil Ānandatīrtha, and the last is Naraharitīrtha, the pupil of Ānandatīrtha. This Naraharitīrtha is considered by some to have been the ruler of Orissa. But this arises from a confusion between him and a king bearing the same name, in the slightly modified form of Narasiṃha,

---

1) Kallianpur in the Uḍipi Tāluka of the district of South Kanara in stated to be the birth-place of Madhva. It was probably the same as the Rajatapīṭha of the Madhvavijaya. (Imp. Gaz. Vol. XIV, page 314.)

2) Ep. Ind. Vol. VI, pp. 260ff.

3) Madhvavijaya, VI. 33.

who was the actual ruler of the country from about Śaka 1191 to 1225. He is mentioned in an inscription at Śrīkūrmam of Naraharitīrtha himself, bearing the date Śaka 1215, which is represented as the eighteenth year of the king's reign [1]). He was Narasiṃha II and was the prince panegyrised in a work on rhetoric, the Ekāvali [2]). Naraharitīrtha's other dates gathered from other inscriptions range between Śaka 1186 and 1212 [3]). All these epigraphical records confirm the truth of the tradition that Naraharitīrtha was sent by Ānandatīrtha to Orissa. He appears to have held a very high position there.

Now if Naraharitīrtha's active period extended from Śaka 1186 to 1215, his master could not have died in Śaka 1119, i. e. fully 67 years before. It seems, therefore, reasonable to take the date given in Madhva's Mahābhāratatātparyanirṇaya, which is 4300 of the Kali age, to be the correct date of his birth. It corresponds to Śaka 1121, which, bearing in mind the fact that some use the current year of an era and some the past, we must regard as equivalent to Śaka 1119, the date given in the lists for Ānandatīrtha's death. But instead of taking it as the date of his death, we shall have to regard it as the date of his birth. He lived for 79 years according to the current account, so that his death must be placed in Śaka 1198 [4]). The two dates may, therefore, be taken as settled. Ānandatīrtha thus lived in the first three quarters of the thirteenth century. He was succeeded, according to the list, by Padmanābhatīrtha who held the pontificate for seven years, i. e. up to Śaka 1205. He was succeeded by Naraharitīrtha who occupied the pontifical seat for nine years, i. e. up to Śaka 1214, or, if we regard 1121 as the date of the first pontiff's birth according to the strict interpretation of the Kali date, up to Śaka 1216; and, as we have seen, his latest date in the inscriptions is Śaka 1215.

§ 51. The Mādhvas follow the method of Vaiśeṣikas and divide all existing things into the categories of substance, qualities, etc., with some modifications of their own [5]). God is a substance. The supreme soul possesses innumerable or an infinite number of qualities. His functions are eight, viz. (1) creation, (2) protection, (3) dissolution, (4) controlling all things, (5) giving knowledge, (6) manifestation of himself, (7) tying beings down to the world, (8) redemption. He is omniscient, expressible by all words, and entirely different from the individual souls and the inanimate world. He possesses the holy form made up of knowledge, joy, etc., independent of every thing, and one only, assuming different forms. All his forms are his full manifestations, and he is identically the same with his incarnations in qualities, parts, and actions. Lakṣmī is distinct from the Supreme Soul, but entirely

---

1) Ep. Ind. Vol. VI, page 262, note.

2) See my note in Trivedi's edition of the work, BSS.

3) Ep. Ind. Vol VI, p. 266.

4) This agrees with the tradition existing in the Maṭha at Phalmāru, near Mulki in South Canara, to the effect that Ānandatīrtha was born in Śaka 1119 and died in Śaka 1199; Ep. Ind. Vol. VI, p. 263, note.

5) This account of the system is abrigded from a work called Madhvasiddhāntasāra by Padmanābhasūri, printed in Bombay by Jāvaji Dādāji, Nirṇayasagara Press, published at Kumbhakonam in Śaka 1815, corresponding to 1883 A. D. The tedious details are omitted.

dependent on him. She is eternal and blessed (Mukta) like the Supreme Soul and is his consort. She has various forms, but no material body, and is thus like the Supreme Soul, and like him is expressible by all words. She possesses the same extension in space and time as the Supreme Soul, i. e. is concomitant with him. Jīvas or individual souls go through the usual succession of existences and are characterised by ignorance or other defects. They are innumerable individually, or as members of groups, such as Ṛjus[1]) who are fit for attaining Brahmahood, and others who are fit for the attainment of the dignity of Rudra, Garuḍa, Asuras, or demons, etc. They are of three kinds: (1) fit for attaining final bliss, (2) always going through the circle of existences, and (3) fit for the condition of darkness. The gods, Ṛṣis, and the manes, and the best of men, belong to the first class, ordinary men belong to the second class, and demons, ghosts, and the vilest of men, etc., to the third class. All these individual souls are distinct from each other and from the Supreme Soul. Creation begins when the Supreme Soul disturbs the equilibrium of the Prakṛti, which then develops into all the other principles of the Sāṃkhya system, as modified by the Purāṇas, until the mundane egg is produced. Then placing the sentient and non-sentient objects into his inside, he enters into the mundane egg. Then, at the end of a thousand celestial years, he produces from his navel a lotus, which is the seat of the four-faced Brahmadeva; and from this last after a long time the ordinary creation takes place.

All knowledge springs from Paramātman, whatever the means by which it is produced. It is of two kinds — that which leads to worldly existence, and that which leads to Mokṣa. Viṣṇu bestows knowledge on the ignorant and Mokṣa on those who have knowledge. The knowledge, or feeling which creates an attachment to the body, child or wife, leads to a worldly life. This is not true knowledge, but ignorance from which results that worldly life; and that ignorance is dispelled by the knowledge of God. Mokṣa is attained by the direct knowledge or perception of Hari by means of a method of service possible to oneself and in a body fitted for it. That direct perception is possible to all good individual souls from Brahmadeva to the best of men. This direct perception is to be attained by many means. What are necessary for direct knowledge, which leads to Mokṣa, are (1) Vairāgya, or the disgust of enjoyments of this world or the next, generated by seeing the vanity of the world and by the company of good persons; (2) equanimity (Śama) and self-control (Dama), etc.; (3) acquaintance with the lore; (4) self-surrender (Śaraṇāgati), in which the mind is devoted to God, as the best of all beings, and is full of the highest love, and in which everything is resigned to God and he is worshipped with devotedness in the three ways, and which is accompanied with the faith that he will unfailingly protect and the feeling that the devotee is his; (5) attendance on a Guru, or preceptor, and propitiation of him, which is necessary for Mokṣa or redemption; (6) acquisition of knowledge from the Guru and not from books or, in the absence of a Guru, from a good Vaiṣṇava, and, in rare cases,

[1]) Ṛjus are a class of gods.

from books also; (7) reflection over what has been taught; (8) devotion, in the order of their merits, to a preceptor and persons better than oneself and deserving respect; (9) love of God (Paramātma-bhakti) consequent on the knowledge of God's greatness and his being the best of all. This love should be firm and higher than that for all others, and this leads to Mokṣa or eternal bliss; (10) sympathy for those who are inferior, but good men, love for those who are equal, as if they were the same as themselves, and respectful love or reverence for superiors; (11) performing rites and ceremonies deliberately without any desire, which has the effect of purifying the soul; (12) the avoidance of prohibited deeds, i. e. sins great and small; (13) resigning every act to Hari as done by him and not by oneself; (14) the knowledge of the comparative position of beings and of Viṣṇu as the highest of all; (15) knowledge of the five distinctions already mentioned; (16) distinguishing Prakṛti from Puruṣa, all beings from Nārāyaṇa down to men with their consorts being Puruṣas and the inanimate world being the Prakṛti; (17) reprobation of false doctrines; (18) Upāsanā or worship. This last is of two kinds, viz. (1) the learning of the Śāstras, (2) meditation. Meditation (Nididhyāsā) is placing Bhagavat before the mind's eye to the exclusion of everything else. This meditation is possible for one who has a distinct knowledge of a thing acquired after the removal of ignorance, doubt and delusion by means of reading or hearing something read and reflection. Some people meditate on Bhagavat as a single spirit and others on him as having four phases as Sat (existence), Cit (knowledge), Ānanda (joy), Ātman (spirit). Then are given meditations resorted to by gods and some of those mentioned in the Brahmasūtras. All these eighteen ways lead to the direct knowledge of God, which is possible for all from Brahmadeva to man. The direct knowledge of God attained by men is comparable with the coruscation of lightning and that attained by gods to the bright disk of the sun. Garuḍa and Rudra have that knowledge in the shape of a reflection, while Brahmadeva has the knowledge of the whole with all its parts, and some have the knowledge of him as dwelling in the universe and limited by the universe. The direct knowledge is simply mental.

§ 52. The followers of Madhva wear a mark on the forehead composed of two white perpendicular lines made with an earth called Gopīcandana above the bridge of the nose, and a dark line in the middle with a reddish spot in the centre. The two white lines are joined by a cross line on the bridge of the nose. They wear on the shoulders and on the other parts of their body prints, made with the same white earth, of the conch-shell, the discus, and other weapons of Viṣṇu. These are impressed occasionally with a heated metallic stamp on the skin, so as to leave a permanent scar. Members of this sect exist in pretty large numbers in the Kanarese districts of the Bombay Presidency, Mysore and on the western coast from Goa to South Kanara, and there are only scattered adherents in Northern India. There are eight establishments, or Maṭhas, for the dissemination and preservation of the creed in South Kanara and three in the inner country. Some of these were founded by Ānandatīrtha himself.

Ānandatīrtha composed thirty-seven[1]) different treatises. He includes among the authorities enumerated by him in support of his system the Pañcarātra-Saṃhitās; but it will be seen from the account given above that in his creed there is no place for the Vyūhas, Vāsudeva and others, and the name by which the Supreme Spirit is spoken of is mostly Viṣṇu. Some of his incarnations, especially Rāma and Kṛṣna, are also adored. But the Gopāla-Kṛṣṇa element seems to be entirely absent from his system, and Rādhā and the cowherdesses are not mentioned. It thus appears that the Pāñcarātra or Bhāgavata system has been set aside by Ānandatīrtha or thrown into the background. The old traditional Vāsudevism of the Bhāgavata school gradually disappeared about his time and made room for general Vaiṣṇavism.

XVII. Nimbārka.

§ 53. We have thus noticed the form which Vaiṣṇavism assumed in the south from the middle of the eleventh century to the middle of the thirteenth. A strong feeling of Bhakti, or love, and a fear of the dangerous consequences of the doctrine of Māyā, or illusion, were the guiding principles of the new development. The influence of this last extended itself to the north, and we can distinguish between two classes of founders of sects, viz. (1) those who wrote in Sanskrit, and (2) those who used the vernacular for the propagation of their creed. The first of the former class we have to notice is Nimbārka. Nimbārka is said to have been a Tailaṅga Brāhmaṇa by birth and to have lived in a village called Nimba[2]), which perhaps is the same as Nimbāpura in the Bellary district. He was born on the 3rd of the bright half of Vaiśākha, and his father's name was Jagannātha, who was a Bhāgavata, and his mother's Sarasvatī[3]). He is believed by his followers to be an incarnation of the Sudarśana, or the discus of Viṣṇu. As to when he flourished we have no definite information, but he appears to have lived some time after Rāmānuja[4]). Nimbārka composed the Vedānta-

[1]) For the names of these see the Granthamālikāstotra in my Report on the Search for Sanskrit Manuscripts during 1882—83, p. 207.

[2]) Manuscript No. 706 of the collection of 1884—7. Nimbārka was the "sun of Nimba".

[3]) Introduction to the commentary on Daśaślokī by Harivyāsadeva. It is to be regretted that the commentator does not give the year of Nimbārka's birth.

[4]) In my Report on the Search for Sanskrit Manuscripts for the year 1882—83, I have given two succession lists of spiritual teachers, one of the sect of Ānandatīrtha (p. 203) and another of that founded by Nimbārka (pp. 208—12). This contains 37 names. There is another list in Manuscript 709 of the collection of 1884—7, which contains 45 names. The two lists agree up to No. 32 Harivyāsadeva. After that, while the first has only five names, the second has thirteen names, and none of these agrees with any of the five, so that after Harivyāsadeva the line appears to have divided itself into two branches. No. 709 of the same collection was written in Saṃvat 1806 corresponding to 1750 A. D., when Gosvāmin Dāmodara was living. He was the thirty-third after Nimbārka in the new branch line. The thirty-third after Ānandatīrtha died in 1879 A. D. Ānandatīrtha according to our revised date died in 1276 A. D., so that his thirty-three successors occupied 603 years. Supposing that the thirty-three successors of Nimbārka occupied about the same period and allowing about fifteen years of life to Dāmodara Gosvāmin, who was living in 1750 A. D., and subtracting from 1765 A. D. 603 years, we have

pārijātasaurabha, which is a short commentary on the Brahmasūtras, and also a small work containing ten stanzas of the name of Siddhāntaratna, usually called Daśaślokī, from the number of stanzas contained in it. Śrīnivāsa, the immediate follower of Nimbārka, wrote a commentary called Bhāṣya on the first, and Harivyāsadeva, the thirty-second in the list of succession, wrote on the second. The thirteenth in the list, Devācārya, wrote the Siddhāntajāhnavī, and his successor, Sundarabhaṭṭa, wrote a commentary on it, called Setu. The thirtieth in the list composed a commentary, or Bhāṣya, on the Brahmasūtras. His name was Keśava Kaśmīrin.

§ 52. Nimbārka's Vedāntic theory is monistic as well as pluralistic. The inanimate world, the individual soul and God are distinct from one another as well as identical. Identical they are in the sense that the first two have no independent existence, but are dependent on God for their existence and action. The theory of the Brahmasūtras that Brahman is the material cause of the universe, is thus understood: To be the material cause of an effect is (1) to possess the capacity of assuming the form of that effect, and (2) to be fitted to do so. Brahman possesses various capacities which are of the nature of the animate and inanimate worlds. These in a subtle form constitute its natural condition. This satisfies the first of the two requirements. The capacities again contain in them the rudiment of the effect, i. e. the world, in a subtle form. This meets the second requirement. By realising these capacities and bringing the subtle rudiment into a gross form Brahman becomes the material cause of the world. Rāmānuja's theory of Brahman forming with the animate and inanimate world a composite personality and of its being the material cause in so far as the bodily portion of the composite personality becomes developed, is rejected by the school of Nimbārka [1]). For a further knowledge of the system I will here give a translation of the Daśaślokī.

I. Jīva, or the individual soul, is knowledge, dependent on Hari, and is in a condition to be associated with, or dissociated from, a body; is an atom; different in different bodies; and is a knower and numberless.

It is called knowledge here to show that it is able to know without the organs of sense, and it is not to be understood here that the soul is the mere phenomenon of knowledge, and not a substance, which is the doctrine of Śaṃkarācārya.

II. The individual soul has his form distorted by its contact with Māyā, or Prakṛti, or the constituent principle with the three qualities which has no beginning. Its true nature becomes known by the grace of God.

Individual souls are of two sorts: (1) those delivered or in a supremely blissful condition; (2) those tied down to the circle of existences. The first are of two kinds: (1) those who are eternally

---

1162, which is about the date of Nimbārka's death, so that he lived after Rāmānuja. This calculation of ours is of course very rough and, besides, the date of the manuscript No. 706, which is read as 1913 by some, but which looks like 1813, conflicts with this calculation, as nine more Ācāryas flourished after Dāmodara. And, if 1813 is the correct date, seven years cannot suffice for these, though 107 may, if the date is read 1913.

[1]) See Keśava's commentary, Br. S. I. 4, 23.

in a supremely blissful condition, such as (a) Garuḍa, Viṣvaksena, and (b) the crown, ear-ornaments and the flute considered as living beings; and (2) those who are freed from the trammels of life. Of these last some attain to the likeness of God and others are content with the perception of the nature of their own soul. Corresponding to these two last are two kinds of Mumukṣu, those who seek deliverance of either kind.

III. The inanimate objects are of three kinds: (1) not derived from Prakṛti; (2) derived from Prakṛti; and (3) time. In the things derived from Prakrti we have the ordinary material objects having the three colours, viz. red, white, and dark.

The first class consists of those which are spoken of figuratively by the use of the names of objects belonging to the second class, such as the sunlike refulgence of the Supreme Soul. It is a refulgence not arising from the Prakṛti. Similarly the body, hands, feet, and ornaments of God, as well as all the surroundings, such as garden, palace, etc., belong to the first class and are of an inanimate nature, though they are not made of matter, i. e., not derived from Prakṛti[1]).

IV. I meditate on the highest Brahman, viz. Kṛṣṇa, who has eyes like the lotus, who naturally is free from all faults, is the store of all beneficient attributes, who has Vyūhas for his parts, and who is adored by all.

The Vyūhas here mentioned are those usually referred to in the Pāñcarātra and Rāmānuja systems. The commentators understand the incarnations also by this expression. One gives a large number of these, divided into classes on certain principles. Kṛṣṇa is called Vareṇya or adored by all, because he has a holy celestial body and bodily qualities, such as beauty, tenderness, sweetness and charm. All these are of course non-material (Aprākṛta), though inanimate according to stanza III.

V. I reflect on the daughter of Vṛṣabhānu (Rādhikā), who shines with a corresponding beauty on the left side (of Kṛṣṇa), is attended on by thousands of female friends, and who always confers all desired objects.

VI. This Parabrahman should be always worshipped uninterruptedly by men in order to be free from the darkness in the shape of ignorance, in which they are enveloped. So was Nārada, who directly perceived the whole truth, taught by Sanandana and others.

VII. All things having Brahman for their souls in accordance with the Śrutis and Smṛtis, the knowledge that [Brahman] is all is true. This is the doctrine of those who know the Vedas, and at the same time the three forms are true as determined from the sacred precepts (Smṛtis) and the Sūtras.

Here is laid down the unity of all things in so far as Brahman is the inner controlling soul of all and is concomitant with them, and their existence and actions are dependent on it, and also pluralism, since there are three distinct substances, which are called forms of

[1]) The physical attributes given to God by Rāmānuja and the rest and to which the word 'celestial' is sometimes prefixed, are to be understood in this sense.

Brahman in the stanza, viz. the inanimate world, the individual soul and the Supreme Soul.

VIII. There appears no way to salvation except the lotus-like feet of Kṛṣṇa, which are adored by Brahmadeva, Śiva and others — Kṛṣṇa, who, at the desire of a devotee, assumes a form easy of meditation and whose power is unthinkable and whose essence cannot be comprehended.

IX. His grace extends itself to those who have a feeling of helplessness and other qualifications, and by that grace is generated Bhakti, or devotion, consisting of special love for him, who has no superior lord. This Bhakti is of two kinds: the highest is one, and the other is that which leads to or is instrumental to it.

By the feeling of helplessness and other qualifications are meant the six modes of Prapatti given in connection with Rāmānuja's system. The Bhakti which is instrumental to that which is the highest, is of the nature of the six or nine modes mentioned in previous sections.

X. These five things should be known by the devotees: (1) the nature of the being to be worshipped; (2) the nature of the worshipper; (3) the fruit of God's grace; (4) the feeling of enjoyment consequent on Bhakti, or love; (5) obstructions to the attainment of God.

The first is the knowing of the nature of the Supreme Being as existence, intelligence and joy (Saccidānanda), of his possessing a celestial body (non-material), of his dwelling in such places as the cow-settlement (Vraja), which is called the celestial city (Vyomapura), of his being the cause of all, omnipotent, tender, merciful, gracious towards his devotees, and so forth. The second consists in knowing the worshipper as an atom, possessing knowledge and joy, and as the servant of Kṛṣṇa, etc. The third is the self-surrender and the giving up of all actions except the service of God, which results in self-surrender. The fourth arises from serenity, servitude, friendliness, affection, and enthusiasm. These states of mind are consequent upon the peculiar relation to God of each individual, as affection was the feeling of Nanda, Vasudeva and Devakī, and enthusiasm, of Rādhā and Rukmiṇī. The fifth are such as regarding the body as the soul, dependence on others than God and one's preceptor, indifference to the commands of God contained in the sacred books, worshipping other gods, giving up one's own peculiar duties, ingratitude, spending one's life in a worthless manner, vilification of good men, and many others.

§ 55. These ten stanzas contain the quintessence of Nimbārka's system. This appears to have Rāmānuja's doctrines for its basis and is a sidewise development of it. It gives predominance to Prapatti or self-surrender of the six kinds alluded to above, and then, by the grace of God, love for Him is generated. His Sādhana Bhakti comprehends all the Yogas of Rāmānuja's system. Rāmānuja, as we have already remarked, changes the original sense of Bhakti and renders it equivalent to the Upāsanā, or the meditation prescribed in the Upaniṣads. But Nimbārka keeps to the original sense. His doctrines make a nearer approach to the Tenkalai, or southern learning, of the Rāmānujīyas. But the great difference between the two teachers is, that, while Rāmānuja confines himself to Nārāyaṇa and his consorts Lakṣmī, Bhū and Līlā, Nimbārka gives almost an exclusive prominence to Kṛṣṇa and his mistress, Rādhā, attended on by thousands of her female companions. Thus the fourth element of Vaiṣṇavism which we have mentioned rises to the surface in Vaiṣṇavism about this time and retains its place in Northern India, including Bengal, except in the case of those sects whose favourite deity is Rāma and not Kṛṣṇa; and to these for the present we will now turn our attention, coming back again to Kṛṣṇaism later on. Nimbārka's system is known by the name of Sanakasaṃpradāya, or the tradition originating with Sanaka. Though Nimbārka was a southerner, he lived at Vṛndāvana near Mathurā, which accounts for the preference given by him to the Rādhā-Kṛṣṇa form of Vaiṣṇavism. His followers are scattered over the whole of Northern India and exist in large numbers near Mathurā and in Bengal. They wear two perpendicular lines of Gopīcandana with a black spot in the middle on the forehead and use a necklace and rosary of the wood of the Tulasī plant. They are divided into two classes, the ascetics and householders. This distinction appears to have originated at the time of Harivyāsadeva, after whom, as I have observed in a note, the successors of Nimbārka were divided into two branches. The reason for the division was probably this new distinction.

XVIII. Rāmānanda.

§ 56. A spirit of sympathy for the lower castes and classes of Hindu society has from the beginning been a distinguishing feature of Vaiṣṇavism. Still, so far as we have advanced, the great teachers kept these castes and classes into, what might be called, an outer court, though they were admitted to the benefits of the new dispensation. They had not, as the pure Vedāntins assert, to do the duties prescribed for their mean position and rise in succeeding lives until they were finally born as Brāhmaṇas, when alone they could avail themselves of the methods laid down for the attainment of Mokṣa, or deliverance. They could attain this even as members of the lowest caste by resorting to devotion, but the Brahmaṇic teachers, Rāmānuja and others, made the methods based on the study of the Vedic literature accessible only to the higher castes, leaving other methods to the rest. But Rāmānanda now began a radical reform and made no distinction between Brāhmaṇas and members of the degraded castes, and all could even dine together, provided they were the devotees of Viṣṇu and had been admitted into the fold. Another reform, which must be traced to Rāmānanda, was the use of the vernaculars for the propagation of the new creed. And a third very important reform made by him was the introduction of the purer and more chaste worship of Rāma and Sītā instead of that of Kṛṣṇa and Rādhā.

Mr. Macauliffe mentions Mailkot as the place of his birth and says that he must have flourished in the end of the fourteenth and the first half of the fifteenth century, which, he states, corresponds with a reckoning which gives 1398 A. D. as the date of the birth of Kabīr. This would rather make Rāmānanda live long before the end of the fourteenth century, as Kabīr was his successor and ordinarily believed to be his pupil [1]). The authority [2]) I have consulted states that he was born at Prayāga as the son of a Kānyakubja Brāhmaṇa, named Puṇyasadana, and his wife Suśīlā. The date of his birth is given as 4400 of the Kali age, equivalent to 1356 of Vikrama-Saṃvat. This corresponds to 1299 or 1300 A. D. and is more consistent with the traditional statement that there were three generations between him and Rāmānuja. The date of Rāmānuja's death is usually given as 1137 A. D., though it makes him out as having lived for 120 years. The lapse of three generations between 1137 and 1300 A. D. is a more reasonable supposition than between 1137 and the end of the fourteenth century. This last date, therefore, given for Rāmānanda is manifestly wrong, and that occuring in the book I have consulted appears to be correct in all probability.

From Prayāga Rāmānanda was sent to Benares for the usual education of a Brāhmaṇa. After he finished this, he became a disciple of Rāghavānanda, a teacher of the Viśiṣṭādvaita school of Rāmānuja. After some time he gave up some of the restrictive practices of the sect, such as that of taking food without being seen by anybody, and separated himself from his preceptor and himself became the founder of a school. As indicated above, he took pupils from the degraded castes also. Thirteen of them became noted and their names are: 1. Anantānanda, 2. Surasarānanda, 3. Sukhānanda, 4. Naraharīyānanda, 5. Yogānanda, 6. Pīpā, 7. Kabīr, 8. Bhāvānanda, 9. Senā, 10. Dhannā, 11. Gālavānanda, 12. Raidās, and 13. Padmāvatī. Of these Pīpā was a Rājpūt, Kabīr was a Śūdra and spoken of also as a Mahomedan following the profession of a weaver, Senā was a barber, Dhannā a Jāṭ, Raidās belonged to the degraded caste of curriers or workers in leather, and Padmāvatī was a woman. With the first twelve he went about the country visiting holy places, conducting disputations with the advocates of the Māyā doctrine, Jainas, Buddhists, etc., establishing his own Viśiṣṭādvaita theory and converting men to his views and admitting them as his disciples. Rāmānanda is stated to have died in 1467 of Vikrama-Saṃvat, corresponding to 1411 A. D. This gives him a life of 111 years, which is rather improbable. Some of his pupils became the founders of different schools, and through them the worship of Rāma spread over an extensive portion of Northern and Central India, successfully competing with that of Gopāla-Kṛṣṇa.

XIX. Kabīr.

§ 57. The few particulars that have come down to us about the birth and life of Kabīr are these. He was the son of a Brāhmaṇa widow who cast him away as soon as he was born, to hide her shame, near the Lahar Tank in Benares. A Mahomedan weaver of the name of Nīrū was passing by the way with his wife Nīmā, when the latter

[1]) The Sikh Religion, etc. by M. A. Macauliffe, Vol. VI, pp. 100—1. 1908 A. D. is said by Macauliffe to correspond to the 510th year of *his* era. By *his* he must mean Kabīr's.

[2]) Chapters from the Agastya-Saṃhitā with a Hindī translation by Rāma Nārāyaṇa Dās, completed in Saṃvat 1960, corresponding to 1904 A. D.

saw the child and carried it home. He was nurtured and brought up by her and her husband Nīrū, and Kabīr, when he had grown up, followed the occupation of a weaver. He showed leanings towards the Hindu faith, and the idea of making Rāmānanda his Guru, or preceptor, arose in his mind. But he conceived it not possible that that sage should receive a Mahomedan as his disciple and therefore had recourse to a contrivance. He laid himself down on the Ghāṭ, or pavement on the Ganges, at which Rāmānanda bathed very early in the morning. On the way Rāmānanda trampled on the boy and exclaimed: "Rāma, Rāma! What poor creature is it that I have trampled upon?" Kabīr rose up and received the exclamation "Rāma, Rāma" as a Mantra communicated to him by Rāmānanda, and he understood that he had thus been made a disciple. Another account is that, being trampled on, Kabīr rose up and cried aloud, when Rāmānanda told him to be quiet and go on uttering the name of "Rāma". Considering that he had thus been accepted as a pupil, Kabīr went on with his adorations of God, proclaiming that he was the disciple of Rāmānanda. Some Hindus went to the latter and asked him whether he had initiated Kabīr. Thereupon Kabīr was sent for and asked by Rāmānanda, when it was that he had been initiated. Kabīr mentioned to him the incident of his having been trampled upon on the Ghāṭ. Then Rāmānanda remembered the matter and clasped Kabīr to his breast. Since that time Kabīr regularly attended at his master's Maṭha and joined him in his disputations with the Paṇḍits. For some time Kabīr lived at Manikapur, as is mentioned in one of his Ramainīs. There he heard of the fame of Shaikh Taqqi and of twenty-one Pīrs. He heard their discourses, condemned their teachings and said: "Oh Shaikhs, of whatever name, listen to me; open your eyes and see the origin and the end of all things and their creation and dissolution". In one of the books of this sect, Shaikh Taqqi is represented as an enemy of Kabīr and a Pīr, or the religious guide, of Sikandar Lodi. At his advice the emperor persecuted Kabīr and used various methods to destroy him. But Kabīr miraculously escaped death and was eventually reconciled to Sikandar Lodi, who received him into his favour. Kabīr died at Maghar, and there was a dispute between the Hindus and the Mahomedans as to the disposal of his dead body, which was covered by a sheet of cloth. When the sheet was removed, the body had disappeared, and in its stead there was a heap of flowers. The Mahomedans took one half of the quantity and buried it at Maghar and erected a tomb over it, and the Hindus took their share to Benares, where it was burnt. Kabīr had a wife of the name of Loi, a son of the name of Kamāl, and a daughter of the name of Kamālī. But there are miraculous stories as to how Kabīr came by them.

As to how much of this account is historical and how much legendary, it is difficult to say. But that he was a Mahomedan weaver at the beginning may be accepted as a fact. And that Shaikh Taqqi, a Mahomedan Pīr, who is mentioned in one of the Ramainīs, as stated above, was his rival and that Kabīr lived about the time of Sikandar Lodi may also be regarded as historical. As to whether Kabīr was a disciple of Rāmānanda, there is some question, as will be presently mentioned. Mr. Westcott considers it not impossible that he should have been both a Mahomedan and a Sūfi [1]), but all his writings show a complete familiarity with the names occuring in Hindu religious literature and Hindu manners and customs, so that it appears to me that there is little or nothing in Kabīr's writings calculated to show that his teachings had a Mahomedan basis. The basis appears to be purely Hindu, though Kabīr was a bold and uncompromising reformer and hurled anathemas at the Paṇḍits, the Brāhmaṇas proud of their caste, and the teachers of the existing sects of the Hindus, and thus appears to have come under the influence of Mahomedanism.

The dates given by various writers for the birth and death of Kabīr are conflicting. Mr. Westcott makes him live for 78 years, from 1440 to 1518 A. D. [2]), and according to Mr. Macauliffe he was born in Saṃvat 1455, corresponding to A. D. 1398 [3]), and he died in A. D. 1518 [4]), having lived for 119 years, five months and twenty-seven days. In a footnote he quotes from an original work the date Śaka 1370, corresponding to 1448 A. D., as the date of his death. Sikandar Lodi was on the throne of Delhi from 1488 to 1517 A. D. The last of the three dates does not harmonise with this, and so it must be given up. Rāmānanda, we have seen, is spoken of as having been born in 1298 A. D. and died in 1411 A. D. If Mr. Westcott's date for Kabīr's birth is true, Kabīr cannot have been a disciple of Rāmānanda. If that of Mr. Macauliffe is accepted, it is just possible that he should have so become, for at the time of Rāmānanda's death Kabīr must have been thirteen years of age, and he is represented in one of the legends to have been but a boy when he was accepted as a disciple by the old sage. The date 1518 A. D. given by both the writers for his death may be accepted as correct. But, if that of his birth given by Mr. Macauliffe is also accepted, we shall have to suppose that Kabīr lived for 119 years; Rāmānanda also according to the dates given in the last section lived for 113 years. Whether both of them lived such long lives might well be questioned. But, until we have more evidence, the dates for Rāmānanda already noticed and for Kabīr as given by Mr. Macauliffe may be provisionally accepted, and thus Kabīr might be considered to have really been a disciple of Rāmānanda, though, of course, being a boy of thirteen, he could not have taken part in his master's disputations with Paṇḍits. In Kabīr's works, however, so far as I have seen them, Rāmānanda's name does not occur, though the name Rāma as that of the Supreme Being and also the relation of the individual soul with Rāma as well as his refutation of the doctrine of God's being Videha or Nirguṇa, i. e. without attributes, must have been borrowed from Rāmānanda's doctrines, which again are based on Rāmānuja's system.

§ 58. We now give a translation of a few passages illustrative of the teachings of Kabīr [5]).

---

[1]) Kabir and the Kabir Panth by Rev. G. H. Westcott. Cawnpore, 1907, p. 44.
[2]) *Ibid.* Chronological Table, p. VII.
[3]) The Sikh Religion, Vol. VI, p. 122.
[4]) *Ibid.* pp. 139—40.
[5]) The edition consulted is that published with a commentary under the orders of Raghurajasimha, Maharaja of Rewah, in Saṃvat 1924.

First Ramainī[1]).

1. There was in the inside a substance called Jīva, or individual soul, the Internal Light illuminated [it]. 2. And then followed a woman of the name of 'desire'; and she was called Gāyatrī. 3. That woman gave birth to three sons, Brahmā, Viṣṇu and Maheśa. 4. Then Brahmā asked the woman who was her husband and whose wife she was. 5. (She replied:) "Thou and I, I and thou, and there is no third. Thou art my husband and I am thy wife." 6. The father and son had a common wife; and one mother has a two-fold character; there is no son who is a good son and who will endeavour to recognise his father.

Second Ramainī.

1. In the light there was sound, which was a woman. 2. And of the woman were Hari, Brahmā and the enemy of the three cities (Śiva). 3. Then Brahmā created an egg and divided it into fourteen regions. 4—6. Then Hari, Hara and Brahmā settled in three regions, and then they arranged the whole Brahmāṇḍa and the six philosophies and ninety-six heresies. Nobody then taught the Veda for his sustenance; and Turuk did not come for making circumcision. 7. The woman brought forth from her womb children. They became distinct individuals and followed different courses of action. 8. Therefore I and thou are of one blood and are one life. Distinctness arises from ignorance. 9. From one woman all sprang, and what knowledge is it that brought about distinctness between them? 13 (Sākhī). Kabīr proclaims: All this ordinary world is destructible; without knowing the name of Rāma all individuals are drowned in the ocean of existence.

Kabīr's account of creation seems to be this. In the light of Rāma there existed a substance which was the subtle element, the sum total of all individual souls. And then that substance was illuminated by that light. Then followed a desire in the shape of a woman, which was at the same time called Gāyatrī and sound (Śabda), and from her the creation took its rise. His idea thus seems to be that individual souls came into being, or were developed out of a substance which was their subtle form, at the will of the Supreme Soul, which (will) was uttered in the form of a sound. That is to say, the Supreme Soul was not the material cause of the world, but a distinct subtle entity. What, in the language of the Upaniṣads, became many was this entity and not the Supreme Soul himself. Kabīr's philosophy is thus not a monism, but dualism. All individuals sprang into existence from the same cause, there was one blood and one life, and consequently the distinction of castes and races was a later fiction. Kabīr thus appears to be an opponent of this distinction.

Fifth Ramainī.

The substance of the first five Caupāīs seems to be that Hari, Hara and Brahmā, taking the two letters (Rāma), laid the foundation of all

[1]) Ramainī is a piece of composition consisting of several Caupāīs (Sk. Catuṣpadī), which are stanzas consisting of four lines with the ends of the first two and of the last two rhyming with each other, and a Sākhī (which is another species of metre) at the end.

learning, and gradually the Vedas and Kitābs (books) came to be composed. 6—8. In all the four ages the devotees devised systems, but were not aware that the bundle they had tied up was torn. Men ran in all directions for salvation, being afraid. Abandoning their lord they ran towards hell.

Eighth Ramainī.

1. The precept "Tat tvam asi" (that thou art) is the message of the Upaniṣads. 2. They lay great stress upon it, and those who are qualified explain it (at great length). 3. Sanaka and Nārada became happy by regarding the highest principle to be distinct from themselves. 4. The colloquy between Janaka and Yājñavalkya comes to the same effect, and that same sweet sentiment was tasted by Dattātreya. 5. Vasiṣṭha and Rāma sang together the same thing, and that same thing was explained to Uddhava. 6. That same thing was substantiated by Janaka and, though he had a body, he was called bodiless (Videha). 7 (Sākhī). No mortal becomes immortal without abandoning the pride of birth. That which one cannot see by experience is to be considered as "unseen" or "unperceived".

In this Ramainī Kabīr shows acquaintance with the Upaniṣads and other branches of Hindu sacred literature, so that he cannot have been a mere "Sūfi and Mahomedan". He rejects the theory of the identity between the Supreme and the individual souls, which is regarded as being laid down in the expression "That thou art" of the Chāndogya-Upaniṣad. The commentator says that by "that" is to be understood the subtle body of sixteen parts and the expression means "Thou art that subtle body". Kabīr takes all the individuals he has named in this Ramainī to have preached duality.

In the fourteenth Ramainī there is a condemnation of the several systems of religion, that contained in the Purāṇas, that of Brahmā, Haṃsa, Gopāla, Śambhu, ghosts and goblins and various forms of worship up to the Nevāja of the Mahomedan.

Thirty-fourth Ramainī.

1. The Paṇḍits were misled by the study of the Vedas which are based on the Guṇas, or qualities, and did not know their own nature and their true friend (God). 2. They practise Saṃdhyā, Tarpaṇa, the six rites and various other such ceremonies. 3. In all the four Yugas Gāyatrī has been taught; ask who obtained salvation (Mukti) by its means. 4. When you are touched by other people, you bathe; tell me who is more degraded than yourselves. 5. You are very proud of your virtues. Too much pride is not good. 6. How can he whose name destroys all pride bear this proud behaviour? 7 (Sākhī). Giving up the traditional mode of worship of the family, they seek the place of Nirvāṇa; having destroyed the seed and sprout, they became an entity without attributes (Videha or Nirguṇa).

Kabīr here condemns the rites, ceremonies and other practices of the Brāhmaṇas, the pride that is generated in them by these, the contempt in which they hold people of other castes, and also their search of Nirvāṇa, or a condition without any attributes, i. e. the Advaita, or a-dualistic, system which they follow.

Fortieth Ramainī.

1. The sea, which is a collection of waters, is a ditch, and in it are the sun, the moon, and thirty-three crores of brothers. 2. In the whirlpools (of such a universe) they (men and gods) have seated themselves and desire happiness, but have not shunned the touch of misery. 3. Nobody knows the secret of misery, and the world has become mad in a variety of ways. 4. Everybody is a fool or a sage in himself and nobody knows Rāma who dwells in the heart. 5 (Sākhī). They themselves are Hari (God), they themselves are lords, they themselves are the slaves of Hari. When there is no guarantee, the lady (Mukti, or salvation) goes away disappointed.

Here again there is a condemnation of various systems and of the self-confidence which has given rise to them and the neglect of God dwelling in the heart.

Sākhīs.

I.

31. The crowds went by the path traversed by the Paṇḍits. Lofty is the ascent to Rāma. Kabīr has climbed it. 135. The whole world has gone astray by partiality for one's own system. He who, becoming free from partiality, adores Hari, is a wise sage. 138. The great ones are lost in their own greatness; pride peers out through every pore; when they are not familiar with a wise preceptor, all the orders of men are of the Camār caste, i. e. the degraded caste of curriers. 182. The Kali is a wicked age; the world is blind and nobody believes in the true word. He to whom a salutary advice is given, becomes an enemy. 211. Three things went to a holy place (the body, the fickle heart, and the mind which is a thief). They did not destroy a single sin, but on the contrary the mind contracted ten others. 260. The Kabīrs (men in general) polluted the path of Bhakti, or faith, by washing pebbles and stones. Keeping poison within, they have thrown out the nectar. 358. "I am the author of the whole creation, there is no other who is superior to me." (This is what some people think.) Kabīr says that, when one does not know what one is oneself, one thinks everything to be contained in oneself. 365. In this world all have passed away considering themselves to be Rāma, but no one actually became Rāma. Kabīr says that those who know Rāma as he truly is, attain all their objects. 366. This world has become mad and has conceived a love for something which can be no matter of experience; and denying all authoritativeness to actual experience, they attach themselves to a soul without attributes (Videha). 372. Seeing a void, men were misled and went about searching in all quarters till they died, but did not find a form without attributes.

II.

91. The bee loiters in the garden, being enticed by the innumerable flowers in it. In the same manner the individual soul loiters among the objects of sense and at the end goes away disappointed. 95. The soul is to the mind as a monkey is to a showman. Making it dance in a variety of ways, it (mind) finally retains it in its own hands.

96. The mind is fickle, a thief and perfect swindler. The gods and the sages fell off in consequence of the mind, and mind finds a hundred thousand openings. 136. If a man gives up his belongings, it does not mean much. Egotism, or self-pride, cannot be given up. Self-pride, which led astray the great Munis, devours all. Running after gold and women, men are burnt by the passion generated by an illusion. Kabīr says, how can they be saved, being like cotton which has come in contact with fire? 147. All became subject to the power of illusion: Brahmā, Viṣṇu, Maheśa, and the four, Nārada, Śārada, Sanaka, and Gaṇeśa, the son of Gaurī. 209. Do not kill a poor living creature; the life of all is the same. You will not be free from (the sin of) killing, even if you hear crores of Purāṇas.

III.

122. He to attain whom the great sages (Munis) go through austerities and whose virtues the Vedas sing, himself gives instruction, but nobody believes. 208. One single poor soul is bound up by many fetters. If the father (God) will not liberate him, what power has the soul himself to do so? 243. I (God) instruct him; but he does not understand and sells himself into the hands of others. I pull him towards myself; but he runs away to the city of death (Yama). 282. If you endeavour to acquire one thing (God), every other thing will come to you; but if you endeavour to acquire every other thing, that one thing will be lost. If you water the root of a tree, you will obtain a sufficiency of flowers and fruits. 310. If you want me (God), give up your desire for every other thing and become mine, and then everything will be yours. 336. He has entered into every body and remains there fully watchful. When one wants a certain accomplishment, he inspires him with the corresponding thoughts (calculated to enable him to achieve success).

Here the first group contains a condemnation of the current religious doctrines; the second gives a specimen of Kabīr's moral teachings; and the third explains the way in which God's grace operates towards the deliverance of man. Kabīr, therefore, was as much a constructive reformer as destructive. In Sākhī 260 of the first group Kabīr, it will be seen, condemns the worship of idols. The religion which he promulgated, therefore, was a pure spiritual theism. The mode of worship used by his followers up to the present day consists of prayers and praises only. Kabīr founded a Pantha, or a sect, and the Maṭhas, or establishments, of that sect exist in several parts of India. The principal one is at Benares, with a branch at Maghar in the Gorakhpur district, where he died. This last is said to be in the charge of a Mahomedan Mahant, or superior. The second was established by Dharmadās, his chief disciple, in the Chattisgarh district of the Central Provinces[1]). The followers of Kabīr's sect are to be found principally among the lower castes, but the sage is highly venerated by all Vaiṣṇavas of whatever caste or class.

---

[1]) For details see Rev. G. H. Westcott's volume on Kabīr referred to above.

XX. Other Rāmānandins.

§ 59. Malukdās, who lived about the end of Akbar's reign, i. e. about the end of the sixteenth century, was a worshipper of Rāma. The tradition that he belonged to the school of Rāmānanda appears to be correct. Like Kabīr, he seems to have been a non-idolater, since in a hymn which I have seen he ridicules men and women who hammer valuable metals into gods, worship them, and, whenever there is a necessity, sell them for the price of the metal, and says that the true way was shown to him by his wise preceptor. The sect founded by him has seven Maṭhas, or establishments, and its adherents follow the occupation of householders.

Dādu was a cotton cleaner at Ahmedabad. At twelve he removed to Sambhar and finally settled at Naraina, about twenty Kos from Jaipur. He flourished about 1600 A. D. at the end of Akbar's reign. His doctrines appear to be similar to those of Kabīr. The only mode of worship was Japa, or the repetition of the name of Rāma. The sect does not worship images of Rāma and it erects no temples. Dādu inculcates faith in, and love of, Rāma and meditation on him. His followers are divided into three classes: (1) Viraktas, (2) Nāgas, and (3) Vistaradhārins. The first live the life of ascetics, the second are bearers of arms and enter into the service of princes as soldiers, and the third lead an ordinary life.

Raidās, a pupil of Rāmānanda, was a founder of a sect the followers of which are to be found in the caste of Camārs, or leather-workers. Nābhājī in his Bhaktamālā tells many legends about him. Under the name of Rohidās he is known and revered even in the Marāṭha country, and Mahīpatī, the Marāṭha writer on saints, devotes a chapter to him.

Senā the barber, a follower of Rāmānanda, is also reported to have founded a sect. He too is known in the Marāṭha country [1]).

XXI. Tulasīdās.

§ 60. Another person who contributed to the propagation of the cult of Rāma over Northern India, was the famous Tulasīdās, whom we will now briefly notice. Tulasīdās belonged to the Saravaryā or Sarayūparīṇa caste of Brāhmaṇas and was born in Saṃvat 1589, corresponding to 1532 A. D., under an inauspicious constellation. He was abandoned by his parents and was picked up by a Sādhu, or a pious man, in whose company he visited many places in India. His father's name was Ātmārāma Śukla Dūbe, his mother's Hulasī, and his own Rāma Bōta. His father-in-law was a man of the name of Dīnabandhu Pāṭhaka, and his wife was called Ratnāvalī. His son's name was Tāraka.

Tulasīdās commenced the composition of his great work, Rāmacaritamānasa, usually known as Rāmāyaṇa, at Ayodhyā in 1574 A. D. and finished it at Benares. He wrote eleven other works, six of which were smaller. Tulasīdās was not a sturdy reformer like Kabīr and

[1]) See Wilson's Hindu Religions.

does not seem to have founded a sect or even to have promulgated a definite Vedāntic theory. In this respect he appears to have been, like a host of other persons who flourished in the country, a teacher of the Bhaktimārga, or the path of devotion, which is based upon a dualistic philosophy with a leaning towards spiritual monism of the Advaita system. Tulasīdās died in 1623 A. D.[1]).

§ 61. I will now give a short specimen of Tulasīdās' teachings from his Rāma-Satasaī, the composition of which, as stated in Dohā 21 of the first chapter, was commenced on Thursday, the ninth of the bright half of Vaiśākha, Saṃvat 1642 = 1585 A. D.

Chapter I.

(Dohā 3) The highest soul, the highest excellent place, than whom or which there is no other, Tulasī understands and hears to be Rāma, the blessed. (Dohā 4) "Rāma whose attributes confer blessings upon all is himself free from all desires. He fulfils all desires, is the benefactor of all. The sages assert this." — So says Tulasī. (Dohā 15) Tulasī sees plainly that in every pore of Rāma there is an endless universe. He is pure, is unchangeable and is irresistible. (Dohā 6) The blessed Jānakī is the mother of the world, and Rāma the father. Both are beneficent. Their grace destroys sin, and creates conscience (confers the knowledge of distinguishing good from evil). (Dohā 44) Where there is Rāma, there is no [evil] desire; where there is [evil] desire, there is no Rāma. Oh Tulasī, the sun and the night do not exist in one place. (Dohā 45) When Rāma is afar, Māyā (illusion or temptation) is strong. When he is known, it becomes tiny or thin. When the sun is at a distance, the shadow is long; when he is on the head, it is below the feet. (Dohā 48) Says Tulasī: "If there is no love for Rāma, all learning is thrown into an oven; and Yama takes away knowledge and devours it; everything burns away, and the very root is destroyed". (Dohā 57) All things by which a man is surrounded, serve as hindrances, and none proves a help (towards the way of bliss); and, in such circumstances, if the end is good, it can become so only through Rāma's grace.

Chapter II.

(Dohā 17) Says Tulasī: "Through the disobedience of God, man brings evil on himself and all his associates. The king of the Kurus, while governing his kingdom, was reduced to dust along with his army and family". (Dohā 18) Says Tulasī: "From sweet words results good on all sides. This is a spell that overcomes everything; avoid all harsh words". (Dohā 19) "A man attains happiness by the grace of Rāma, and it escapes one without it", says Tulasī, "though they know this, bad men neglect to adore Rāma."

Chapter IV[2]).

82 (89 B. I.). The excellent retentive faculty is called Girā or Sarasvatī, and the immutable Dharma is a Vaṭa tree. Dharma con-

[1]) For details see Dr. Grierson's articles in the Indian Antiquary, Vol. XXII.
[2]) The editions consulted are those published by Navalkiśora at Lakhnau in 1886 and in the Bibliotheca Indica in 1897.

sists of a triad of confluent rivers destroying sin. Oh Tulasī, conceive no dislike for these and accept these.

The triad is given by the commentator as action, knowledge, and Bhakti, or devotion.

83 (90 B. I.). One becomes clean by bathing (in these three confluent rivers), i. e. grasping the triad by the understanding. The dirt in the shape of immorality is washed off, and then there is no doubt as to the easy attainment of the place of Rāma. 84 (91 B. I.). Forgiveness is holy Vārāṇasī. Bhakti, or devotion, is like the river of gods (Gaṅgā), and clear knowledge is like Viśveśvara. These together with compassion, which is power (Pārvatī), shine.

The commentator remarks that just as Benares with the other three brings about deliverance, so do forgiveness, devotion, knowledge, and compassion.

85 (92 B. I.). Vārāṇasī is not far from him whose heart dwells in the house which is Kṣamā (forgiveness) — Vārāṇasī, in which shines, oh Tulasī, the celestial river in the shape of Bhakti, which results in numerous virtuous deeds. 86 (93 B. I.). Kāśī is the bright half of a month and Magaha, or Magadha, is the dark half in which dwell covetousness, infatuation, intoxication, and lust. Oh Tulasī, considering which is beneficial and which is injurious, do [choose where to] reside during all the watches of the day.

Kāśī is associated with the four virtues mentioned above, and Magadha with the vices noticed here. So one is told to practise what is beneficial and to avoid what is injurious.

87 (94 B. I.). What has gone away will not come again. Therefore do acquire knowledge. The same thing that you have to-day you will have to-morrow; therefore, oh Tulasī, give up all infatuation.

The idea seems to be: Do not waste time by procrastination; begin your devotions at once.

88 (95 B. I.). The past and the future hang together on the present. Oh Tulasī, do not entertain any doubt; get through that which is before you at present.

89 (96 B. I.). A good soul is like the Mānasa (lake), and in it is the pure water of the sweet glory of Rāma. Sin is washed off and the heart becomes pure (by bathing in that water); and this calm water is not inaccessible to the wise.

The idea seems to be that in a good soul a taste for devotion to Rāma springs up and, when it is cultivated, the soul becomes pure.

From these extracts it will be seen that according to Tulasīdās Rāma is the supreme God, and that through his grace man becomes holy and blessed. He should, therefore, be adored; where he is, sin is not, and therefore, for the purification of the mind, he should always be thought of and meditated on. The ways to God usually followed are, he says, inefficacious and as such may be thrown into the fire.

XXII. Vallabha.

§ 62. We will now turn our attention to the more extensive and almost exclusive cult of the Kṛṣṇa of Gokula. The founder of it was

Vallabha. He was the son of a Tailaṅga Brāhmaṇa named Lakṣmaṇa Bhaṭṭa, who was a student of the Black Yajurveda and lived at a village named Kānkarava in the Telugu country. On one occasion Lakṣmaṇa Bhaṭṭa went on a pilgrimage to Benares with his wife, Elamāgāra. On the way she gave birth to a son on the eleventh of the dark half of Vaiśākha of the Vikrama year 1535, corresponding to 1479 A. D. [1]) That son was known as Vallabha. Vallabha lived for some time in Vṛndāvana and for some time at Mathurā. About that time it is alleged that Gopāla-Kṛṣṇa manifested himself on the Govardhana hill by the name of Devadamana, called also Śrī-Nāthajī. The God told Vallabha in a dream to come and see him, informing him that his companions in the cow-settlement, when he became incarnate as Kṛṣṇa, were born again in the present age and commissioned him to make them his attendants, that he might sport with them as in the former age. Accordingly, Vallabha went and saw Devadamana or Śrī-Nāthajī. Śrī-Nāthajī commanded him to erect a shrine for himself and to promulgate the method of worshipping him, without which a man would not be admissible to the Puṣṭimārga, or the path of divine grace, which Vallabha had founded. The meaning of this seems to be that Vallabha connected his system with a special manifestation of Kṛṣṇa known by the name of Śrī-Nāthajī [2]).

Vallabha's Vedāntic theory is the same as that of an earlier author of the name of Viṣṇusvāmin. This Viṣṇusvāmin is said to have been the son of the councillor of a Draviḍa chief dependent upon the emperor of Delhi [3]). Nābhājī in his Bhaktamālā makes Jñāndeva, Nāmdeva, Trilocana, and lastly Vallabha his successors [4]). The first was Jñāndeva, who is represented as a follower of his system (Saṃpradāya). He was one of three sons born to a man, who became a householder after he had assumed the order of an ascetic. He was, therefore, excommunicated and was not allowed to learn the Vedas. But he himself by his miraculous power made a male buffalo repeat the Vedas. This story is the same as that related of the Jñāndeva of Mahārāṣṭra, the author of a vernacular commentary on the Bhagavadgītā. But the Marāṭhas do not know of Viṣṇusvāmin as his Guru, or teacher, or of Jñāndeva being his successor or follower. If, however, the tradition reported by Nābhājī is correct, Viṣṇusvāmin must have lived about the middle of the thirteenth century. The date of the commentary above alluded to is Śaka 1212, corresponding to 1290 A. D.

The Vedāntic theory of Viṣṇusvāmin which is the same as that of Vallabha is as follows. The one primeval soul was not joyful, because he was alone (BU. I, 4, 3), and, desiring to be many, he himself became the inanimate world, the individual soul, and the inward controlling soul. These sprang from him like sparks from a burning fire and are his parts (MU. II, 1). By his own inscrutable power he rendered the properties of intelligence and joy imperceptible in

[1]) Yajñeśvara, Āryavidyāsudhākara.

[2]) See Harirāya Mahārāja's Govardhanaprākaṭyakī Vārtā, published in Saṃvat 1935, p. 11.

[3]) Yajñeśvara, Āryavidyāsudhākara, p. 228.

[4]) Ed. by Khemarāj, Bombay, Śaka 1827 (1905 A. D.), pp. 95—98.

the first, and his joy alone in the second, while the third has all the attributes perceptible in it. Simple Brahman as such has perceptible joy prevailing in it [1]).

§ 63. The following particulars have been gleaned from two works belonging to Vallabhācārya's sect [2]). The whole world has Brahman for its material cause. The perception of forms apparently different from the Brahman is due to ignorance or delusion and to the true nature of Brahman being rendered imperceptible. The individual soul is identical with Brahman, a part of Brahman and atomic. From the Akṣara composed of existence, intelligence, and joy (Saccidānanda) particles come out as sparks from fire. From the predominance of the Sat portion in them the joy portion is concealed, and thus we have the individual souls possessing Sat, existence, and Cit, intelligence. The individual soul is not a form of the Supreme Soul altered by a third thing being involved in it, such as the Māyā (illusive power), but is itself the same substance as the Supreme Soul with one attribute rendered imperceptible. The relation between the two is thus that of identity (Advaita), both being in the pristine unchanged form, i. e. identity of untransformed souls (Śuddhādvaita).

The individual soul is of two kinds: (1) going through the circle of existences, and (2) delivered from the trammels of life. The first is subject to misery in consequence of his delusion that his body and senses are his soul. He remains in this condition till he acquires knowledge, sees the vanity of the world and devotes himself to meditation and the love of God, when he is delivered. The delivered souls are: (1) those who have become so, while in their previous condition, by the termination of ignorance or delusion, such as Sanaka and others; and (2) those who dwell in the world of the Bhagavat, other than the pervading Vaikuṇṭha [3]), where they attain the condition of pure Brahman by the favour of the Bhagavat; (3) there are others, who, having the divine nature in them and coming in contact with good men, resort to various ways of Bhakti, or the propitiation of God, until perfect love alone for him comes to dwell in their heart, and finally become the associates of the Bhagavat in his eternal sports and amusements. This last is the highest Mokṣa, or deliverance. That class of worldly souls who have no divine nature in them and in whom evil predominates, are ever moving in the circle of existences. The souls who have the divine nature in them are of two kinds: (1) those who subject themselves to certain moral discipline (Maryādājīva), and (2) those who depend entirely on God's grace (Puṣṭijīva). Both attain final deliverance, but there is a difference which corresponds

1) Sakalācāryamatasaṃgraha by Śrīnivāsa, Chowkh. Series.

2) Śuddhādvaitamārtaṇḍa by Giridhara, and Prameyaratnārṇava by Bālakṛṣṇa Bhaṭṭa, Chowkh. Series.

3) I translate the word Vyāpi-Vaikuṇṭha thus. The Vyāpi-Vaikuṇṭha is above the Vaikuṇṭha of Viṣṇu, the protector of the world. There dwells Puruṣottama, who manifests himself variously to his various devotees. To those in whom Bhakti has risen to the highest pitch and has become a haunting passion he manifests himself as the sportive Kṛṣṇa. In a portion of the Vyāpi-Vaikuṇṭha there is the Goloka with Vṛndāvana in which there are extensive trees, bowers of creepers, and the river Yamunā. The highest Bhaktas are transferred to this Vṛndāvana, and Kṛṣṇa sports with them there.

to that between (2) and (3) above and which will be further explained below.

Śrīkṛṣṇa is the highest Brahman. He has hands and feet not made up of ordinary matter (Aprākṛta), but celestial. His body consists of Sat, existence; Cit, intelligence; Ānanda, joy. He is called Puruṣottama, as the most excellent of all beings, and has all attributes which are not ordinary, but celestial. All his sports are eternal. He, with his four arms or two arms, sports with his various devotees, or Bhaktas, in the extensive Vaikuṇṭha, which contains Vṛndāvana with its large forests. Kṛṣṇa is, therefore, the highest joy (Paramānanda). By his will his Sattva portion overcomes the Ānanda or joy portion and, becoming Akṣara, or unchangeable, he is the cause of all causes and creates the world. Then Akṣarabrahman is of two kinds: (1) that which is recognised by the devotees as the place of Puruṣottama, which has the attributes of the extensive Vaikuṇṭha and others; (2) to the enlightened it appears in the form of existence, intelligence and joy, infinite in time and space, self-manifesting and devoid of all qualities. Therefore, in the form in which the enlightened see it all the positive qualities are hidden or rendered imperceptible by the inscrutable power referred to above, and therefore they are not to be regarded as non-existing. When Brahman is spoken of as devoid of all qualities, what is meant is just this. There are thus three forms of the Supreme Being, Puruṣottama and the two kinds of the Unchangeable here mentioned. To explain the controlling of all by Puruṣottama, that form of his that dwells in the sun, the gods, the earth, etc., is called Antaryāmin (the inward controller). It is this inward controller that becomes incarnate in the various forms usually mentioned. The celestial Sattva quality of Kṛṣṇa becomes Viṣṇu, and in this form he becomes the protector of all. Similarly the qualities of Rajas and Tamas assume the forms of Brahmadeva and Śiva for discharging the functions of creation and destruction.

Puṣṭi is the grace (Anugraha) of God which is to be inferred from its fruit or the results, which are ordinary, or of this world, and extraordinary, or of the next world. Mahāpuṣṭi, or the highest grace, is that which removes great obstacles and conduces to the attainment of God himself. Puṣṭi enables one to attain the four objects of life. Extraordinary, or special Puṣṭi, conduces to Bhakti, which leads to the attainment of God. The Bhakti, or devotion generated by this special grace, is called Puṣṭibhakti. The frame of mind generated by this kind of devotion is the desire of the attainment of God to the exclusion of everything else. This Puṣṭibhakti is of four kinds: (1) Pravāha-Puṣṭibhakti, (2) Maryādā-Puṣṭibhakti, (3) Puṣṭi-Puṣṭibhakti, (4) Śuddha-Puṣṭibhakti. The first is the path of those who, while engaged in a worldly life with its *me* and *mine*, which is compared to a stream (Pravāha), do acts calculated to bring about the attainment of God. The second is of those who, withdrawing their minds from worldly enjoyments, devote themselves to God by hearing discourses about him, singing his name, and such other processes. The third is of those who already enjoying God's grace are made by another grace competent to acquire knowledge useful for adoration; and thus they come to know all about the ways of God. The followers of this path have to depend on their own efforts for the acquisition of knowledge referred to. The fourth is of those who through mere love devote themselves to the singing and praising of God as if it were a haunting passion. This Bhakti is generated by God himself and does not depend upon man's will as the third, mentioned above, does. First a liking for himself is generated by God in the mind of a man to whom his grace extends. Then a man sets about acquiring knowledge about God, and all this is called Premabhakti (love adoration). Now the stages in the development of this are as follows: (1) love or liking (Preman), (2) attachment or addictedness (Āsakti), (3) a haunting passion, which is the mature condition of the first two (Vyasana). The haunting passion leads to the attainment of the end, that is, the highest bliss. Those in whom Bhakti has attained to this pitch reject with scorn the four kinds of Mukti and choose the eternal service of Hari, as noticed in the section on the Pāñcarātra system. By the haunting passion about Hari he is seen everywhere, and therefore everything becomes an object of love, and the devotee identifies himself with everything. Then the inner and the outer world is, for the devotee, full of Puruṣottama, or the highest soul. The final fruit of this devotion is admission to the eternal sports of Kṛṣṇa. The Bhaktas join in these sports, assuming the forms of cows, beasts, birds, trees, rivers, etc., and enjoy the company of Puruṣottama, which confers boundless joy. These eternal sports are like those which Kṛṣṇa went through when he became incarnate in Vraja and Vṛndāvana. Some of the devotees become in the celestial Vṛndāvana Gopas and Gopīs and join in the sports. The Maryādābhaktas attain Mukti called Sāyujya, which consists in being one with Hari. The Puṣṭibhaktas reject it with scorn and seek for participation in the sports of Hari.

§ 64. These are the doctrines of the school of Vallabha. We will now proceed to give a short description of the practical modes of worship. Vallabha had a son named Viṭṭhaleśa, and they are spoken of respectively as Ācārya and Gosāiṃ or Gosvāmin. The latter had seven sons of the names of Giridhara, Govindarāya, Bālakṛṣṇa, Gokulanātha, Raghunātha, Yadunātha, and Ghanaśyāma. The Gurus of this sect ordinarily called Mahārājas are descendants of these seven. Each Guru has a temple of his own, and there are no public places of worship. The devotee should visit the temple of his Guru at stated intervals, which are eight in number during the day. The mode of worship is as follows. The conductor of the worship should rise early in the morning, utter the name of Bhagavat and rinse his mouth and then drink a little of the washings of the feet [of Bhagavat] and, with his face to the north or the east, should utter the name of the Ācārya and pray to him and make a bow. The same should be done to Viṭṭhaleśa and the names of his seven sons should be uttered, as well as of one's own Guru, and then a bow should be made to Kṛṣṇa after uttering the names Govardhana and others. Then the river Yamunā should be remembered and bowed to, and six stanzas of a poem called Bhramaragītā should be repeated; and then the Gopīs, or cowherdesses, should be adored. After this the worshipper should answer the call of nature, wash his hands, feet and face, and then drink a portion of the washings of the feet of Kṛṣṇa, and eat the residue of the betel leaves supposed to be eaten by Kṛṣṇa. Then he should besmear his body with oil and bathe. After bathing he should drink in a little water, after repeating the name of Nārāyaṇa. Then he should make a perpendicular mark on his forehead with white earth, the mark of a lotus on the bosom and of a bamboo leaf on the arms, etc., twelve in all, to represent the twelve forms of Viṣṇu, Keśava, Nārāyaṇa, Mādhava, etc. He should then print the forms of the various weapons of Viṣṇu on his body, and then, saluting Vallabhācārya, should adore Kṛṣṇa with the Gopīs. He should then open the door of the temple and, going into the sleeping apartments, bring out the wreaths of flowers and all other things used on the previous day, and then sweep and clean the apartments. He should then brush the throne and make all the arrangements necessary for the reception of Kṛṣṇa awakened from sleep. He should then approach the bed-room and sing a song calling upon Kṛṣṇa to rise from sleep, to take the refreshments prepared for him and to go with his companions to the forest for grazing the cows. Kṛṣṇa should be brought out and placed on the throne. Rādhā should be placed to his left hand, and then the worshipper should prostrate himself before her. The refreshments already prepared should then be placed before them, and they should be requested to eat them. Then the bed should be dusted and cleaned and then Kṛṣṇa should be made to wash his mouth. Other refreshments should be then placed before the two. And at the end of all an Āratī, or waving of lamps, should be gone through with a song. Vallabhācārya should then be saluted. Then comes the bath of Kṛṣṇa. After bathing saffron paint should be applied. Then he should be dressed and milk given to him. Afterwards by the churning of milk froth should be prepared and offered to Kṛṣṇa. He should be then told to wash his mouth with water. Then betel leaves should be offered to him. Then a cradle should be adorned and Kṛṣṇa should be told to get into it, and then it should be rocked and toys should be got ready for the divine boy. Afterwards the mid-day dinner should be prepared. A Caukā, or a small four-legged table, should be placed before him and viands of all kinds in cups should be put on the table. The lord should then be told to eat them. A little rice should be placed in a small plate and, mixed with ghee, five or seven mouthfuls should be held before him. Then lamps should be waved about him. Subsequently all the other dishes should be offered. In this manner the ceremonies go on. A meal is again prepared at night and Kṛṣṇa is laid on the sleeping cot and made to sleep again. Thus the order of the ceremonies is as follows: (1) the ringing of the bell, (2) the blowing of the conch-shell, (3) awakening of the Lord (Ṭhākurjī) and offering morning refreshments, (4) waving of lamps, (5) bathing, (6) dressing, (7) Gopīvallabha food, (8) leading the cows out for grazing, (9) the mid-day dinner, (10) waving of lamps, (11) after the last the screen is drawn up and the God cannot be seen; this interval is called Anosara or Anavasara, i. e. no time for seeing him, (12) the finishing up, (13) the evening meal, (14) going to bed.

Besides the ordinary worship detailed above, the followers of this sect hold a number of feasts and festivals, some of which are in honour of Vallabhācārya, his son and seven grandsons. The influence exercised by Vallabha and his successors over their adherents seems to have been immense, and this has come down to their descendants or existing Gurus of the sect also. This is kept up by the fact that the God cannot be worshipped independently in a public place of worship, but in the house and temple of the Guru or the Mahārāja, which therefore has to be regularly visited by the devotees with offerings. The followers of this system consist principally of the trading classes of Gujarāt, Rājputāna and further to the north about Mathurā. The principal doctrine which these latter are taught is that all their belongings should be dedicated to their Guru; and this doctrine is not seldom carried to an extreme. Among the different kinds of Bhakti mentioned above there is only one which contemplates non-attachment to worldly objects. The highest Bhakti as well as the others are generated in the heart of man by the grace of God; and the first even ripens into a haunting passion. This grace of God one may enjoy even while engaged in a worldly life. The Maryādā-Puṣṭi, which is one of the four forms and requires the restraint of passions, does not conduce to the attainment of the highest bliss, which consists in joining in the eternal sports of Hari in the Goloka. The spirit of this system, therefore, seems to be sportive enjoyments and it cannot but be expected to influence the ordinary life of its followers. Moral rigidity culminating in indifference to worldly enjoyments and self-abnegation does not appear to be a characteristic of this school. Vallabhacārya himself was a married man, and so were all his successors and so are all the Gurus of the sect, who are as much men of the world as their followers.

§ 65. From the account we have given it will be seen that the fourth element of Vaiṣṇavism, that we have described in a preceding section, alone constitutes the religion of Vallabha. The sportive boy Kṛṣṇa of the cow-settlement with all his pranks is the highest god of this school; and his mistress Rādhā, who is mentioned only in the later books and dignified into his eternal consort, as will be mentioned further on, is the object of the deepest adoration. This sportive Kṛṣṇa with his Rādhā is transferred to a heaven which is in a region higher than the ordinary Vaikuṇṭha of Nārāyaṇa or Viṣṇu and is called Goloka. The highest aim of man's life is to get to this place and join in the sports. Thus the doings of Kṛṣṇa in Gokula and his relations with the men and women as well as the inferior animals, trees and even the river Yamunā constitute the basis of Vallabha's system and also its goal when transferred to Goloka.

XXIII. Caitanya.

§ 66. About the same time as Vallabha there flourished in Bengal another propagator of the religion of Rādhā and Kṛṣṇa, who is known by the name of Caitanya. The prominent distinction between the two appears to be, that while Vallabha and those who followed him developed the ceremonial side of the religion, Caitanya and his successors devoted themselves to the cultivation of the emotional side. Caitanya endeavoured to win the hearts of man by instituting Kīrtanas or the fervent singing of songs about the love of Rādhā and Kṛṣṇa and other devotional matters. The love of the cowherd god and his mistress had already become the subject of bewitching songs by Jayadeva in Sanskrit and by other poets in the vernacular. Caitanya also was a more courageous reformer in so far as he cried down the mechanical religious ceremonial of the prevalent Hinduism and preached spiritual devotion and at the same time condemned the distinctions of castes and admitted all, including even Mahomedans, as his pupils.

§ 67. Caitanya's original name was Bisambhar (Viśvambhara) Miśra, and his father's name was Jagannātha Miśra and mother's Sacī Debī. The father lived originally in Sylhet in Eastern Bengal, but had emigrated to Nadiya (Nabadvīpa) before the birth of Bisambhar, his youngest son. The eldest son's name was Bisvarūpa, who is called Nityānanda in the history of Caitanya. These were the only two sons of Jagannātha, and between these were eight daughters, who died young. Caitanya was born on the full-moon day of Phālguna in the year 1407 of the Śaka era, corresponding to 1485 A. D. He was afterwards called Kṛṣṇa Caitanya and was considered by his disciples an incarnation of Kṛṣṇa himself. As such he is reported to have played pranks with the women of the village, which, however, cannot be considered as historically true. Caitanya is also known by the name of Gaurāṅga, i. e. possessed of a fair and not a dark body, and Gauracandra, or fair moon. When he was eighteen years of age, he married a wife of the name of Lachmī Debī and began to live the life of a householder, taking pupils and giving them secular instruction. Soon after he took to a wandering life and visited many places in Eastern Bengal. Begging and singing were his occupation, and he is said to have collected a great deal of money. During his peregrinations his wife died, and on his return home he married another. When he was about twenty-three years of age, he went to Gayā to make offerings to his manes and on his return he began the mission of his life. He condemned the ritualistic system of the Brāhmaṇas and preached faith in Hari and the love of him as well as singing his name as the only effectual ways to salvation. He also preached the doctrine of the brotherhood of men, denouncing the system of castes. It is stated that the doctrine of faith and love had been preached before Caitanya by a person of the name of Advaitācārya, whose practice it was, after the performance of the usual Brahmaṇic rites, to go to the banks of the Ganges and call out for the appearance of God to substitute the doctrine of faith and love for that of the performance of various rites. It is also said that this Ācārya was at first the instructor of Caitanya and afterwards became his pupil. Whatever it may have been, the new doctrine was first publicly proclaimed to the exclusion of others by Kṛṣṇa Caitanya. He was assisted by his brother Nityānanda, who was regarded as an incarnation of Balarāma, the brother of the god Kṛṣṇa. Caitanya now began to hold meetings for the singing and glorification of the name of Hari. These were at first private and held in the house of a pupil named Srībāsa. The doings of these devotees met with scorn and ridicule, especially at the hands of the worshippers of Kālī, one of whom put red flowers and goat's blood on the steps of the door of the house in which the Vaiṣṇava meetings were held. The fervour displayed at these Kīrtanas, or singing of the name of Hari, gradually increased in intensity, until the loud singers and principally Caitanya himself swooned away and dropped senseless on the ground. In the year 1510 Caitanya became a Saṃnyāsin, or an ascetic, and was initiated into the order by Keśab Bhāratī of Katva. After this he first went to Purī to visit the shrine of Jagannātha, and thence wandered about the country for six years preaching his new faith [1]. On one occasion he went to Benares, where he is reported to have held a disputation with Prakāśānanda, a teacher of the monistic Vedānta of Śaṃkarācārya. Caitanya condemned Śaṃkara's commentary on the Vedāntasūtras and said that it mystified the sense of the original. Śaṃkarācārya did not give the plain ordinary sense of the words of Bādarāyaṇa, but forced his own views into them. The doctrine of development (Pariṇāmavāda) was held by the author of the Sūtras, while Śaṃkarācārya rejects it and brings in his doctrine of illusion (Vivartavāda). The former alone is true according to Caitanya. After these wanderings he returned to Purī, where he spent the last eighteen years of his life, and died in Śaka 1455, corresponding to 1533 A. D.

§ 68. Some of the doctrines attributed to Caitanya are as follows. Kṛṣṇa is the highest god and is so beautiful that he excites love for himself even in the heart of the God of love, and is enamoured of himself. His Parabrahmaśakti (power) pervades the universe and assumes a corporeal form by his wonder-creating power (Māyāśakti), though he is the soul of all. He possesses a self-multiplying power (Vilāsaśakti) which is of two kinds. By one of these, in sporting with the cowherdesses, he became as many Kṛṣṇas as were sufficient to give one to every two of them (Prābhavavilāsa). By the other self-multiplying power (Vaibhavavilāsa) he assumes the forms of the four Vyūhas, or forms of Vāsudeva, Saṃkarṣaṇa, etc., Vāsudeva representing intelligence, Saṃkarṣaṇa, consciousness, Pradyumna, the love, and Aniruddha, sportiveness. Here, it will be seen, the functions of the four Vyūhas are changed, and the principle of love is attributed to Pradyumna, instead of that of the mind as in the older system, and that of sportiveness, instead of self-consciousness which is transferred to Saṃkarṣaṇa, is attributed to Aniruddha. This change is in consonance with a system of which love and sport form the distinguishing characteristics. All the usual incarnations spring from one or other of the Vyūhas. According as the quality of Sattva, Rajas, or Tamas predominates, Kṛṣṇa becomes Viṣṇu, Brahmadeva, or Śiva, respectively. The sports of Kṛṣṇa go on always, as the rising and setting of the sun. His eternal sports are carried on in the Goloka. Kṛṣṇa has three powers: the internal which is intelligence, the exter-

[1]) The above is an abstract of the account given by J. Beames in his paper published in Ind. Ant. Vol. II, pp. 1 ff.

nal which generates appearances, and the differentiated which forms the Jīva, or individual soul. His chief power is that which creates dilatation of the heart, or joy. This appears to be the power of love. When this love becomes settled in the heart of the devotee, it constitutes Mahābhāva, or the best feeling. When love attains to the highest pitch, it constitutes itself into Rādhā, who is the most loveable of all and full of all qualities. She was the object of the highest love of Kṛṣṇa and being idealised as love, some of the agreeable feelings of the heart are considered her ornaments. The sports of the cowherdesses were due to simple love (Preman), and this it was that Uddhava and other devotees sought to attain. The Supreme Soul (Paramātman) is boundless and is full intelligence itself. The individual soul is an atom having intelligence. They are necessarily connected together and this connection can never be destroyed. Kṛṣṇa is the support (Āśraya) and Jīva rests on him (Āśrita). The relation between the two is identity as well as difference. Thus the Vedāntic theory of Caitanya's system is the same as that of Nimbārka. As the bee is distinct from the honey and hovers about it and, when it drinks it, is full of it, i. e. is one with it, so the individual soul is at first distinct from the Supreme Soul, seeks the Supreme Soul consistently and continuously and, when through love he is full of the Supreme Soul, he becomes unconscious of his individual existence and becomes, as it were, absorbed in him. Herein is described the ecstatic condition in which the individual soul becomes one with God, though they are really distinct. Kṛṣṇa is the lord of the power of delusion, or ignorance (Māyā), and Jīva is the slave of it. When the latter cuts off its shackles, he distinctly sees his own nature and his true relation to God. Kṛṣṇa is to be approached and attained by Bhakti alone [1]).

§ 69. Kṛṣṇa Caitanya, Nityānanda and Advaitānanda are called the three Prabhus, or masters of the sect. The descendants of Nityānanda live at Nadiya, and those of Advaita at Śāntipur. They are the spiritual heads of the sect. Nityānanda was appointed by Caitanya himself as the superior of the church. His female descendants live at Bālegor and male ones at Khordu near Barrackpur. There are temples belonging to Caitanya's followers at Mathurā, Vṛndāvana, and three principal ones in Bengal: one at Nadiya dedicated to Caitanya, the other at Ambikā, to Nityānanda, and the third at Agradvīpa, to Gopinātha. There is a shrine dedicated to Caitanya in the vicinity of Dhākādakṣiṇa in Northern Sylhet, where his father originally lived. It is visited by pilgrims from all parts of the district and even from Bengal. At Khetur, in the Rajaṣāhi district, a temple is erected in his honour, where a religious fair is held in the month of October, which is attended by about 25,000 persons.

The sectarian marks worn by the followers of Caitanya are two white perpendicular lines on the forehead joined together at the bridge of the nose and a line continued up to the tip of the nose. They also use necklaces of three strings of Tulasī beads and a rosary of the same,

---

[1]) See Gaurāṅgatattvasaha Gaurāṅgacarita by Prasanna Kumāra Vidyāratna, printed at Calcutta.

as a help in the muttering of Hari's name. The worship of Gurus, or spiritual heads, as gods characterises this system. Most of Advaita's followers observe caste distinctions, but a minority rejects them. This minority consists of Bairāgis, or recluses. In one branch of the sect there are monks as well as nuns. They live in the same convent. And there is only a platonic relation between them. A person of the name of Rām Saram Pāl of the Sadgopa caste founded about two hundred years ago a branch of the sect called Kartābhājas, or worshippers of the Kartā, or headman. It admits of recruits from all castes and observes no distinction. The founder, also called Kartā Bābā, died at Ghoṣapur, and his votaries assemble periodically to do honour to him. The spiritual teachers of Caitanya's sect, whether male or female, are celebates.

The three Prabhus, or masters, did not leave any compositions. But Caitanya's pupils, especially Rūpa and Sanātana, wrote a great deal. A work by the latter entitled Rasāmṛtasindhu contains an analysis of the feeling of love, or Bhakti, explaining the states of mind which lead to it and its various forms. A considerable body of literature has grown up round this system of religion.

XXIV. Debasement of Vaiṣṇavism.

§ 70. The worship of Rādhā, more prominently even than that of Kṛṣṇa, has given rise to a sect, the members of which assume the garb of women with all their ordinary manners and affect to be subject even to their monthly sickness. Their appearance and acts are so disgusting that they do not show themselves very much in public, and their number is small. Their goal is the realisation of the position of female companions and attendants of Rādhā; and hence probably they assume the name of Sakhībhāvas (literally, the condition of companions). They deserve notice here only to show that, when the female element is idolised and made the object of special worship, such disgusting corruptions must ensue. The worship of Durgā in the form of Tripurasundarī has led to the same result.

Though the Vaiṣṇava systems of Nimbārka, Vallabha and Caitanya are based on the fourth element of Vaiṣṇavism that we have pointed out in a preceding section, still that element has undergone an important modification. Before, Kṛṣṇa was a person who had amorous dalliances with the Gopīs generally. But now Kṛṣṇa had a definite consort in Rādhā, who had a large number of female companions, who were probably the original Gopīs. She is indissolubly united with him in the creed of the worshippers. This Rādhā is not mentioned by name in the Harivaṃśa, Viṣṇu-Purāṇa and the Bhāgavata. In the last, however, among the cowherdesses engaged in Kṛṣṇa's amorous sports in Vṛndāvana on an autumnal moonlight night, there was one with whom the youthful god carried on his dalliance further, after he had become invisible to the rest. This woman became proud of Kṛṣṇa's special attachment for her, whereupon the god disappeared from her also. Here was contained a suggestion which probably led to the creation of Rādhā in later times. In the apocryphal Nāradapañcarātra-

Saṃhitā, as mentioned before, the one single lord is represented to have become two, one a woman and the other a man, who was he himself. He then had amorous intercourse with her. The woman was Rādhā. In the Brahmavaivarta-Purāṇa she has been made to spring from the primordial body of Kṛṣṇa, forming its left side, and is eternally associated with him in his amorous sports in this world as well as the world of cows (Goloka). The name of Rukmiṇī occurs in the ordinary forms of Kṛṣṇaism, but in the systems named above it is entirely absent. The introduction of Rādhā's name and her elevation to a higher position even than Kṛṣṇa's operated as a degrading element in Vaiṣṇavism, not only because she was a woman, but also because she was originally a mistress of the cowherd god, and her amorous dealings were of an overt character.

In the Rāma cultus Sītā is a dutiful and loving wife and is benignant towards the devotees of her husband. She holds a position entirely subordinate to Rāma, while Rādhā is often preferred to Kṛṣṇa. There is no amorous suggestion in her story as in that of Rādhā, and consequently the moral influence of Rāmaism is more wholesome. Kabīr does not, so far as I know, mention the name of Sītā at all. He was a strict monotheist and his Rāma was the supreme lord (Sāheb) only. Those other teachers who followed him maintain the same attitude, so that the Rāma cultus represents a saner and purer form of Hindu religious thought than Rādhākṛṣṇaism.

XXV. Nāmdev and Tukārām.

§ 71. The popular Vaiṣṇavism of the Marāṭha country centres itself round the shrine of Viṭhobā at Paṇḍharpur, which is a city situated on the banks of the Bhīmā or Bhīmarathī. The full name of the god is Viṭṭhal, which is not a Sanskrit name, but the etymology is clear enough. It is stated that the corruption of the Sanskrit name Viṣṇu in the Canarese language is Viṭṭhu, and this looks probable, since Kṛṣṇa is corrupted into Kuṣṭa in the Goanese dialect and Kuṭṭa, Kiṭṭi, or Kṛṣṭa in the Canarese, and we have seen that Viṣṇu, the first portion of the name of the Hoysala prince Viṣṇuvardhana, was corrupted to Viṭṭi or Biṭṭi[1]). The terminations *bā* and *la* are appended to the name Viṣṇu or Viṭṭhu to indicate additional sense such as tenderness or reverence. When the shrine was established we have not the means of determining, but we have clear evidence of its being in existence in the middle of the thirteenth century. In a copperplate inscription of the reign of Kṛṣṇa of the Yādava dynasty of Devagiri it is stated that Malliseṭṭi a general and viceroy of the king made, while engaged on a military expedition, the grant of a village in the Belgaum district at Pauṇḍarīkakṣetra, a holy place situated on the Bhīmarathī, in the vicinity of the god Viṣṇu, in the year 1171 of the Śaka era corresponding to 1249 A. D.[2]) Now if the Pauṇḍarīkakṣetra was situated on the Bhīmarathī or Bhīmā river, it is certainly not unreasonable to suppose that is was the same as Paṇḍharī which

[1]) See above, p. 52.

[2]) Indian Antiquary, Vol. XIV, p. 68 ff.

is the alternative name of Paṇḍharpur; and the god in whose vicinity the grant was made must therefore have been Viṭṭhal, or Viṭhobā, here mentioned by his Sanskrit name and not the popular Canarese corruption. In another inscription on stone existing at Paṇḍharpur itself and dated 1192 Śaka, which corresponds to 1270 A. D., Bhānu, the son of Keśava, is represented to have performed an Aptoryāma sacrifice in Pāṇḍuraṅgapura in consequence of which crowds of people and Viṭṭhala together with the gods were greatly gratified[1]). Here we have another name of Paṇḍharpur and that was probably given to it because it was the city of Pāṇḍuraṅga. Paṇḍaraṅga, or Paṇḍuraṅga, is according to Hemacandra a name of Rudra or Śiva[2]). And we have a temple of Śiva at Paṇḍharpur and pilgrims have to visit it first before going to that of Viṭhobā or Viṭṭhal. Pāṇḍuraṅga, which is the same as the Paṇḍuraṅga of Hemachandra, is however in modern times a popular name for Viṭṭhal. Whether then the city was called Pāṇḍurangapura on account of it containing the temple of Viṣṇu, or Viṭṭhal, or that of Śiva is doubtful. But from the wording of the inscription in which Viṭṭhala and Pāṇḍuraṅgapura are mentioned independently it would appear as if Viṭṭhal had no connection with the name and that it was given to the city on account of its containing a Śiva temple. But when Viṭhobā's importance increased in later times so vastly that Śiva was thrown entirely into the shade, Pāṇḍuraṅga became identical with Viṭṭhala. The name Pauṇḍarīka occuring in the first inscription seems to owe its origin to a man named Puṇḍarīka, the popular legend about whom is to the following effect. The region about Paṇḍharpur was, it is said, a forest of the name of Ḍiṇḍiravana. There lived a man of the name of Puṇḍalīka, who spent all his time in the service of his aged parents, and the god Kṛṣṇa was pleased with his devotion to them. In the meantime, while Kṛṣṇa was living at Dvārakā, he remembered Rādhā, who was the object of his fervent love while he was in Gokula. Rādhā, who had after Kṛṣṇa's leaving Gokula betaken herself to a residence in the Himālaya mountain for the practice of austerities in consequence of her separation from Kṛṣṇa, came to know of this through her innate cognitive power and came at once to Dvārakā and sat on the lap of Kṛṣṇa. Some time after, Rukmiṇī, the wedded wife of Kṛṣṇa, came to the place, and Rādhā did not rise up to honour her as every other woman in similar circumstances did at her approach. Kṛṣṇa even did not take Rādhā to task for this dishonour of Rukmiṇī, and Rukmiṇī got offended, left Dvārakā and wandered about, until she came to Ḍiṇḍiravana and rested there on the site of the modern Paṇḍharpur. Kṛṣṇa was filled with sorrow at the disappearance of Rukmiṇī and went about in quest of her to all parts of the country, until he came to the place where Rukmiṇī was lying. After some explanations she was reconciled to him, and Kṛṣṇa then went to the hut of Puṇḍalīka to reward him for his devotion to his parents by personal manifestation.

[1]) Early History of the Dekkan, Second Ed., p. 115, in which, however, Keśava, the father of Bhānu, is by mistake represented as the sacrificer.

[2]) Deśīnāmamālā VI, 23.

Puṇḍalīka being engaged in attending to the wants of his father and mother was not able to greet him at once and threw back a brick (Marāṭhī: vīṭ) and asked him to stand on it and wait for him until he finished what he was engaged on. Kṛṣṇa stood on the brick and there he was joined by Rukmiṇī, and thus the shrine of Paṇḍharpur grew up.

Puṇḍalīka has been referred to as the originator of the Viṭṭhal cult of devotion both by Nāmdev and Tukārām, and that is the popular belief. The legend points to this fact and we may therefore take him to be the person who promulgated the cult of Viṭhobā, or Viṣṇu, in the Marāṭha country. He established himself at Paṇḍharpur and it must be on that account that the city is called the holy place (Kṣetra) Pauṇḍarīka, which I identify with the modern name Paṇḍharī in the first inscription. The Pāṇḍuraṅgapura of the second may have become the later Paṇḍharpur.

There is another historical significance in this legend, and that appears to be this. At first, no woman was connected with the Kṛṣṇa worship, as we have seen in the case of the pure Pāñcarātra or Bhāgavata system. Then came Rādhā to be associated with him in the north, as we have seen, in the systems of Nimbārka, Vallabha and Caitanya, while Rukmiṇī, the lawful wife, was united with him in the Marāṭha country. The Kṛṣṇa of Paṇḍharpur is almost exclusively known by the name of Viṭṭhala or Viṭhobā, and Rukmiṇī by the name of Rakhamāī or Rakhamābāī. In the religious literature of the country Viṭṭhala, or Kṛṣṇa, is almost exclusively spoken of as Rukmiṇīpati or Rukmiṇīvara, the lord or husband of Rukmiṇī, and not as Rādhāvallabha, or the lover of Rādhā. Thus the Vaiṣṇavism of the Marāṭha country, associated as it is with these two names, is more sober and purer than that of the three systems named above. Rāhī, the Marāṭhī form of Rādhikā, is not unknown, but an insignificant place is assigned to her. The sports of Kṛṣṇa in Gokula are also represented occasionally in the mode of worship, but very little importance is attached to them. This Vaiṣṇavism of the Marāṭha country found a fertile soil among the lower classes, though it has had followers among Brāhmaṇs and other higher classes also. Like the Vaiṣṇavism of the disciples of Rāmānanda, it had no learned or Sanskrit-knowing promulgators, but its prophets were Śūdras, who, however, had the true religious instinct and possessed a clear spiritual insight. Such were Nāmdev and Tukārām.

§ 72. The family of Nāmdev originally lived at a village called Narasi Vāmaṇī, situated near Karhāḍ in the Sātāra district, and now known by the name of Bhayē-Narsingpur or Kolem-Narasingpur. It belonged to the tailor caste and followed that occupation or of dealers in cloth. The name of Nāmdev's father was Dāmā Śeṭ, and that of his mother, Goṇābāī. They migrated to Paṇḍharpur, where Nāmdev was born in the Śaka year 1192, corresponding to 1270 A. D. Nāmdev received ordinary education, but showed little capacity for the usual occupation of his family. He became a devoted worshipper of Viṭhobā and had for his Guru a person named Visobā Khecar, who appears to have been a non-idolater. For Nāmdev says of him that he gave him the following instruction: —

No. 191 [1]. "A stone-god never speaks. What possibility then of his removing the disease of mundane existence? A stone image is regarded as God, but the true God is wholly different. If a stone-god fulfils desires, how is it he breaks when struck? Those who adore a god made of stone, lose everything through their folly. Those who say and hear that a god of stone speaks to his devotees, are both of them fools. Those who extol the greatness of such a god and call themselves his devotees, should be regarded as worthless persons and their words should not be heard by the ear. If, by chiselling a stone, a god is made of it and is worshipped with care for many years, will he be of use at any time? Do reflect on this well in your mind. Whether a holy place is small or large, there is no god but stone or water. In the village of Dvādaśī (Bārsī) [2] instruction was given that there is no place which is devoid of God. That God was shown to Nāma in his heart, and thus Khecar conferred a blessing on him."

The omnipresence of God and his being neither stock nor stone are well brought out here. The omnipotence of God Nāmdev brings out in the following: —

No. 151. "The Veda has to speak by thy might and the sun has to move round; such is the might of thee, the lord of the universe. Knowing this essential truth, I have surrendered myself to thee. By thy might it is that the clouds have to pour down rain, mountains to rest firm and the wind to blow. Nothing moves at all (without thee). Oh lord Pāṇḍurang, thou art the cause of all."

It will thus be seen that, though Nāmdev worshipped the idol at Paṇḍharpur, he had full knowledge of the true nature of God, as given in treatises like the Upaniṣads; and this God it was that he tried to attain.

No. 1029. "Your mind is full of vices. What is the use of the pilgrimages you make? What is the use of austere practices, if there is no repentance? The sins resulting from a mental act cannot be effaced by the highest holy place (literally: the father of the holy places). The essence of the matter is very simple: Sin is effaced by repentance", so says Nāmā.

No. 887. "Vows, fasts, and austerities are not at all necessary; nor is it necessary for you to go on a pilgrimage. Be you watchful in your hearts and always sing the name of Hari. It is not necessary to give up eating food or drinking water; fix your mind on the feet of Hari. Yoga or sacrificial ceremonies or giving up objects of desire is not wanted. Realise a fondness for the feet of Hari. Neither is it necessary for you to contemplate (lit. dwell in) the one without attributes. Hold fast to the love of the name of Hari; says Nāmā, be firm in singing the name and then Pāṇḍurang will render himself manifest to you."

In these two songs Nāmdev urges upon his hearers the total inefficacy of the usual modes of purification and of the attainment of God, such as pilgrimages, vows, fasts, or meditation on the absolute, and sacrifices.

---

[1] Tukārām Tātyā's edition, published in Bombay in 1894.

[2] Bārsī is a town near Paṇḍharpur.

No. 245. "Recognise him alone to be a righteous man, who sees Vāsudeva in all objects, eradicating all pride or egoism. The rest are entangled in the shackles of delusion. To him all wealth is like earth and the nine species of gems are mere stones. The two, desire and anger, he has thrown out and cherishes in his heart (lit. house) quietude and forgiveness. He constantly repeats the name of Govinda, not desisting even for a moment."

No. 1004. "Firmly grasp the truth which is Nārāyaṇa. Purity of conduct should not be abandoned; one should not be afraid of the censure of people and thus accomplish one's own purpose. Surrender yourself to your loving friend (God), giving up all ostentation and pride. The censure of people should be regarded as praise and their praise not heeded. One should entertain no longing for being respected and honoured, but should nourish in oneself a liking for devotion. This should be rendered firm in the mind and the name of God should not be neglected even for a moment."

In these songs Nāmdev describes the holy condition of him who is a devotee of Vāsudeva and sees him everywhere, and preaches self-surrender to him, regardless of the criticism of the world.

This is a short specimen of the teachings of Nāmdev. Purity of heart, humility, self-surrender, forgiveness, and the love of God form the sum and substance of it. Nāmdev wrote songs in Hindī also and some of these are incorporated in the Grantha-Sāheb, or the bible of the Sikhs. I will here translate two of these [1]: —

No. 2352. "He is one, [but] fills and encompasses many; wherever you look you find him there. There is scarcely one who understands him, all being deluded by the variegated picture drawn by Māyā (delusive power). Everything is Govinda, everything is Govinda, there is nothing without Govinda. Just as there is one thread and on it are woven breadthwise and lengthwise hundreds of thousands of beads, so is everything woven in the lord. The waves, the foam, and the bubbles of water are not different from water. All this extent of the universe is the sport of Parabrahma and, when we think of it, is not different from it. Illusive phantoms and the objects seen in dreams are regarded as real. When by the instruction of my Guru my mind awoke, I accepted the truth. Reflecting in your mind, see this all to be the creation of Hari, says Nāmdev; in the inside of every individual thing there is one Murāri alone without any interstice."

No. 2353. "The pitcher is filled and the water brought to bathe the god. There were forty-two hundreds of thousands of animals in it; there was already Viṭṭhal in them. Whom shall I bathe? Wherever we go there is Viṭṭhal and he ever sports in joy. Flowers have been brought and wreaths woven of them for worshipping God. First of all the flowers were smelt by the bees, there was Viṭṭhal there; what shall I do? Milk has been brought and cooked for the offering of Khīr [2]) to God. The milk was first tasted by the calf, in it was

[1]) Tukārām Tātyā's edition.

[2]) A preparation of milk and rice mixed with sugar.

Viṭṭhal, what shall I do? Here is Viṭṭhal, there is Viṭṭhal, there is no world without Viṭṭhal. This place and that thou hast filled. Thou hast filled the whole world, says Nāmā humbly"[1]).

In these hymns God's omnipresence is described by Nāmdev.

§ 73. The date assigned to the birth of Nāmdev is, as we have seen, Śaka 1192, that is, 1270 A. D. This makes him a contemporary of Jñāndev, the author of the Jñāndevī, which was finished in 1290 A. D. But the Marāṭhī of the latter work is decidedly archaic, while that of Nāmdev's writings has a considerably more modern appearance. Nāmdev's Hindī too looks more modern than that of the thirteenth century, when the poet Canda flourished[2]). What this is due to, it is difficult to say. But it appears probable that the traditional date of Nāmdev's birth, Śaka 1192, has been pushed backwards and that he is represented as a contemporary of Jñāndev. We have seen in a former section that Nābhājī in naming the successors of Viṣṇusvāmin places Jñāndev first and Nāmdev afterwards. If we are to judge from Nāmdev's Marāṭhī and Hindī, his date must be put later by about a century.

Some conception, however, of the time when Nāmdev flourished may be formed from the strong and definite sentiments as to the futility of idol-worship, which his instructor is represented, in one of the hymns translated, to have expressed. Khecar, or Visoba Khecar as he is usually called, appears to have been an uncompromising opponent of idol-worship from the accounts given of him in the existing biographies. All previous writers, including Rāmānuja, as well as a great many that followed, excused idol-worship in some way or other. If then Khecar's attitude towards it was definitely hostile, he and his pupil Nāmdev must have flourished when the Mahomedan influence had for the first time become very powerful. The Mahomedans established themselves in the Dekkan in the beginning of the fourteenth century of the Christian era, and their hatred of idol-worship must have taken about a hundred years to make its way into the understanding of religious Hindus. But a more direct evidence for the fact that Nāmdev flourished after the Mahomedans had established themselves in the Marāṭha country is afforded by his mention in a song (No. 364) of the destruction of idols by the Turaks, i. e. Turks. The Mahomedans were often called Turaks in early times by the Hindus. Nāmdev, therefore, probably lived about or after the end of the fourteenth century. It will thus be seen that the date of Nāmdev's birth given with such details is quite wrong. Unfortunately the historical spirit has by no means been the distinguishing feature of the intellectual life of us Indians, and we often confuse different persons together and attribute to one what belongs to another. Some such confusion must have taken place in the present case.

§ 74. Tukārām was born and lived at a village called Dehu, which is about fourteen miles to the northeast of Poona. The name of the family to which he belonged was More. It was a family of the Marāṭha

[1]) These two hymns have been translated by Macauliffe in Vol. VI, pp. 41-42 of the Sikh Religion. The readings in the Bombay Ed. have been compared with those in the Grantha-Sāheb, pp. 427—28 of the Lucknow Ed. of 1893.

[2]) See my Report on the Search for Sanskrit Mss., 1887-1891, page LXXX.

caste, which caste may have sprung from the old order of Kṣatriyas, but is considered to belong to the Śūdra order. Nothing specific is known about the date of his birth, but there is no reason for doubting the truth of the date traditionally assigned to his death, which is Śaka 1571, corresponding to 1649 A. D. His biographer, Mahīpati, represents him to have become a bankrupt at the end of the first half of his life, when he was twenty-one years of age. From that it is inferred that he lived for 42 years, and he is thus understood to have been born in 1607-8 A. D.

Seven of Tukārām's ancestors were devoted worshippers of the god Viṭhobā. Of these Viśambhara was the first who made regular pilgrimages to Paṇḍharpur, but after some years he constructed a temple in his own village and, placing the idols of Viṭhobā and Rukmāī in it, dedicated it to their worship. Tukārām's father's name was Bolhojī and he followed the occupation of a petty trader. When he became old, he proposed to entrust the affairs of his family and his business to Sāvjī, his eldest son. But Sāvjī was a man for whom a worldly life had no interest, and he declined to undertake the business. It was, therefore, made over to Tukārām, who was then thirteen years of age. Tukārām managed the affairs somehow, till he became seventeen years old, when his father died. He naturally felt desolate when this occurred and, being a man of simplicity and liable to be imposed upon by designing persons, his affairs got into disorder and he incurred loss in his trade. Tukārām was at first married to a wife who was sickly, and some time later he married another of the name of Jijābāī or Āvalī, the daughter of a well-to-do trader in Poona. When his affairs got into confusion, Āvalī procured a loan for him and set him up again. A short time after, he made a profit in his new trade, and, while coming back from the place to which he had gone for the sale of his goods, he met a man who was being carried about by the agents of his creditor and who was crying out for assistance to relieve him from his debt and the impending imprisonment. To this man Tukārām gave all that he possessed, the capital and the profit that he had made. He returned to Dehu empty-handed, and soon after there was a famine, which made him a thorough bankrupt, and his first wife died of hunger. Tukārām then made up his mind to renounce his business, but his younger brother Kānhyā protested against it. Then, sitting on the banks of the Indrāyaṇī, he told his brother to bring all the documents, deeds and bonds relating to their business, divided them into two parts, gave one to Kānhyā and told him to live separately from him, and his own share he threw into the river. Henceforward he devoted himself to the contemplation of God and singing his praises, spending the day on the top of a hill near Dehu and the night at the temple of Viṭhobā in the village. He read the Marāṭhī works on religious subjects of the saints and sages who had flourished before him. The idea of giving expression to his thoughts and feelings by composing songs in Marāṭhī soon arose in his mind. The metre used by him was that which is known by the name of Abhaṃg, the measure of which is by no means strict or regular, but which is characterised by the use of rhyming words at specific intervals. A single-minded piety and the desire to be of service to all, even by executing their errands, became settled points in his character. Family matters had to be attended to by his wife, Āvalī, who often found herself in great straits. Tukārām's chief occupation was the performance of Kīrtans, which consist of religious discourses interspersed with the singing of songs. These discourses gradually became very attractive and drew in crowds of people. The songs he sung at these had been often prepared by himself, and some were composed by him extempore while engaged in the discourse. Tukārām's fame spread about not only in his village, but in the surrounding country, and it evoked jealousy, especially in the minds of Brāhmaṇs, who had set themselves up as religious teachers; and he was subjected to persecution. He, however, maintained an evenness of temper throughout, though there were struggles in the mind. His fame reached the ears of the rising prince, Śivājī, the future king of the Marāṭhas. He was eager to hear Tukārām's Kīrtans and on one occasion invited him into his presence, sending him messengers with torches, umbrella and horses, as emblems of high honour. Tukārām, however, declined to go and sent him a letter written in his usual metre. On another occasion Śivājī attended his Kīrtan at Lohagaon, about six miles from Poona, and placed before him a plate full of golden coins. Tukārām, of course, declined to receive them, and they were distributed among the Brāhmaṇs there. When his end approached, he is reported to have gathered together a large body of his followers and to have proceeded to the banks of the Indrāyaṇī, all singing loudly and enthusiastically the praises of God and fully absorbed in it. When they approached the river, Tukārām suddenly disappeared. No further account of his death has been handed down.

§ 75. It has been already stated that Tukārām had acquired a great facility in composing Abhaṃgs. He spoke in Abhaṃgs and wrote in Abhaṃgs. Some of these only could be written and were written, and others were neglected by him or his immediate followers, but retained in the memory of others. The collections, therefore, of his pieces cannot be expected to be of the same size. There are two such printed in Bombay, one containing 4621 pieces and the other 8441. This latter collection is uncritically made and oftentimes one same piece is given a second time with the opening lines omitted. Still, this is a larger collection and contains Abhaṃgs which are not to be found in the first collection, but are quite in the style of Tukārām with the usual fervent devotion and purity of thought. We will now give a few specimens.

First collection, No. 2869. "When the auspicious juncture of Siṃhastha [1]) comes, it brings fortune only to barbers and priests. There are crores of sins in the heart, but externally a man shaves the hair on the head and the beard. What has been shaved off, has disappeared. Tell me what else has changed. The vicious habits are not changed, which might be regarded as a mark of the destruction of

[1]) When Jupiter is in the sign of Leo, the period is considered favourable for the washing away of sins, and Hindus go to holy places, such as Nāsik, shave their heads and mustaches and bathe in the river.

sins; says Tukā, without devotion and faith everything else is useless trouble."

Second coll., No. 4733. "What hast thou done by going to a holy river? Thou hast only outwardly washed thy skin. In what way has the interior been purified? By this thou hast only added a feather to thy cap (lit. prepared a decoration for thyself). Even if the bitter Vṛndāvana fruit is coated with sugar, the settled quality of the interior (bitterness) is in no way lessened. If peace, forgiveness, and sympathy do not come in, why should you take any trouble?"

First coll., No. 90 (1—2). "Sesamum seeds and grains of rice thou hast burnt by throwing into fire, but desire and anger are as mischievous as before. Why hast thou taken trouble in vain, giving up the adoration of Pāṇḍurang?"

Here Tukārām condemns religious practices which concern the body only, and mechanical rites, such as giving oblations, and enforces the necessity of striving for the attainment of spiritual virtue and of the adoration of God.

In No. 2383 (first coll.) Tukārām condemns the worship of goddesses, Jākhāī, Jokhāī, of gods like Bhairava and even Gaṇapati, and of ghosts and goblins, and earnestly recommends the adoration of him whose consort is Rakhamāī. Tukārām was thus a devotee only of Viṭhobā of Paṇḍharpur and a monotheist in this sense. Though he worshipped the idol at the place, still he had always before his mind's eye the great Lord of the universe, as the following will show: —

First coll., No. 4361. "Thy greatness is unsearchable. Even the Vedas became silent and the power of the mind becomes stunted. What possibility is there of my mental power reaching him whose light it is that the sun and the moon display? Even the thousand-tongued (the great serpent) is unable to expound thy greatness. How then shall I be able to do so? Says Tukā, we are thy children, thou art our mother, place us under the shadow (protection) of thy grace."

First coll., No. 4419. "All the world says that there is not a space so minute as a sesamum seed without thee. The old Ṛṣis, sages, pious and holy men said that thou art in the heart of all these things . . . . . Thou hast filled up numberless universes and also a residue still remained. But to me thou hast become inaccessible."

First coll., No. 1870. "God is ours, certainly ours, and is the soul of all souls. God is near to us, certainly near, outside and inside. God is benignant, certainly benignant, and fulfils every longing even of a longing nature. God protects us, certainly protects us, and subdues strife and death. God is merciful, certainly merciful, and protects Tukā."

This great God is to be attained only by devoted love and by no other means: —

First coll., No. 810. "This thy nature is beyond the grasp of the mind or of words; and therefore I have made devoted love a measure. I measure the Endless by the measure of love; he is not to be truly measured by any other means. Thou art not to be found by processes of concentration (Yoga), sacrificial rites, practice of austerities, and any bodily exertions, nor by knowledge. Oh Keśava, accept the service which we render to thee in the simplicity of our hearts."

There is peace and pure indescribable bliss in seeing God: —

Second coll., No. 1411. "Oh Nārāyaṇa, the peace arising from rest is truly not to be attained without thy feet; even if modes and methods are followed for crores of Kalpas[1]), bliss will not ensue: The bliss of bliss, which is interminable and boundless, which is enjoyed by Hari and Hara, manifest to me, oh thou, the sustainer of my soul, oh omniscient, those feet of thine [which produce it]."

But this God is not to be seen by those whose passions are unrestrained: —

First coll., No. 4420. "The Endless is beyond, and between him and me there are the lofty mountains of desire and anger. I am not able to ascend them, nor do I find any pass. Insurmountable is the ascent of my [mountain-like] enemies. What possibility is there of my attaining Nārāyaṇa, my friend? Pāṇḍurang is lost to me; says Tukā, it is now plain that this valuable life of mine has gone for nothing."

To curb these passions becomes now his great and earnest aim. He examines his heart carefully and on all occasions in life finds them present there in one shape or another; with all his efforts he fails to restrain them; and addresses fervent prayers again and again to God to help him. The number of these is very large: —

Second coll., No. 1430. "With whose support shall I gird up my loins? Oh Pāṇḍuraṅg, I feel depressed. All wicked persons abide in my frame and my mind is subdued by them. All my efforts have proved fruitless. What shall I do? Thou art the only mother of the helpless; says Tukā, those wicked persons will not leave my frame without thy might."

The wicked persons are the passions.

When in the course of years Tukārām became famous and was praised everywhere, he found a glow of satisfaction gathering strength in his heart. This he recognised as pride or conceit, and he was greatly afraid of it and again and again prayed to God to free him from this pride and bestow humility of spirit: —

First coll., No. 1779. "I have become an expert in the unrestricted use of words. The root of the whole matter I have not attained. Therefore, oh king of Paṇḍharī, my mind is afflicted. Who knows what is in my heart? I am respected or worshipped, and this has given rise to conceit; and my further progress (towards perfection) has been arrested; says Tukā, I do not know the true way and find myself in the hands of egotism." Again: —

First coll., No. 1133. "What shall I do with fame and worldly honour and greatness? Do show me thy feet. Do not bring about this (result), that thy servant should go for nothing. If I become great and bear the burden of ostentatious knowledge, I shall go away from thy feet farther and farther. What possibility is there of people knowing the internal condition? A man is judged by his external

[1]) A long fabulous period.

appearances. Even adversity will be sweet to me, if it leads me to thy feet."

He thus goes on cultivating the virtue of humility, until at last he comes to speak of the death of the self in him as in the following: —

First coll., No. 3474. "I have surrendered my soul to thee and then I have abandoned my individuality (dwelling). Now thy might alone prevails here. I being dead, thou hast established thy station here. Now nothing like m e and m i n e remains here."

Here he speaks of his having abandoned the self and God's having come to dwell in his heart instead of the self. And more distinctly: —

First coll., No. 2668. "I have seen my own death with my eyes. The result is incomparable rapture. The three worlds are filled with joy. And I have enjoyed as the soul of all. By my sense of individuality I was confined to one place and by its abandonment I have become all-reaching. The pollution arising from birth and death is at an end and I am free from the littleness resulting from the feeling of m e and m i n e. Nārāyaṇa has now given me a place to dwell in; putting my faith in him I have remained at his feet; Tukā says, the fulfilment of what I undertook I have manifested to the world."

Here he speaks of the dying of the lower man in himself and the coming to life of the higher man. There is a large number of pieces conveying instruction to men seeking spiritual advance. A few specimens will now be given.

First coll., No. 3800. "Therefore one should surrender oneself to God with all one's heart. He will carry one to the opposite bank of the river of life, which is difficult to be crossed. He whose name is Ananta, or Endless, is very merciful; Tukā says, I have experienced this and therefore announce it to all."

Second coll., No. 5383. "Fortunate, indeed, are those persons, in whose heart dwells forgiveness and to whom, when there is occasion, courage and strength do not fail; who do not criticise other people by calling them good or bad and who think nothing of worldly greatness or superiority; who internally and externally are alike pure like the Gaṅgā and whose heart is tender; Tukā says, I will wave my body round them and place my head on their feet."

First coll., No. 2397. "For all beings entertain no hostile feeling. This one alone is the excellent way. Thus alone will Nārāyaṇa accept thee. All talk without this is useless trouble. Relatives as well as the evil-disposed should be regarded as alike and the mind devoted to the doing of good to others; Tukā says, when the mind is pure everything becomes efficacious."

First coll., No. 1368. "Do not give up food; do not betake yourself to a forest-dwelling; in all your sufferings and enjoyments think of Nārāyaṇa. A child sitting on the shoulders of its mother feels no trouble. Put an end to all thoughts different from this. Do not get entangled in worldly enjoyments nor abandon them; dedicate everything you do to God, and have done with it; Tukā says, do not ask me again and again; nothing else is to be taught but this."

Here Tukārām dissuades men from giving up the world and becoming recluses and advises them instead to dedicate their lives to the service of God and do everything in a manner to propitiate him.

The question has often been discussed among Marāṭhas whether Tukārām followed the Vedāntic theory of Śaṃkarācārya and regarded everything as an illusion except one soul. There are some Abhaṃgs which exhibit the closest possible approach to that theory, such as the following: —

First coll., No. 300. "What means crossing a mirage to reach the yonder bank? Children play with golden coins which are but pot-sherds. Is there any profit or loss by those transactions? Little girls perform marriage (of dolls). Is the relation thus established real? The happiness or misery experienced in a dream is seen not to be true when a man awakes. The expressions, one is born, one is dead, are all false; and the saying that persons are in bondage or are delivered is a mere waste of breath, so says Tukā."

Here the illusive nature of everything is set forth quite in the style of Śaṃkarācārya's world-illusion. Again: —

First coll., No. 1992. "A sugar crystal and sugar powder differ only in the name. There is no difference when sweetness is to be judged. Tell me, oh Pāṇḍuraṅg, how thou and I are distinct. Thou hast moved the world and m e and m i n e are the results. Gold in the form of ornaments is worn on the foot, the hands, nose and the head. When all these are thrown into the crucible, where remains the distinction? Profit and loss are real in a dream when one goes to sleep; both vanish when one is awakened, so says Tukā."

Here there is a mixture of the two opposite theories, that of Pariṇāma, or development, as in the case of gold and ornaments made of it, and that of Vivarta, or illusion, as in the case of things seen in a dream. The latter alone is held by Śaṃkarācārya. Again: —

First coll., No. 2482. "When salt is dissolved in water, what is it that remains distinct? I have thus become one in joy with thee and have lost myself in thee. When fire and camphor are brought together, is there any black remnant? Tukā says, thou and I were one light."

Here the losing of self-consciousness in moments of ecstasy appears to be what is meant, and not quite a perfect identity of God and man. Nāmdev and Tukārām were not learned Paṇḍits like Rāmānuja and Madhva and cannot be expected to formulate a consistent metaphysical theory of the relations between God, man, and the world. On the other hand, Tukārām was such a devout and sincere lover of God that the idea of such a distinctness between the three as would render such a love possible, was constantly present in his mind, and there are a great many Abhaṃgs in which he condemns the theory of spiritual monism as in the following: —

First coll., No. 1471. "His words should not be listened to, who expounds useless (unsubstantial) knowledge without Bhakti, or devotion. When monism is expounded without faith and love, the expounder as well as the hearer are troubled and afflicted. He who calls himself Brahma and goes on in his usual way, should not be spoken to and is a buffoon. The shameless one who speaks heresy in opposition to the Vedas is an object of scorn among holy men. Even an outcast is superior to him who cuts off the relation between God and his devotee (by asserting them to be identical), so says Tukā."

Here is an uncompromising denunciation of spiritual monism which leaves no scope for Bhakti, or devotion. It is considered as opposed to the Vedas and as a heresy. Again: —

First coll., No. 3753. "For me there is no satisfaction in the doctrine of monism. Sweet to me is the service of thy feet. Confer this gift upon me making it fit (to be given by thee). Thy name and singing of it are dear to me. The relation between God and his devotee is a source of elevated joy. Make me feel this, keeping me distinct from thee. All this belongs to thee. Confer it upon me some day."

Here in his confutation of spiritual monism he takes his stand on the heartfelt charms of the love of God. He sets the innate feelings of his heart against the sophism of the advocates of the Advaita-vedānta.

First coll., No. 1589. "I will make the mouth of the knowers of Brahma to water (in longing) and make the delivered ones to abandon the pristine condition (attained in consequence of deliverance). In singing the whole bodily frame becomes instinct with Brahma and the good fortune (resulting from it) consists in making God a debtor. I will bring indolence on him whose practice it is to repair to holy places and make the enjoyment of a life in heaven bitter. I will make the man who practises austerities give up his pride and put to shame sacrificial rites and charities. I will accomplish the great object of life, viz. love and wealth of devotion, which constitutes the true treasure of Brahma and its substance; and I will make people say that it was by good fortune that they saw Tuka and became blessed."

Here his enthusiasm for the love and devotion for God becomes so great, that he instinctively, as it were, out of the strength of his feelings declares all other ways of reaching God, including the monistic Vedānta, as worthless and inefficacious. Lastly I will here translate the Abhaṃg in which Tukārām sets forth the mission of his life: —

First coll., No. 520. "We lived in the Vaikuṇṭha and have come for this very reason, viz. for bringing into practice truly what the Ṛṣis taught. The world is overgrown with weeds; we will sweep clean the paths trodden by the righteous and accept what has remained. The old truths have disappeared. Mere verbal knowledge has brought about destruction. The mind (of man) is eager for worldly enjoyments and the way to God has been wholly obliterated. We will beat the drum of Bhakti which carries terror to this sinful age; Tukā says, proclaim victory with joy[1])."

The above extracts from a voluminous collection will give some indication of the manner in which Tukārām endeavoured to execute his mission. He denounced the merely mechanical rites and practices, enforced humility and the purification of the heart and a single-minded devotion to God.

[1]) The readings of this piece have been compared with those handed down orally and corrected.

XXVI. Résumé.

§ 76. We have thus completed our survey of Vaiṣṇavism from about the fifth century before Christ to the middle of the seventeenth. It first appeared as a religious reform, like Buddhism and Jainism, but based on theistic principles. Its early name was Ekāntika Dharma, or the religion of a single-minded love and devotion to One. In its back-ground stood the Bhagavadgītā, a discourse professing to be preached by Vāsudeva-Kṛṣṇa. It soon assumed a sectarian form and was called the Pāñcarātra or Bhāgavata religion. It was professed by a tribe of Kṣatriyas of the name of Sātvata and was noticed by Megasthenes about the end of the fourth century before Christ as the religion of such a specific people. This faith mingled itself with the existing one in Nārāyaṇa, the fountain from which all men have sprung, and with that in Viṣṇu, whose traces were visible in this world, and who at the same time had a mysterious nature. In the Bhagavadgītā itself were embodied some of the teachings of the Upaniṣads and a few general doctrines of two kinds of philosophy, the Sāṃkhya and the Yoga, which, however, had not yet assumed the character of definite systems. Soon after the beginning of the Christian era another element was contributed to this system of religion by the Ābhīras, or cowherds, who belonged to a foreign tribe, in the shape of the marvellous deeds of the boy-Kṛṣṇa, who came to be regarded as a god, and of his amorous dalliances with cowherdesses. So constituted, Vaiṣṇavism went on till about the end of the eighth century, when the doctrine of spiritual monism and world-illusion was promulgated and disseminated by Śaṃkarācārya and his followers. This was considered as destructive of the Bhakti, or love, which Vaiṣṇavism enjoined. And the feeling of hostility to spiritual monism gathered to a head in the eleventh century, when Rāmānuja made strenuous endeavours to put it down and spread the religion of Bhakti in a reinvigorated form. He was followed in the north by Nimbārka, who, however, gave prominence to the fourth or cowherdess element of Vaiṣṇavism and enjoined the worship of Kṛṣṇa's mistress Rādhā also, Rāmānuja having passed them over in severe silence. The attacks on spiritual monism and world-illusion were continued in a determined and definite manner in the thirteenth century by Madhva or Ānandatīrtha, who established the doctrine of pluralism and brought into prominence the name of Viṣṇu as that of the supreme God. In the north, Rāmānanda gave a new turn to Vaiṣṇavism by bringing in the name of Rāma, while Rāmānuja, from whom his metaphysical doctrines are derived, laid particular stress on the name Nārāyaṇa. The preachings of Rāmānanda and his disciples were carried on in the vernacular. Rāmānanda's religious activity is to be referred to the fourteenth century. He was followed by Kabīr in the fifteenth century, who preached strict monotheism, the name of his God being Rāma, and condemned idolatry. Vallabha in the sixteenth century preached the worship of the boy-Kṛṣṇa and his mistress Rādhā. Caitanya about the same time promulgated the worship of the grown up Kṛṣṇa, for ever associated with Rādhā, who was idealised into an image of pure love. The increasing ardency in the love and devotion of God sought for realistic expression and the conception of Rādhā deepened and acquired an exclusive prominence and importance. The devotion of Caitanya and his followers was sincere and fervent, and even bordered on the frantic; but that of Vallabha and his school was more dramatic than real. Ultimately this conception led to the degradation of Vaiṣṇavism. In the Marāṭha country, Nāmdev, whose date is uncertain, but who probably lived about the end of the fourteenth century, and Tukārām, in the first half of the seventeenth century, preached the worship of Viṭhobā of Paṇḍharpur as the supreme God and, discarding Rādhā-Kṛṣṇaism, cultivated a more sober line of devotion. They also resorted to the vernacular for the dissemination of their ideas. They, as well as Kabīr and, to a certain extent, Caitanya also, condemned the formalism which prevailed in the religion of their day and preached pure love of God. The two Marāṭha saints and Kabīr also laid particular stress on the purification of the individual's heart and moral elevation as means to a single-minded and devoted love of God and as necessary for the attainment of eternal bliss.

The points of contact between these various Vaiṣṇava systems are that their spiritual elements are essentially derived from the Bhagavadgītā, that Vāsudeva as the name of the Supreme Being stands in the back-ground of all, and that spiritual monism and world-illusion are denounced by them equally. The differences arise from the varied importance that they attach to the different spiritual doctrines; the prominence that they give to one or other of the three elements that were mingled with Vāsudevism; the metaphysical theory that they set up; and the ceremonial which they impose upon their followers. The Bhagavadgītā was supplemented in later times by the Pāñcarātra Saṃhitās and the Purāṇas such as the Viṣṇu and the Bhāgavata, and other later works of that description. These occasionally elucidated some of the essential doctrines, laid down the ceremonial and brought together a vast mass of legendary matter to magnify the importance of their special teachings and render them attractive.

Part II.

ŚAIVISM AND MINOR RELIGIOUS SYSTEMS.

I. Introductory.

Formation of the Conception of Rudra-Śiva.

§ 77. Some of the phenomena of external nature are pleasing, vivifying and benignant; others are terrible, dispiriting and destructive. In the dawn the old Āryas found the lovely goddess Uṣas, pursued by her lover Sūrya, or the Sun (RV. I, 115, 2). In the rising sun they found Mitra, a friendly god, who roused them from sleep and set them to do the work of the day (RV. III, 59, 1; VII, 36, 2). And in the sun, who visibly at rising stretched forth his rays as if they were his arms, filling the heaven and the earth, vivifying the world at the end of the night and placing it in the course assigned to it by him, they found Savitṛ (RV. IV, 53, 3). The dreadful and destructive phenomena are usually the storms that uproot trees and even demolish houses, accompanied by the thunderbolt which strikes down men and beasts dead in a moment; and the epidemics that rage and carry off numbers of men. In these the old Āryas saw Rudra, who went about howling with the stormy winds (Maruts), who were his sons (Rudriyas). But human beings do not believe in a purely malignant power reigning in the universe. The dreadful phenomena are attributed to the wrath of a god, which, however, can be appeased by prayer, praise and offerings. Then the god becomes Śiva, or the benignant. This appears to be the natural process by which a belief in such a god as Rudra-Śiva became established in India in ancient times. We will now trace the development of the idea of this god until he became the supreme creator, ruler, and pervader of the universe, a knowledge of whom contributed to eternal bliss.

II. The Development of the Idea of Rudra-Śiva.

§ 78. Rudra is represented as discharging brilliant shafts which run about the heaven and the earth (RV. VII, 46, 3) and as possessing weapons which slay cows and men (RV. I, 114, 10). Here the destructive agency of lightning seems to have been clearly in view. He is prayed to by the singers to keep these away from them and to protect the two-footed and four-footed beings belonging to them (RV. I, 114, 1). When, in consequence of the prayers or in the natural course of things, the cattle go unharmed, Rudra is represented to be Paśupa, or protector of the cattle (RV. I, 114, 9). Rudra is prayed to not to afflict children with disease (RV. VII, 46, 2) and to keep all in the village free from illness (RV. I, 114, 1). Rudra was thus believed to cause diseases, and when men recovered from them or were altogether free from them, that also was attributed to the agency of Rudra; and he is consequently spoken of as possessing healing remedies (RV. I, 43, 4) and as the best physician of physicians (RV. II, 33, 4) and as possessed of a thousand medicines (RV. VII, 46, 3). The singers also pray for the acquisition of those pure and salutary remedies belonging to the Maruts and Rudra, which father Manu desired (RV. II, 33, 13). The general character of the prayers addressed to Rudra is well brought out in the following: "Oh Rudra, do not, out of thy anger, injure our children and descendants, our people, our cattle, our houses, and do not kill our men. We invoke thee always with offerings" (RV. I, 114, 8). By his power he perceives all earthly beings and by his universal sovereignty he perceives divine beings (RV. VII, 46, 2). Here even in the Ṛgveda, Rudra is raised to supreme power.

§ 79. The character of Rudra appears in a much more developed form in the Śatarudriya (TS. IV, 5, 1; VS. chapter 16). His benignant form (śivā tanuḥ) is distinguished from its opposite, the malignant. He is called Giriśa and Giritra, "lying on a mountain", probably because the thunderbolt that he hurls, springs from a cloud, which is often compared to a mountain and in which he was believed to dwell. The cowherds and the female bearers of water see him as he creeps along with his blue neck and red complexion, that is, these simple folk working in the open field see a black cloud tinged red by the soft glow of the lightning. Representing, as Rudra does, the darker powers of nature, he may be expected to dwell away from the habitations of men, and therefore he is called the lord of the paths, of the forests and of those who roam in them, of thieves and highway robbers who frequent and move about in lonely places to prevent being detected, and also of outcasts who live away from the usual dwellings of men.

In his character as a healer he appears here as the lord of medicinal herbs and is called a heavenly physician. Being the lord of the open fields or plains, he is the lord of cattle (paśūnāṃ patiḥ) which roam in them. The name Paśupati became in later times a special appellation of this God. In this manner the range of Rudra became so wide that he came to be called the "lord of the quarters". He is called Kapardin, or the wearer of matted hair, which epithet is probably due to his being regarded as identical with Agni, or fire, the fumes of which look like matted hair. The names Śarva (arrow-wielder), and Bhava also, occur, and when his wrathful nature is thoroughly appeased, he becomes Śaṃbhu or benignant, Śaṃkara or beneficent, and Śiva or auspicious, which names occur at the end of the Śatarudriya. He is also represented as wearing a hide (kṛttiṃ vasānaḥ). How the epithet arose it is difficult to say. But, being represented as roaming in forests and other lonely places, the idea of investing him with the skin-clothing of the savage tribes may have suggested itself to a poet. The Niṣādas, a forest tribe, are compared to Rudras, which fact lends support to this view.

The name Rudra has been generalised and many Rudras are

spoken of, and a wish is expressed that they may be far away from the singer. Here the signification of the common name appears to be an evil spirit. In another place also the name is generalised, but the signification is much better. The Rudras are called Gaṇas or tribes, and Gaṇapatis or leaders of tribes, workmen, potters, cart-makers, carpenters, and Niṣādas or men of the forest-tribes. Thus these followers of handicraft and also the forest-tribe of Niṣādas are brought into close connection with Rudra; probably they were his worshippers, or their own peculiar gods were identified with the Āryan Rudra. This last supposition appears very probable, since the groups of beings, whose Pati, or lord, he is represented to have been, dwelt in or frequented open fields, forests and waste lands, remote from the habitations of civilised men.

§ 80. In AV. the conception of Rudra is further developed, and he is elevated to a higher platform. Several other names, by which he was known in later times, are also given, but the bearers of these are spoken of and addressed as separate gods. Bhava and Śarva are treated as two distinct deities and spoken of as ruling (īśāthe) over two-footed and four-footed beings (IV, 28, 1). They are styled the swiftest of all archers, and to them belongs what is near as well as remote. They are called thousand-eyed. Their range is far and wide (3). Their stroke can not be avoided by any man or god (5). They are invoked to launch their thunderbolt against the Yātudhāna, or evil spirit (6). They are implored to deliver the singers from calamity (7). Śarva is called the archer, and Bhava the king (rājan), and obeisance is made to them, and they are desired to remove their deadly poisons to other places (VI, 93, 2). Obeisance is made to Rudra who is in Agni, who is in the waters, who has entered into the herbs and plants, and who has formed all these beings (VII, 87, 1). This verse occurs in AU. (VI) and also in ŚU. (II, 17), where, however, it appears in a somewhat altered form, the word Deva being used instead of Rudra. In describing a particular ox Mahādeva is spoken of as his two arms (IX, 7, 7). Bhava and Śarva are invoked to launch the lightning against the doer of wickedness (X, 1, 23). They are called Bhūtapati (the lord of spirits) and Paśupati (the lord of beasts) (XI, 2, 1). They are reverenced as being in their domains in the sky and in the middle regions (XI, 2, 4). Five distinct species of animals, kine, horses, men, goats, and sheep, are marked off as belonging to Paśupati (XI, 2, 9). To Ugra, the fierce, belong the four intermediate quarters, the sky, the earth, and the wide atmosphere, and that which has spirit and breathes on the earth (XI, 2, 10). Bhava sees everything on earth. Nothing is far or near to him. He destroys things in the farther ocean, being himself in the preceding ocean (XI, 2, 25). Rudra is implored not to bring on consumption, poison, and celestial fire (XI, 2, 26). Bhava is the lord (īśa) of the heavens, the earth, and fills the whole atmosphere (XI, 2, 27). Bhava is addressed as king (rājan) (XI, 2, 28). A wish is expressed that the arrows of Bhava, Śarva, and Rudra, who is Paśupati (the lord of beasts), may be always propitious (sadāśiva) (XI, 6, 9). Savitṛ is called Aryaman, Varuṇa, Rudra, and Mahādeva (XIII, 4, 4). All the stars and the moon are under Rudra's control (XIII, 4, 28). The gods made Bhava the archer, the protector of the Vrātyas, or outcasts, in the intermediate space of the eastern region, Śarva of the southern region, Paśupati of the western region, Ugra of the northern region, Rudra of the lower region, Mahādeva of the upper region, and Īśāna of all the intermediate regions (XV, 5, 1—7).

§ 81. In ŚB. (VI, 1, 3, 7) and KB. (6, 1, 9), Rudra is mentioned as the son of Uṣas; and, after he was born, Prajāpati gave him, as he grew up, eight names, seven of which are the same as those given above from the AV. and the eighth is Aśani, or the thunderbolt. It would be seen that the AV. regards the seven as different though allied gods, though once Rudra is identified with Paśupati. As in the case of the sun-god the several ways of looking at him gave rise to the conception of several sun-deities such as Savitṛ, Sūrya, Mitra, Pūṣan, etc., so the same terrible and destructive agency in nature, with its benignant and gracious counterpart, looked at from different points of view, gave rise to the belief in the seven different gods mentioned in the AV. They are all regarded as the names of one god in the ŚB. and KB., and an eighth name is introduced. Of these eight names, four, Rudra, Śarva, Ugra and Aśani, are indicative of the destructive energy, and the other four, viz. Bhava, Paśupati, Mahādeva or Mahān devaḥ, and Īśāna, of its benignant counterpart. It will have been observed that the AV. brings in a new element, that of poisons which the terrific god was believed to send forth and of his shafts being unfailing and unavoidable by gods and men. On the other, or the benignant side, Bhava is represented to be a shining king (rājan). Rudra is the lord of all creatures. His range is far and wide. He controls the stars and the moon. He reigns in the sky and the middle regions. He is in fire and water, in plants and herbs, and in all beings; and he is the protector of Vrātyas in all quarters; and he is pre-eminently the ruler (Īśāna). Thus the terrible and the destructive God became, when he was propitiated by men in a variety of ways, a benignant God and attained to the whole majesty of the godhead by the time of the YV. and AV., and it is on this majestic form of the god that the theosophic speculations of ŚU., which we will notice further on, are based.

§ 82. But the darker side of the nature of this god was never forgotten. A sacrifice called Śūlagava is mentioned in most of the Gṛhyasūtras. A bull is sacrificed to Rudra to appease him (AG. IV, 9). The rite should be performed beyond the limits of a village, and its remains should not be brought into it, which rule sufficiently indicates the inauspicious character of the rite. The Vapā, or omentum, should be sacrificed to Rudra by uttering twelve names, seven of which are the same as the first three in the first group given above and the four in the second group. Aśani is omitted, and we have the following five additional names, Hara, Mṛḍa, Śiva, Bhīma, and Śaṃkara. Or the Vapā may be thrown into the fire by uttering six specific names only or the single name Rudra. This Śūlagava sacrifice should be performed in a cow-shed when a cattle disease has to be averted. In

PG. (III, 8) the names uttered in throwing the oblations are the same eight as those in the two groups above. with the addition of Agni. There are also oblations to the wives, Indrāṇī, Rudrāṇī, Śarvāṇī, and Bhavānī. HG. (II, 3, 8) has the same deities as the eight above-mentioned, Bhīma being substituted for Aśani; and oblations are given to the wife of each by repeating the formula "bhavasya devasya patnyai svāhā" (to the wife of God Bhava) etc. and not by uttering their proper names.

Directions are given in PG. (III, 15) to render obeisance to Rudra and pray for safe conduct when traversing a path, coming to a place where four roads meet, crossing a river, getting into a ferry-boat, entering a forest, ascending a mountain, passing by a cemetery or by a cow-shed and such other places. Similarly HG. (I, 5, 16) directs that a traveller should adore Rudra by repeating the specific formula given by him, when he comes to the crossing of four roads or to a heap of cattle-dung, when serpents creep, and when he is overtaken by tornado or is entering a river or comes to a variegated scene, sacrificial site or an old large tree.

It will thus be seen that, in the time of the Gṛhyasūtras, Rudra was still a terrible god, who had to be appeased. He was the god that held sway over regions away from home, over fields, wildernesses, cemeteries, mountains, old trees and rivers. Whenever a man came to anything which inspired awe and terror, Rudra was the god thought of and prayed to to protect. Herein lies the reason which rendered him in later times the omnipresent supreme lord of the universe to the exclusion of all other Vedic gods except Viṣṇu. Many are the occasions in the life of man, which excite fear; there are epidemics and other diseases, poisons, serpents, storms, thunderbolts and wild and awful scenes, and consequently the god who brings on these occasions and protects when appeased will be thought of oftener than other gods. The lovableness of the works of God, his greatness and majesty and his mysterious nature are also matters which strike the mind of man; and these appear to have operated in bringing Viṣṇu into prominence. What contributed to the formation of Vaiṣṇavism were the appearances and occurrences which excited love, admiration and a spirit of worship; while in Rudra-Śaivism the sentiment of fear is at the bottom, howsoever concealed it may have become in certain developments of it, and this sentiment it is that has worked itself out in the formation of various Rudra-Śaiva systems of later times. In the monotheistic religions of other countries the same god is feared and loved; in India the god that is loved is Viṣṇu-Nārāyaṇa-Vāsudeva-Kṛṣṇa, while the god that is feared is Rudra-Śiva.

III. Śvetāśvatara and Atharvaśiras Upaniṣads.

§ 83. Before we proceed to the consideration of the Rudra-Śiva sects, we must devote some time to the consideration of a religio-philosophic treatise which represents the farthest point in the development of the idea of Rudra-Śiva as a god worshipped by the Indian Āryas generally. This is the Śvetāśvatara-Upaniṣad. It does not appear to be composed in a sectarian spirit. The elevated notions about the nature of God and his relations to man and the world, which had been reached in the time of the early Upaniṣads, have been disentangled from their connection with the impersonal Brahman and transferred to the God who had at the time when the Upaniṣads were written, acquired a living and active personality in the minds of the people. This god was Rudra-Śiva, who, as we have seen, had by the time of AV. attained to the dignity of the supreme god. After the preliminaries, the doctrinal points that occur in the first chapter are these: that there are three unborn elements in the world; of these the all-knowing and the ignorant, the ruler and the ruled, are two, and there is a third which has in itself materials of enjoyment and suffering (9). Brahman is of three kinds, viz. the sufferer or enjoyer, what is enjoyed or suffered, and the dispenser or mover. There is nothing further to be known (12). Pradhāna is changeable, the immortal is unchangeable; Hara, the one lord, rules over the changeable and the soul. By meditating on him, by devoting oneself to him, by realising him, the whole ignorance is dispelled (10). By making one's body the lower block of wood, the syllable "Oṃ" the upper, and by the act of meditation, which is (like) the rubbing of the two blocks against each other, one should perceive the hidden god (14). One finds that soul in oneself who seeks him by means of truth and exertion, as oil in seeds, butter in curds, or water in a spring (15).

The three elements mentioned in 9 and 12 are adopted by Rāmānuja in his system, and these texts are quoted by writers of that school. What is set forth in the tenth is similar to that which occurs in the sixteenth and seventeenth verses of chap. 15 of the BhG.

In the second chapter there is first of all a short mention of the Yoga processes, which lead to the perception of the supreme soul and the purity of the self. When by the purified nature of the individual self, as by a lamp, is known the nature of Brahman, or the god who is unborn, unchangeable, pure in every way, one is free from all bondage (15). The chapter closes with the verse which we have noticed as occurring in the AV.

In the third chapter we have in the beginning a stanza which sets forth that those become immortal who know him who, possessing a net, rules by his ruling powers, rules over all the worlds by his ruling powers, who alone is the cause of production and growth (1). There is only one Rudra — and they do not recognise another — who rules these worlds by his ruling powers, who is the inmost soul of all men, who contracts everything on the final day, and, creating all beings, protects them (2). He has his eyes everywhere, his face everywhere, as in RV. X, 81, 3 (3). May Rudra, the cause of the production and growth of the gods, the lord of the universe, the great prophet, and who formerly created Hiraṇyagarbha, endow us with a holy will (4). Then follow two verses from the Śatarudriya, praying Rudra to look at the singer with his gracious countenance and not to do harm to men, etc. (5, 6). Knowing the lord (Īśa), who is the highest Brahman and the greatest of all, who dwells in the inside of all beings whatever their form, and who encompasses the whole universe, men become immortal (7). Then follow similar verses expressive of the attributes of the supreme God and prescribing a knowledge of him as the door to immortality. As formerly remarked, a verse and a half in this chapter occurs word for word in the thirteenth chap. of the BhG. It also deserves remark that the proper names of the supreme being that occur are Īśāna, Īśa, and Śiva; and the epithet Bhagavat, that is used also, deserves notice (11, 12, 15, 17, 20). In verse 20, which occurs also in the MU., there is Īśam for Ātmanaḥ which is indicative of the peculiarity of this Upaniṣad which we have noticed. There are two verses from the Puruṣasūkta (RV. X, 90).

The fourth chapter opens with the expression of the desire that he who, himself being without form, creates many forms with a certain purpose, in whom in the end as well as in the beginning the universe exists, may endow the adorers with a holy will. Then follows the identification of this supreme soul with fire, sun, wind, moon and a variety of other objects (2—4). We have then the metaphor of one male goat lying down with the female goat and another male goat abandoning her after enjoyment, which represents the soul in the worldly and the delivered conditions (5). We have next the verse about two birds, the friends and companions of each other, resting on the same tree, one eating the fruit of that tree and the other simply looking on without eating, which occurs in the RV. (I, 164, 20) and in the MU. (III, 1, 1). The next verse about the weak soul being deluded and in grief and being delivered from his sorrows when he sees the other soul, who is the ruler (Īśa), occurs in the MU. also (III, 1, 2) but not in the RV. After two verses there is another, in which Māyā is called Prakṛti, and he who uses this Māyā is called Maheśvara (10). Maheśvara is a name of Śiva. Having known the boon-giver, Īśāna, who presides over every productive organ and in whom and from whom are all things, one attains eternal peace or serenity (11). Then there is a repetition here of a verse in the previous chapter (III, 4) with an unimportant difference of reading (12). Then occurs the second part of the verse in RV., which represents Hiraṇyagarbha to be the lord of two-footed and four-footed animals (X, 121, 3), the first part of the latter being paraphrased here (13). This verse was probably suggested by the occurrence of the name of Hiraṇyagarbha in the previous verse. Having known Śiva (the auspicious), who is minuter than the minute, the creator of the universe, of many forms, and who alone encompasses the universe in this medley of the world, one attains eternal peace (14). That same lord of the universe concealed in all objects is the protector of the world in time. Devoting themselves to him and knowing him thus, the Brahmarṣis and the deities cut away the nooses of death (15). Knowing Śiva, concealed in all beings, who is as subtle as the essence of milk other than the butter, knowing the god who alone encompasses the universe, one is free from all nooses (16). This god — this great soul — whose work is the universe always dwells in the hearts of men. He is determined by the heart, the intelligence, and internal consciousness; those who know this become immortal (17). When there was simple darkness and no day or light, no entity or nonentity, Śiva alone existed. He was the one unchangeable thing, and he was the bright light of the sun, and from him sprang all intelligence (18). Here appears an idea similar to that expressed in RV. X, 129. No one can seize him above, transversely or in the middle. There is not another like him. Great is his glory (19). His form is invisible. Nobody sees him with the eye. Those who see him, dwelling in the heart, by the heart and the internal consciousness, become immortal (20). This verse is the same as in KU. (VI. 9), excepting in the third line, which there is the same as the third line of v. 17 above. The chapter ends with two verses containing a prayer to Rudra to protect, the latter of which is the same as RV. I, 114, 8.

In the first verse of the fifth chapter are mentioned two indestructible beings, Brahman and the other, who are endless, in whom there lie, unobserved, knowledge and ignorance. Ignorance is destructible, knowledge is indestructible; and there is another who rules over knowledge and ignorance (1). In the next verse is mentioned the birth of Kapila and his being fed with knowledge by him who presides over every productive energy (2). Giving various forms to each group (lit. net), the god resolves everything into the original principle. Creating again the lords of beings, he, the great soul, the ruler, wields sovereignty over all (3). As the sun illuminates all quarters, upper and lower and transversal, so also the god, the Bhagavat, presides over the natures of all productive energies (4). The original cause of the world makes natural powers develop and brings to a mature condition those who are capable of development. He presides over this universe and puts into operation all the qualities (5). That is concealed in Upaniṣads, which contain the secret of the Vedas. That origin of Brahman, Brahmadeva knows. All the ancient gods and Ṛṣis, who knew that, being absorbed in it, became immortal (6). The Upaniṣad then proceeds to mention the individual soul, the lord of the vital airs, who performs actions and enjoys or suffers their fruit, possesses three qualities and follows three ways and goes through a succession of births in consequence of his actions (7). He is as big as the thumb, bright like the sun, is conscious of himself and wills, is as minute as the hundredth part of the hundredth part of the point of a hair and is endless. In himself he is not a female nor a male nor sexless. This depends on the body assumed by him (8, 9, 10). He assumes many gross and subtle forms in accordance with his qualities and the qualities of his actions and of the self. But he who effects their union, is another (12). Then follows a verse similar to IV, 14 and the latter part of 16 (13). In the last verse Śiva, the God, the creator and destroyer, is said to be knowable by Bhāva (faith, love, or the pure heart) (14).

The sixth chapter appears to be a sort of resumé of what precedes. Among other things it is stated that He who promotes virtue and dispells sin, should be known as existing in oneself (6); that the one God is concealed in all beings, is all-pervading, the internal soul of all beings, presiding over all actions, the support of all beings, the witness of all, the life-giver, absolute and without qualities (11); and that, knowing the cause which is to be understood by means of the Sāṃkhya and the Yoga, a man is free from all nooses (13). After this follows a verse to the effect: "nor the sun nor the moon nor the stars nor lightning illuminate him (i. e. make him known); when he shines, everything shines after him, and by his light all this is rendered visible, or is illuminated" (14). This verse occurs in KU. (V. 15) and in MU. (II, 2, 10). The work ends with an expression of the author's self-surrender to the god, who shines forth in one's own intelligence, who first created Brahmadeva, and who sent forth the Vedas — the god who has no parts, who does not suffer change, who is all peace, has no defects and is unpolluted, the bridge for crossing over to immortality, and who is like fire that has burnt fuel (18, 19).

§ 84. From this short summary it will be seen that this Upaniṣad contains verses from the Saṃhitās of the RV. and YV. and others, which must have been in a floating condition and were appropriated by the Muṇḍaka and Kaṭha Upaniṣads as well as by this; and a great many others, which have not been traced elsewhere, are original. All these contain truths about the nature of God, the individual soul and the inanimate world and the relations between them. The way to redemption is meditation on the supreme soul, which way is characteristic of the Upaniṣad doctrine in general. Certain Yoga processes are prescribed to render this meditation effective, and the final result is a perception of the supreme soul as existing everywhere, and this perception constitutes eternal bliss. This treatise contains the theism of the Upaniṣad period in its most mature form with a God distinctly personal at the centre. The attributes of the supreme soul are often given in very general terms, and he is referred to by the non-sectarian general name Deva, but as often that Deva is identified with Rudra, Siva, Iśāna and Maheśvara, and his powers are spoken of as Iśanīs; but there is no indication whatever that these names have been given for the purpose of raising Rudra-Siva to the supreme godhead to the exclusion of another god. Names indicative of Rudra-Śiva appear to have been used, since he was invested with a personality perceived and acknowledged by all. This Upaniṣad, therefore, is not a sectarian treatise like others promulgated in later times, and is often quoted by Śaṃkarācarya, Rāmānuja and other writers of the different schools, and not by those of one school only. It must have been composed before the BhG. since the latter contains, as already stated, a verse and a half from it, and the nature of the religio-philosophic speculations contained in it, though essentially Upaniṣadic, make a nearer approach to the later Bhakti school than those of any of the older treatises of the class. The description of the godhead and of the final pure serenity are instinct with the glow of love and admiration and the treatise ends with an expression of self-surrender to the god, who makes himself manifest in one's own intelligence. The Śvetāśvatara-Upaniṣad, therefore, stands at the door of the Bhakti school, and pours its loving adoration on Rudra-Śiva instead of on Vāsudeva-Kṛṣṇa as the BhG. did in later times when the Bhakti doctrine was in full swing. Vāsudeva-Kṛṣṇa had a historic basis; and the circumstances which led to his being invested with the supreme godhead, occurred in later times, while in the age, in which the Śvetāśvatara-Upaniṣad was composed, Rudra-Śiva was alone in the field as the supreme god, and the germs of Bhakti, or love, which manifested themselves at the time, were directed towards him; but when Vāsudeva-Kṛṣṇa also came into the field, he appealed more to the hearts of men as the god who had come to dwell amongst them; consequently the germs of Bhakti speedily developed, and he became the object of the heightened feelings in preference to the other.

§ 85. Up to the time at which we have arrived we meet with no mention of the wife of Rudra or Śiva, but in the Kena-Upaniṣad, which is certainly one of the earlier Upaniṣads, the name of Umā occurs. She is called Haimavatī, or the daughter of Himavat, but she is not mentioned in the KnU. as the wife of Rudra or Śiva, though in later times she was known to be so. The story is: — Brahman conquered the enemies of the gods for them, but the gods took credit to themselves for the victory and were proud of their achievements. Agni, Vāyu and Indra were sitting together, engaged in joyous conversation, when there appeared at some distance a spirit. Agni first went out to see what it was. The spirit asked him the nature and extent of his power and laid down a blade of grass, which it asked him to burn away. Agni was not able to do this and returned baffled. Then went Vāyu, who also was not able to blow away the blade of grass; afterwards went Indra, and at his approach the spirit disappeared. Indra was disappointed, but he saw a beautiful woman of the name of Umā-Haimavatī and asked her who the spirit was. She said it was Brahman. The story represents that condition of things, in which the old Vedic gods had lost their power or hold over men, and Brahman had come into prominence as the supreme spirit. Since it was Umā that disclosed the nature of the spirit, it may be understood that the Brahman mentioned was Rudra-Śiva and Umā was his wife. It would thus appear that she had come to be so regarded some time before the Upaniṣad was composed.

§ 86. The Atharvaśiras is another Upaniṣad appertaining to Rudra. It is a much later work as is shown even by the very variant texts before me, commented on by Nārāyaṇa and Śaṃkarānanda. The gods, it is said, went to heaven and asked Rudra who he was. He said that he alone was, is, or will be, and nothing else. He is in all the quarters, he is Gāyatrī, man, woman, etc., and thus a number of things are mentioned with which he is identical. Then Rudra was invisible to them, and they raised their arms and praised him saying: "He who is Rudra, is Bhagavat, and who also is Brahmadeva, a bow to him". In the similar sentences that follow, instead of Brahmadeva we have Viṣṇu, Maheśvara, Umā, Skanda, Vināyaka, etc. The sun and the constellation are also included. Then Oṃkāra is mentioned, to which many epithets and epithets of epithets expressive of divine attributes are given, and lastly it is called the one Rudra, who is Īśāna, Bhagavat, Maheśvara and Mahādeva. Then follow the etymologies of the epithets or names. The only Rudra he is called, because he alone creates and absorbs everything. He is called Īśāna, because he rules by the powers called the Īśanīs. Then follow four or five verses from ŚU. with different readings in some cases. The substance of what follows is thus given by Śaṃkarānanda. For the knowledge of Rudra one should use moderate food, devote himself to reading (Śravaṇa), thinking (Manana), etc., become a Paramahaṃsa, or a single-minded devotee, and spend his time thus. One should undertake the Pāśupata vow (Vrata), which is of the following nature. Greed and anger should be given up. Forgiveness should be realised. The muttering of Oṃ should be practised, and meditation resulting in Avagati, or perception, should be resorted to. The text, of which this is the explanation, may be generally rendered thus: — "In the inside of the heart exists the subtle body, in which there are anger, greed and forgiveness. Destroying greed, which is at the bottom of human motives, and concentrating the mind on Rudra, who is one and eternal, one should be moderate in eating and drinking". Then follows a precept to besmear the body with ashes by repeating the words: "The ash is fire, the ash is water, the ash is earth, everything is ash, the ether is ash, the mind, the eyes and other senses are ash." This is the Pāśupata vow (Vrata), enjoined for the removal of the noose with which the Paśu, or the individual soul, is tied."

Here the besmearing of the body with ashes after repeating a formula, or Mantra, is prescribed as a vow for the devotees of Paśupati, or Rudra-Śiva, calculated to effect a deliverance from the trammels of life. The expression "Paśupāśavimokṣaṇa", which means the loosening of the noose tied round the necks of beings, is a characteristic of the Pāśupata sect. This Upaniṣad therefore belongs to that sect. Before, however, we pass on to the consideration of this sect, we must cast a glance at the position which Rudra-Śiva holds in the Mahābhārata.

IV. Rudra-Śiva in the Mahābhārata and Liṅga Worship.

§ 87. At the beginning of the Bhīṣmaparvan Kṛṣṇa advises Arjuna to make an obeisance to Durgā before the commencement of the battle and pray for success. Arjuna does so after repeating a hymn in honour of Durgā, containing the names of Umā, mother of Skanda, Kātyāyanī, Karālī, and a number of others. In the Vanaparvan Arjuna is represented to have gone to the Himālaya and practised austerities there. Some time after, Śiva appears dressed like a Kirāta, and a severe fight ensues between them. Arjuna is overpowered in the end and lies on the ground exhausted. He then praises Śiva, and, having made an altar of earth, puts flowers on it in the name of Śaṃkara. These, however, appear as placed on the head of the Kirāta, whereupon Arjuna makes him out as Śiva the object of his adoration, and surrenders himself to him. Śiva becomes pleased and offers him whatever he wishes. Arjuna asks for the weapon presided over by Paśupati (Pāśupatāstra), which possesses the power of destroying all formidable enemies (chaps. 38—40). In the Droṇaparvan again (chaps. 80, 81) the attainment of the Pāśupatāstra, which appears to be of another kind, consisting of a bow and arrow, by Arjuna, is mentioned.

Arjuna and Kṛṣṇa are spoken of as having gone to the Himālaya in a vision and seen Śaṃkara at his dwelling. They bow their heads before him, sing a hymn in his praise, in which they call him the unborn, the creator of the universe, the unchangeable and utter the names which we have given as occurring in earlier works, and thus propitiating him ask for the Pāśupata weapon. They are directed to a lake where the Astra had been thrown. There they saw two venomous serpents, which, however, assumed at the time the forms of a bow and an arrow, and these Arjuna took away. In the Sauptikaparvan (chap. 7) Aśvatthāman is mentioned to have propitiated Śaṃkara and obtained a sword from him. Śiva himself enters into his body, and Aśvatthāman carries havoc and destruction with the terrible sword in the camp of the Pāṇḍus, killing all their progeny, and even Dhṛṣṭadyumna, who had cut off the head of his father Droṇa. Yudhiṣṭhira asks Kṛṣṇa how he was able to effect all this. Kṛṣṇa says that he did it through the power of Śaṃkara and relates another story about him. Brahmadeva once told Śaṃkara not to create. Whereupon Śaṃkara concealed himself under water for a long time. When, therefore, there was no creation for such a long period, Brahmadeva created another Prajāpati, who brought into existence a large number of beings. These beings, being afflicted with hunger, went to Prajāpati to devour him. He, being afraid, went to Hiraṇyagarbha, who created two kinds of food for those beings and then they were quieted. After some time Mahādeva rose out of the water, and seeing that new beings had been created and were in a flourishing condition, he cut off his organ of generation as no more necessary, and it stuck into the ground. He then went away to perform austerities at the foot of the Muñjavat mountain. There is a similar story about Mahādeva's having ceased to create and become a Yogin in the Vāyu-Purāṇa (chap. 10). Brahmadeva told Nīlalohita (Mahādeva) to create, and bringing to mind his wife Satī, he created thousands of beings exactly like himself, who were immortal. Thereupon he stopped and rendered himself incapable of procreation. He then resorted to all those processes of the Yoga which in the Purāṇa is called the Pāśupata-Yoga. In the Sauptikaparvan Kṛṣṇa continues the story of Mahādeva and tells Yudhiṣṭhira that when the gods created the rite of sacrifice and assigned no oblation to Rudra, he was full of wrath and destroyed the sacrifice; whereupon they assigned him a portion and the god was pleased. In the Anuśāsanaparvan (chap. 14) Kṛṣṇa is introduced as recounting the glories of Mahādeva. He says, Jāmbavatī, one of his wives, expressed a desire for as good a son as Rukmiṇī, his chief consort, had. To procure such a son he had recourse to Mahādeva, through whose favour only his wishes could be fulfilled. He then went to the Himālaya, on which Śiva lived. On the way he saw the hermitage of Upamanyu. Upamanyu enters into a long discourse on the beneficent deeds of Mahādeva. A list is given of persons, including many Daityas, who obtained their desired objects, such as sons, weapons, powers, etc., through the favour of Mahādeva, whom they had propitiated by rigid austere practices and other ways. One of these was Śākalya, to whom was granted the boon that he would be an author and would obtain immortal glory and his son would be the composer of Sūtras. The persons alluded to here must be the compiler of the RVS. and the author of the Pada text. Upamanyu began to practise austerities to propitiate Śiva at the instance of his mother, who, in describing the god's power and beneficence, spoke of him as dancing nakedly and of his having the quarters for his clothing (Digvāsas). In the course of his austerities, Mahādeva, to test Upamanyu's devotion, appears before him in the form of Indra and offers him many magnificent boons, which Upamanyu refuses and declares that he would have boons from Śaṃkara alone, and that he would become a worm or a butterfly at the command of Śaṃkara, but did not desire even the sovereignty of the three worlds given by Indra. In the course of his narrative Upamanyu says that Mahādeva was the only god, whose organ of generation (Liṅga) is worshipped by men. He and Umā were the real creators of animals, as these bear the marks of the two, and not the discus or the conch-shell or marks of any other god. Eventually Śiva and Umā appeared before Upamanyu, seated on a strong towering ox, attended on the one side by Brahmadeva seated on the swan, his vehicle, and on the other by Nārāyaṇa on Garuḍa with the conch-shell, lotus, etc., and conferred on him all the blessings he desired. At his instance Kṛṣṇa also entered on a long course of austerities, at the end of which Mahādeva with Umā appeared before him in the same manner as they did to Upamanyu. The god conferred eight boons upon him, and his consort eight more; besides she promised him sixteen thousand wives, and altogether the number of boons he obtained was twenty-four inclusive of the birth of such a son as he wanted.

§ 88. The characteristics of Śiva, or Mahādeva, as brought out by these accounts appear to be these. He was a powerful, wrathful and impetuous god, but generous and bountiful, and spared nothing when he was propitiated. Whenever a man conceived a desire for anything, he was the god to be appealed to for its fulfilment. He lived on the Himālaya with his wife Umā, Pārvatī, or Durgā, who had a number of other names such as Kālī, Karālī, etc., and was attended by a number of beings called his Gaṇas, or hosts. His vehicle was an ox. He had, of course, all the attributes of the supreme godhead. He is represented as having betaken himself to the processes of Yoga, or contemplation, when he had ceased to be creative. It will be seen that the object of worship in Śaivism is the Liṅga, or phallus. We have found no trace of this characteristic in the earlier literature, so far as we have examined it[1]), and the first time we meet with it is in this passage from the Anuśāsanaparvan. We have had occasion in a previous section to remark that Rudra-Śiva had a close connection with stragglers in the forest, with Vrātyas, or those who were not included in the Āryan community, and with the wild tribe of the Niṣādas, and also observed

[1]) I do not, however, deny the possibility that when the ŚU. in IV, 11 speaks of the god Īśāna as presiding over every Yoni and in V, 2 of the lord as presiding over all forms and Yonis, an allusion to the physical fact of the Liṅga and Yoni connected together may have been meant as typifying the philosophical doctrine of gods presiding over every creative cause.

that the gods of these last were amalgamated with Rudra. Rudra's partiality for serpents and his being the lord of spirits, or Bhūtas, were probably due to the influence of the serpent-worship and the devilry of the savage tribes. There are two places in the RV., in one of which Indra is prayed to not to allow those whose god is Siśna to disturb the rites of the singers (VII, 21, 5); and in another he is represented to have conquered the riches of a city after killing those whose god is Śiśna. Here evidently those whose god was Śiśna, or phallus, are meant as the enemies of the Vedic Āryas, who disturbed their holy rites. Notwithstanding all that is said about the matter, my own belief is that the persons here referred to were really some tribe of the aborigines of the country, who worshipped the phallus. Just then as the Rudra-Śiva cult borrowed several elements from the dwellers in forests and stragglers in places out of the way, so it may have borrowed this element of phallic worship from the barbarian tribes with whom the Āryas came in contact. This element, however, does not appear to have come in all at once, especially among the learned classes, whose beliefs are represented in the literature which we have examined. The Liṅga worship had, it appears, not come into use at the time of Patañjali, for the instance he gives under P. V, 3, 99 is that of an image or likeness (pratikṛti) of Śiva as an object of worship, and not of any emblem of that god. It seems to have been unknown even in the time of Wema-Kadphises, for on the reverse of his coins there is a human figure of Śiva with a trident in the hand; and there is also an emblem, but it is Nandin, or the bull, and not a Liṅga, or phallus. But this element must have crept in early enough among ordinary people who were in closer communication with the uncivilised tribes, and gradually made its way to the higher clasess, of whose creed it subsequently became an article. And it is this final stage of its adoption by the higher classes that is represented in Upamanyu's discourse in the Mahābhārata. From all that we have brought forward from the post-Saṃhitā literature it will appear that Rudra-Śiva was a deity whose worship was common to all the Āryas, and who was not at first a sectarian god. As above remarked, he was in charge of the field before the Vaiṣṇava or Vāsudevic deities came in to contest his supremacy. The Gṛhyasūtras, which, as we have seen, give directions as to the adoration of Rudra under various circumstances, can not be considered as belonging to any Śaiva sect. In the time of Patañjali, images of Śiva, Skanda and Viśākha, made sometimes of precious metals, were kept for common worship by certain religious persons who derived an income from them [1]. The images of Śiva here alluded to cannot have been meant for the use of a particular sect.

V. Origin and Diffusion of the Śaiva Sects and the Several Classes of Śiva Worshippers.

§ 89. A Śaiva sect is, however, mentioned even by Patañjali. The members of it were known as Śivabhāgavatas, or devotees of

[1]) See his comment on P. V, 3, 99.

Śiva, the Bhagavat. Śiva, we have seen, is called Bhagavat in AU. A Śivabhāgavata carried in his hand an iron lance as an emblem of the deity he worshipped (under P. V, 2, 76).

In the Nārāyaṇīya section of MBh., the Pāśupata is mentioned as one of five schools of religious doctrines (Śāntiparvan, chap. 349, v. 64). Śiva-Śrīkaṇṭha, the consort of Umā, the lord of spirits and the son of Brahmadeva, is represented to have revealed the tenets of that school (verse 67). Whether this statement is to be understood in the sense that its founder was a human being afterwards recognised as an incarnation of Śiva, or whether it is a mere general statement like that contained in the BU. (II, 4, 10) that the Ṛgveda, Yajurveda, etc. are the breath of this great being, meaning nothing more historically than that the system gradually came into existence without any special individual being concerned with it, is a question somewhat difficult to answer definitely; but there is evidence in the Purāṇas and inscriptions of the existence of a belief in favour of the first supposition. The Vāyu-Purāṇa (chap. 23) and the Liṅga-Purāṇa (chap. 24) represent Maheśvara to have told Brahmadeva that when, at the time of Kṛṣṇa-Dvaipāyana during the twenty-eighth repetition of the Yugas, Vāsudeva, the best of Yadus, would be born of Vasudeva, he would incarnate himself as a Brahmacārin by the name of Lakulin after entering a dead body thrown into a cemetery; the place where this would occur, would be called Kāyāvatāra or Kāyāvarohaṇa, and he would have four pupils of the names of Kuśika, Garga, Mitra and Kauruṣya. These Pāśupatas, with their bodies sprinkled with ashes, resorting to the Yoga of Maheśvara, would in the end go to the world of Rudra. Now in an inscription in the temple of Nātha near that of Ekalingji, 14 miles to the north of Udaipur, Rājputāna, it is stated that Śiva became incarnate as a man with a club (lakula) in his hand in the country of Bhṛgukaccha, being propitiated by Bhṛgu. Sages, Kuśika and others, conversant with the Pāśupata Yoga and using ashes and wearing bark-dress and matted hair, are mentioned. There is another inscription, usually called the Cintra Praśasti, which states that Śiva became incarnate in the form of Bhaṭṭāraka Śrī-Lakulīśa and dwelt at Kārohaṇa in the Lāṭa country. There appeared in bodily form four pupils of his of the names of Kuśika, Gārgya, Kauruṣa and Maitreya for the strict performance of the Pāśupata vows, and they became the originators of four branches. The date of the first inscription is Vikrama 1028, or 971 A. D., and the second was composed between A. D. 1274 and 1296. In another inscription dated 943 A. D. found at Hemāvatī in the Sira Tāluka, Mysore, Lakulīśa is represented to have been born again as Munīnātha Chilluka to preserve the memory of his name and doctrines [1]).

Mādhava calls the Pāśupata system that he explains in his Sarvadarśanasaṃgraha, Nakulīśa-Pāśupata, and quotes a few words from what appears to be a work attributed to him. From all this it appears that there lived a certain person of the name of Lakulin (the holder of a lakuṭa, or laguḍa, or lakula, i. e. a club) who founded a Pāśupata system. Four schools sprang out of it, and their reputed founders,

[1]) See Jour. B. B. R. A. S. Vol. XXII, pp. 151—153.

whether historical or legendary, were considered his pupils. Lakulin is the same as Nakulin, and the fact that his rise has been represented by the Purāṇas to be contemporaneous with Vāsudeva-Kṛṣṇa points to the inference that traditionally the system was intended to take the same place in the Rudra-Śiva cult that the Pāñcarātra did in the Vāsudeva-Kṛṣṇa cult. We may, therefore, place the rise of the Pāśupata school mentioned in the Nārāyaṇīya about a century after that of the Pāñcarātra system, i. e. about the second century B. C.

§ 90. Before we proceed further we will notice the extent of the diffusion of the creed. At the end of the commentary on the Vaiśeṣika-sūtras, the author Praśastapāda makes his obeisance to Kaṇāda, the author of the Sūtras, and characterises him as having composed the Vaiśeṣikaśāstra after propitiating Maheśvara by the greatness of his Yoga (meditation or concentration) and Ācāra (practice). These two ways are common to both the Pāśupata and Śaiva systems, as will be seen hereafter, and Kaṇāda, therefore, may have been a follower of the Pāśupata or Śaiva system. Bhāradvāja, the author of the Uddyota, or a gloss on Vātsyāyana's Nyāyabhāṣya, is called Pāśupatācārya, or a teacher belonging to the Pāśupata school, at the end of his work. Wema-Kadphises, a powerful prince of the Kuṣana race, who ruled over a large part of northern and northwestern India about the middle of the third century A. D., styles himself on the reverse of his coins a devotee of Maheśvara, or a member of the Māheśvara sect, and an image of Nandin and another of Śiva with a trident in his hand occur on the obverse. Varāhamihira in the latter part of the sixth century lays down the rule that the priests to be employed for the installation of an image of Śambhu should be Brāhmaṇas besmearing their bodies with ashes. By these he means members of a Śaiva sect, since, in the case of other gods, the names mentioned are those of the sects founded in the names of those gods.

Haribhadra, an old Jaina author, speaks in his Ṣaḍdarśanasamuccaya of the schools of Gotama and Kaṇāda as professing the Śaiva faith. But his commentator Guṇaratna, who flourished in the latter part of the fourteenth century [1]), calls the Vaiśeṣikas Pāśupatas and the other school Śaivas. This last must be a mistake, since Bhāradvāja of the Nyāya school is specifically spoken of as a Pāśupatācarya, as we have seen The Chinese traveller Hiuen Tsiang in the middle of the seventh century mentions the Pāśupatas twelve times in his book. In some places he says that there were temples of Maheśvara at which the Pāśupatas worshipped; in one or two temples, he says that they resided. And at Benares he found about ten thousand sectaries who honoured Maheśvara, besmeared their bodies with ashes, went naked and tied their hair in knots. These and those who lived in temples must have been like the Bairāgis, or ascetics, of modern times, who had given up the world; but probably the others mentioned by him were the followers of the Pāśupata faith who lived the ordinary life of householders In the copper-plate charter of Nāgavardhana, nephew of Pulakeśin II of Mahārāṣṭra, who ascended the throne in 610 A. D.

---

[1]) Ind. Ant. Vol. XI, pp. 255—256.

and was living in 639 A. D., a grant is recorded of a village near Igatpuri in the Nāsik district for the worship of the god Kāpāleśvara, i. e. the lord of the wearers of garlands of skulls, and for the maintenance of the Mahāvratins residing in the temple. It will hereafter be shown that the name Mahāvratin, or observer of the great vow, designated the Kāpālikas or Kālāmukhas. Thus there is evidence of the existence in the middle of the seventh century of the sect of Kāpālikas in Mahārāṣṭra[1]). In the Karhāḍ grant of Kṛṣṇa III of the Rāṣṭrakūṭa dynasty, the king mentions his having granted in Śaka 880 (= 958 A. D.) a village to Gagaṇaśiva, the practiser of great austerities, who was fully versed in all the Śivasiddhāntas and was the pupil of Īśānaśiva, who was an Ācārya, or preceptor, and the head of the establishment at Valkaleśvara in Karahāṭa. These holy men and their establishment seem to have belonged to the Śaiva sect and not to the Pāśupata. The evidence for the existence of the Kālāmukha and Śaiva sects in Mysore in the latter part of the twelfth century will be given in the next section.

Here it seems necessary to make another distinction. Bāṇa in the Kādambarī represents Pāśupatas with red clothing to have been among those who waited to see Tārāpīḍa's minister Śukanāsa at the door of his house for some private purposes of their own; but in another place he represents Vilāsavatī, the queen of Tārāpīḍa, to have gone to the temple of Mahākāla on the fourteenth (of the dark half of the month) to worship the god. Bhavabhūti in the Mālatīmādhava (Act III) represents Mālatī to have gone with her mother to the temple of Śaṃkara on the fourteenth of the dark half of the month. This fourteenth day still continues to be sacred to Śiva when special worship is performed. Now Vilāsavatī and Mālatī and her mother can hardly have been meant to be members of that sect, some followers of which, with a red clothing, were waiting at Śukanāsa's door. It, therefore, appears to be clear that all worshippers of Śiva were not members of any of those sects the names of which have come down to us, as observed in a previous section. Rudra-Śiva had gradually from the earliest times grown to be a god commonly worshipped by the Indians, and he has continued to be their ordinary god to this day. The sects that subsequently arose were based upon specific methods of redemption, when religious and philosophic thought was advancing or perhaps declining, but the old god was resorted to by ordinary people without reference to them. And it must be remarked that those sects must have had a clerical or ascetic class as well as a class of lay followers or householders — and probably in some cases at least Hiuen Tsiang means these last by his Pāśupatas — and a class of Śaiva religious men, as distinct from lay followers, existed in Karahāṭa as we have noticed. There were thus three classes of Śiva worshippers: — (1) clericals or ascetics, (2) their lay followers, and (3) ordinary people who had no particular connection with any sect. The poets Kālidāsa, Subandhu, Bāṇa, Śrī-Harṣa, Bhaṭṭa-Nārāyaṇa, Bhavabhūti and several others adore Śiva at the beginning of their works. They may have been the lay followers of any of the sects, but, in all likelihood, they belong

[1]) Jour. B. B. R. A. S. Vol. XIV, p. 26.

to the third class. For of these Subandhu, Bāṇa and Bhaṭṭa-Nārāyaṇa invoke Hari or another form of Viṣṇu at the same time, thus showing that they were not exclusive adherents of one of the two gods. The many temples of Śiva constructed by the early Cālukyas and the Rāṣṭrakūṭas and the Kailāsa and other cave temples at Ellora excavated by the latter contain no indication of their being intended for a specific Śaiva sect, and therefore they may be regarded as pointing to the diffusion of the general worship of Śiva in Mahārāṣṭra from the seventh to the tenth century.

VI. Names and Doctrines of the Śaiva Sects.

§ 91. The older Śaiva sects had and have a literature of their own, the so-called Āgamas attributed to Śiva himself and a number of works by human authors. But the literature has not yet been published nor even discovered. I have, therefore, necessarily to resort to the stray notices about the sects and their doctrines, contained in works not written by the followers of the systems except in one case. With the more modern sects the case is different, their literature having recently become available.

Śaṃkara says that the Māheśvaras maintain that Paśupati has revealed five topics (Br. S. II, 2, 37). Thus the sects were known by the general name of Māheśvara, and Paśupati, or the god Śiva, was believed to be their founder. Rāmānuja under the same Sūtra, which, however, is numbered 35, speaks of the systems as the tenets of Paśupati. Keśava Kāśmīrin calls the sects the followers of the "tenets of Paśupati". Śrīkaṇṭha-Śivācārya calls them the "believers in the Āgamas revealed by Parameśvara, or the great god". The name Māheśvara is the old name as is evident from the fact that Wema-Kadphises, as noticed above, and several later princes, especially of the Valabhī dynasty, called themselves Māheśvaras. Hiuen Tsiang, too, as we have seen, mentions temples of Maheśvara, at which the Pāśupatas worshipped. It also follows that all these sects were at the same time known by the name of Pāśupata sects; and the founder of them all was believed to be the god Paśupati.

The same conclusion is to be deduced from the Mysore inscriptions that have been published, the only difference being that the original teacher is called Lakulin or Lakulīśa. In one inscription dated 943 A. D., referred to above, it is stated that Lakulīśa, being afraid that his name and doctrines would be forgotten, became incarnate as Muninātha-Cilluka [1]). This appears to be a general name applicable to all systems. In another dated 1078 A. D. one ascetic is called an ornament to the Lākula school and another is spoken of as "a hand to Lākula" [2]). This appears to be the general name and does not point to a specific sect. In a third dated 1103 A. D. Someśvara-Sūri is spoken of as having caused the Lākula doctrine (Siddhānta) to bloom. He is called a Naiyāyika and Vaiśeṣika [3]). This shows that he belonged to the specific

1) Ep. Carn. Vol. XII, p. 92 (Translation).
2) Ep. Carn. Vol. VII, Śikarpur Taluq No. 107.
3) Ep. Carn. Vol. VII, Pt. I, p. 64 (Translation).

Pāśupata sect. In a fourth dated 1177 A. D. certain ascetics are called upholders of the Lākulāgamasamaya, i. e. the system based upon a work of Lakulin, and adherents of Kālāmukhas[1]). Here evidently the Kālāmukhas are called Lākulas, which is the same as Pāśupatas. The names of the ascetics mentioned in this inscription end in the word śakti and jīya, which appear to be characteristic of the Kālāmukha sect. In a fifth dated 1183 A. D. is noticed a grant to Nāgaśiva-Paṇḍita, who is called an upholder of the Lākula system, and the names of his preceptors in the two preceding generations end in the suffix śiva. Nāgaśiva is praised for eminence in Āgama and in Śivatattva[2]). From the ending suffix śiva in these names and the mention of a proficiency in Āgama and in Śivatattva, it appears that Nāgaśiva was a follower of the Śaiva school and at the same time he was a Lākula, or Pāśupata. A sixth dated 1199 A. D. notices a grant of land to Bammadeva, son of Nāgarāśi, the promoter of the system based upon the work of Lakulin[3]). The suffix rāśi is found in a great many names of the devotees of Śiva. Whether it is a characteristic of a specific sect is not clear, but it appears that the bearers of it belong to the Pāśupata, or the Kālāmukha school. In a seventh dated 1213 A. D. a certain religious man is represented as the upholder of the system known by the name of Vāgi-Lākula, i. e. the system of the learned Lakulin[4]). In an eighth dated 1285 A. D. the grantor is called a supporter of the new system of Lakulin[5]). This perhaps refers to the later school of Liṅgāyats. Thus it will be seen that Lākula was the general name by which the Śaiva sects were called, and the specific name Kālāmukha is associated with the general name in one case. This general name has for its basis the historical fact, noticed above that a person of the name of Lakulin or Lakulīśa founded a Śaiva system corresponding to the Pāñcarātra system, which the Vāyu- and Liṅga-Purāṇas consider to be contemporaneous with it. The other general name Pāśupata arose by dropping the name of the human individual Lakulin and substituting that of the god Paśupati, whose incarnation he was believed to be, as is done in the texts of the MBh. quoted above. But that the Śaiva system had a human founder is confirmed by the fact that the name of his work, the Pañcādhyāyī, or Pañcārthavidyā, has been handed down, as will be shown immediately below, and probably the work is extant, even if it has not yet been discovered, as Mādhava

[1]) Ep. Carn. Vol. V, Pt. I, p. 135 (Translation).

[2]) Ep. Carn. Vol. V, Arsikere Taluq No. 89. Another holy person of the name of Nāga with the suffix rāśi instead of śiva is mentioned in inscr. No. 69 Arsikere Taluq (Ep. Carn. Vol. V, p. 137). A grant is therein recorded to Mādhajīya, a disciple of Nāgarāśi, who belonged to the Kālāmukhas and was himself the disciple of Padmaśiva-Paṇḍita. Another Nāgarāśi is mentioned in inscr. No. 48 (Ibid.). The grantee in this case is Kalyāṇaśakti, disciple of Śivaśaktideva, who was himself the disciple of Nāgarāśi, "bound to the Kālāmukhas". This Nāgarāśi, or these two Nāgarāśis, appear to me to be different from the Nāgaśiva mentioned in the text. And the use of the termination rāśi in his case, he being a Kālāmukha, and of the word śakti in the case of two of the pupils, strengthens my supposition that these were characteristic of the Kālāmukha sect, the former being applicable to the Pāśupata also.

[3]) Ep. Carn. Vol. V, Arsikere Taluq No. 103.

[4]) Ep. Carn. Vol. V, Arsikere Taluq No. 46.

[5]) Ep. Carn. Vol. XII, p. 45 (Translation).

mentions a gloss on the perpetual commentary (Bhāṣya) on it, which also will be noticed below. The conclusion therefore appears to be that a certain historical person was the founder of the main Śaiva system which was the same as that explained by Mādhava as Nakulīśa-Pāśupata, and that three other systems arose out of it in later times.

The commentators of Śaṃkara state that there were four of these schools bearing the names of Śaiva, Pāśupata, Kārukasiddhāntin and Kāpālika. Vācaspati, however, calls the third Kāruṇikasiddhāntin. Rāmānuja and Keśava Kāśmīrin mention the same four schools, but call Kārukasiddhāntin by the name of Kālāmukha. The word Kāruka is probably a corruption of Kauruṣya, the name of the third of the four (according to the Purāṇas) pupils of Lakulīśa, or this last name may be the Sanskritised form of the original Kāruka [1]). A work of the name of Pañcādhyāyī, dealing with the five topics alluded to above and attributed to Paśupati, is mentioned by Keśava Kāśmīrin and is quoted by Rāmānanda on Kāśīkhaṇḍa [2]). This must be the same work as that which is quoted from by Mādhava in the section on Nakulīśa-Pāśupata and attributed by him to Nakulīśa, or Lakulīśa.

VII. The Pāśupata System.

§ 92. The five topics mentioned by Śaṃkara and explained by his commentators are these (1) Kārya, or effect, which is Mahat and the rest produced from Pradhāna; (2) Kāraṇa, or the cause, which is Īśvara or Maheśvara and also Pradhāna; (3) Yoga, which is absorption in meditation or the muttering of the syllable Oṃ, contemplation, concentration, etc.; (4) Vidhi, bathing (in ashes) at the three points of time, i. e. the beginning, the middle and the end of the day, and the rest up to Gūḍhacaryā, i. e. incognito movement; (5) Duḥkhānta, which is final deliverance. This is amplified by Mādhava in the section on the Pāśupata sect.

I. Effect (Kārya) is that which is not independent. It is of three kinds: (1) cognition (Vidyā), (2) organs (Kalā), and (3) individual soul (Paśu). Of these cognition is the property of the individual and is of two kinds: (1) external, and (2) internal. External cognition is

---

[1]) These four schools are mentioned in the Vāyavīyasaṃhitā of the Śiva-Purāṇa (II, 24, 177). The Śaiva school, however, is called Siddhāntamārga, and the Kālāmukhas are called Mahāvratadharas.

[2]) See Aufrecht's Cat. Cat. The Vāyavīyasaṃhitā (II, 24, 169) also mentions this work, which it characterises as the highest theosophy (Vidyā) of Śiva and gives Pañcārtha as its name, i. e. Pañcārthavidyā. This Pañcārtha appears to be alluded to by Mādhava when he refers his reader to the Pañcārthabhāṣyadīpikā in his section on Nakulīśa-Pāśupata. In an inscription in the temple of Harṣanāth, which exists in the Sīkar principality of the Jaipur state, a person of the name of Viśvarūpa is mentioned as the teacher of the Pañcārtha-Lākulāmnāya, i. e. the sacred book of Lakulin, called Pañcārtha. The inscription is dated V. E. 1013 = A. D. 957, so that there can be no question that the Pāśupata system was attributed to a human author named Lakulin, the work composed by him being called Pañcārtha (Ep. Ind. Vol. II, p. 122).

The occurrence of the names of the schools and of this book in the Purāṇa shows that its composition was later than the foundation of the schools, which, therefore, must be considered as owing nothing to it.

of two kinds: (1) distinct, and (2) indistinct. Distinct external cognition, which is educed by the instruments of knowledge, is called conceptual operation (Citta). For by the conceptual operation every man reduces to definiteness the thing that has been apprehended definitely or indefinitely by the aid of the light in the shape of the external object. The internal cognition is of the nature of virtue or vice, which forms the objective of the individual and determines for him the body of precepts he has to follow. Organs are dependent on the cognitive individual and are themselves insensate. They are of two kinds: (1) effects, and (2) causes. The effected organs are of ten kinds: the five elements, earth and others, and the five qualities, colour and others. The organs, which are causes, are of thirteen kinds: the five senses, and the five organs of action, and the three internal organs, viz. intelligence, egoism and mind, the functions of which are the determination of the will, the consciousness of the self, and the formation of a plan respectively. The individual (Paśu) is that which has individualism (Paśutva). It is of two kinds: (1) impure, and (2) pure. The impure individual is that which is connected with the body and the organs, while the pure one is unconnected with them. The details should be seen in the Pañcārthabhāṣyadīpikā and other works.

II. The cause (Kāraṇa) is that which effects the destruction of the whole creation and its prosperity or promotion. Though it is one, still on account of its various properties and functions it has many forms, such as lord (Pati), naturally powerful (Sādya), etc. To be the lord means to have the unbounded power of knowing and acting. He is, therefore, the eternal ruler. To be a Sādya is to be possessed of supreme sovereignty, which is not incidental, but natural.

III. Yoga is the connecting of the individual soul with god through the conceptual faculty (Citta). It is of two kinds, consisting in (1) action, and (2) cessation from action. The first consists in muttering syllables and formulas, meditation, etc. The second, or cessation from action, consists in mere feeling (Saṃvid).

IV. Vidhi, or process, is an operation which effects or brings about righteousness. It is of two kinds: (1) primary, and (2) secondary. The first, or primary, is conduct (Caryā) which induces righteousness directly. That conduct is of two kinds: (1) vows, and (2) means or doors. The vows consist in besmearing the body with ashes and lying down in ashes, definite practices (Upahāra), muttering and circumambulation. Thus has Nakulīśa said: "One should besprinkle one's body at the three points of the day and lie down in ashes". The definite practices are six. These have been stated by the author of the Sūtras to be laughing, singing, dancing, Huḍukkāra, prostration, and inaudible repetition. With these he says one should worship. Laughing is the making of the sound 'hā! hā! hā!' by the forcible stretch of the throat and the lips. Singing is the contemplation of the attributes of Maheśvara in accordance with the rules of the science of music. Dancing should be resorted to by contracting and stretching forth hands, feet, etc. and all other principal and subsidiary limbs accompanied by the representation of feeling in accordance with the science of dancing and gesticulation. Huḍukkāra is a holy sound resembling that of an ox made by striking the tongue on the palate. Huḍuk is an inimitative sound like the sacrificial Vaṣaṭ. When there is a crowd of people, all this should be done so as not to be observed.

The means, or doors, are these: (1) Krāthana, i. e. affecting to be asleep when one is awake; (2) Spandana, which is the moving or the shaking of the limbs as if they were paralysed; (3) Mandana, or the walking as if one's legs and other limbs were disabled; (4) Śṛṅgāraṇa, which is showing oneself to be in love by means of amorous gestures as if on seeing a beautiful young woman; (5) Avitatkaraṇa, which is doing a thing condemned by all as if one were devoid of the sense of discrimination between what should be done and what should be avoided; (6). Avitadbhāṣaṇa, which is speaking nonsensical and absurd things.

Secondary processes are those which are intended to help the conduct (Caryā), such as besmearing with ashes after worship, and to remove the sense of indecency or impropriety attaching itself to begging and eating the remnant of what others have eaten. For this purpose the author of the Sūtras has laid down that one should besmear his body after the worship and wear the faded flowers and leaves which had been removed from the god and a Liṅga (the image of the phallus).

V. Duḥkhānta, or final deliverance, is of two kinds: (1) total destruction of misery, and (2) an elevated condition consisting in the possession of the power of knowing and acting. The power of knowing is of five kinds: (1) Darśana, or seeing all objects which are atomic, concealed or are at a distance, and touching them; (2) Śravaṇa, or the miraculous hearing of all sounds; (3) Manana, or the miraculous knowing of all objects of thought; (4) Vijñāna, or the miraculous knowledge of all the sciences with that of the treatises on them and the matter contained in these last; and (5) Sarvajñatva, or the miraculous knowledge of the principles (of a science), whether mentioned or unmentioned, succinct and detailed, with their divisions and peculiarities. The peculiarities of the present system are such as these: In other systems the destruction of misery is final deliverance; in this system the attainment of the highest powers is also to be added. With others, that which comes into existence from non-existence is an effect; here the effect is eternal such as Paśu, or the individual soul. In other systems the cause depends for its operation on a subordinate cause; here the great lord acts independently. With others, the fruit of the Yoga, or concentration, is the attainment of an absolute condition; here it is the attainment of the highest powers. With others, Vidhi, or process, has for its fruit heaven and other places, from which there is a return to mortal life; in this system the fruit is proximity etc. (to god), from which there is no return.

The power of acting, though one, is regarded as threefold: (1) Manojavitva, or the power of doing anything instantly; (2) Kāmarūpitva, or the power of assuming variety of shapes and forms or bodies and senses without an effort; (3) Vikramaṇadharmitva, or the possession of great power, even when the operation of the senses is suspended. Thus then a man acquires these miraculous powers of knowledge and action at the end of a long course of conduct and discipline prescribed by the Pāśupata system.

It will be seen how fantastic and wild the processes prescribed in this system for the attainment of the highest condition are. Rudra-Śiva was the god of the open fields and wild and awful regions away from the habitations of men and worshipped by aberrant or irregular people. This character did impress itself on the mode of worship for his propitiation, which was developed in lat ertimes. The ŚU. endeavoured to humanise Rudra-Śiva; but the wild and outlandish character of the god prevailed. We will now proceed to the consideration of the Śaiva system which seems to have been established in later times. Here also Mādhava will be our main guide, since the many works that he quotes from are not available.

VIII. The Śaiva System.

§ 93. There are three principles: (1) the lord (Pati), (2) the individual soul (Paśu), and (3) fetters (Pāśa); and the whole system has four Pādas, or parts, which are knowledge (Vidyā), action (Kriyā), meditation (Yoga), and conduct, or discipline (Caryā). The first part contains an explanation of the nature of the individual soul (Paśu), fetters (Pāśa), and god (Īśvara), and determines the importance of formulas (Mantra) and the lord presiding over the formulas (Mantreśvara). This leads to initiation (Dīkṣā), which is necessary for the acquisition of the highest object of life. The second part contains an explanation of the process of initiation (Dīkṣāvidhi), which is of many forms and has many parts. The third part explains meditation, or concentration, along with its subsidiary processes. The fourth teaches discipline, or conduct, consisting in doing what is prescribed and avoiding what is proscribed. Without this Yoga is not possible.

I. Now the lord (Pati) is Śiva. Śiva acts, being impelled thereto by the deeds (Karman) of souls, and produces things to be enjoyed or suffered and their means. The exercise of his creative power thus depends on the Karman of man. He does everything; therefore, he is omniscient. God has not a body like that of an individual soul which has the fetters of taint and Karman, etc.; but he has a body made up of powers, certain specific five formulas (Mantras) [1]) being imagined to be the different parts of his body. These five are his powers and are also considered his different forms, and by these he does the five actions, which are creation, existence or protection, destruction, concealment, and benefaction. The following four partake of the nature

[1]) These five formulas, or Mantras, are contained in the TA. (X, 43—47) and in the Mahānārāyaṇīya Up. 17. The commentator considers these to refer to the five faces of Śiva, respectively. They are Sadyojāta, Vāmadeva, Aghora, Tatpuruṣa and Īśāna. They are also called forms of Śiva. One of the Dānas, or charitable gifts, mentioned by Hemādri (Dānakhaṇḍa Vol. I, pp. 789—792 Bibl. Ind.) consists of five images made of gold or other metal fashioned in a particular manner of these five forms of Śiva. In giving each a certain verse has to be repeated. These five forms are identified in a Śaiva treatise with the earth, water, fire, wind and ether, respectively, and they are considered as the creators of these elements in another, viz. Vīra-Śaiva-Cintāmaṇi, Sholapur 1908 A. D.

of Śiva: (1) formulas (Mantras), (2) the deity presiding over the formulas (Mantreśvara), (3) the great god (Maheśvara), and (4) delivered souls (Mukta).

II. The Paśu is the individual soul, who is atomic and known by the name of Kṣetrajña (self-conscious) and others. It is eternal and all-pervading. It is not incapable of action nor is it one only, as is maintained by other schools of philosophy. When the fetters are removed, he becomes Śiva, possessing eternal and boundless knowledge and power of action. The Muktas, or delivered ones, are Śivas, who have so become by the favour of him who is eternally Mukta, and is a person with five formulas (Mantras) for his body, i. e. he is identified with the god Śiva himself. Though they become Śivas, they are not independent, but depend upon the eternal god, Śiva. Paśu is of three kinds: (1) Vijñānakala, who has shaken off his connection with all the organs (Kalāḥ) [1]) in consequence of the destruction of the impression of deeds done, by means of knowledge, meditation, asceticism, or by the enjoyment or suffering of the fruit (Bhoga), and has simple taint (Mala). The second is Pralayākala, whose organs are destroyed by the dissolution of the world. He has both impression of deeds (Karman) and taints (Mala). The third is Sakala, who has all the three fetters, taint (Mala), impression of deeds (Karman), and material cause (Māyā). Vijñānakala is of two kinds: (1) one whose taint (Kaluṣa) has ended, and (2) another whose taint (Kaluṣa) has not ended. The first are those, whose taint (Kaluṣa) having ended, are elevated to the position of Vidyeśvaras. The Vidyeśvaras are eight and are as follows: (1) Ananta, or endless, (2) atomic, (3) the most excellent Śiva, (4) the one-eyed, (5) the one Rudra, (6) he with the three forms, (7) Śrīkaṇṭha, and (8) Śikhaṇḍin. Another author says that Śiva invests the Samāptakaluṣa (one whose taint has ended) with Vidyeśatva, which is of eight kinds, and the Asamāptakaluṣa (one whose taint has not ended) he raises to the dignity of formulas (Mantras) which are seven crores. Pralayākala is also of two kinds. The first is one whose two fetters have matured (and about to be shaken off), and the second is different from him. The first attains Mokṣa, and the second, entangled with Puryaṣṭaka, undergoes many births in accordance with his impression of deeds (Karman). The Puryaṣṭaka is a subtle body, which is composed of elements which are variously enumerated. Of those who have the Puryaṣṭaka, some, who are virtuous, are raised to Bhuvanapatitva by Maheśvara Ananta. Sakala is also of two kinds: (1) one whose taint (Kaluṣa) is matured, and (2) one whose taint (Kaluṣa) is not matured. The first is raised to the dignity of Mantreśvara of 118 Mantras, i. e. of so many kinds. Parameśvara, assuming the form of his preceptor by the process of initiation and the use of power calculated to counteract the matured taint, confers Mokṣa. Those Aṇus, or atomic souls, whose taint has not ripened (i. e. is not in a condition to be wiped away) are made to suffer or enjoy in accordance with their Karman.

III. Pāśa (fetter) is of four kinds: (1) Mala, or taint, (2) Karman, or the impression of deeds, (3) Māyā, or material cause, and (4) Rodhaśakti,

[1]) See previous section.

or obstructive power. Mala, or taint, is that which conceals the knowing and acting power of the soul and is like the husk enveloping a grain of rice. Karman is the impression of deeds done for the attainment of fruit. It is righteous or unrighteous. It is unbeginning, ever continuing in succesion in the manner of seed and its sprout. Māyā is that into which the whole creation resolves itself at the time of dissolution and from which it springs out at the time of recreation. The obstructive power is the power of Śiva, which, because it regulates the three other fetters and conceals the true nature of the soul, is itself called a fetter. It performs its function, because it is the principle of speech by means of which names are given to things and thus their nature is determined [1]).

§ 94. This constitutes the first part of the system (Vidyāpāda), the nature of the other three parts has been succinctly given above. A few details are these [2]): The second part (Kriyāpāda) treats of the accomplishment of Mantra, the twilight adorations, worship, muttering of formulas (Japa), throwing oblations into the fire, occasional ceremonies for the attainment of eternal bliss, anointing of the preceptor and of the person entering on a course of action for final emancipation (Sādhaka), and one's own initiatory ceremonies necessary to fit one for a wordly and for an eternal life. In the third, or the Yoga part are mentioned the thirty-six principles; the deities presiding over them; the lords of the different worlds; the individual soul; the all-ruling soul; the power (Śakti); the direct perception of Māyā and Mahāmāyā, which are the causes of the world; the attainment of the miraculous powers, minuteness, lightness, etc. for those who concern themselves with the worldly element; the methods of the restraint of the breath, abstraction, meditation, concentration, and absorption in thought (Samādhi); and the positions of the circles in the body beginning with the root-circle (Mūlādhāra, or navel). The fourth part treats of penances, a purificatory ceremony (Pavitrāropaṇa), the foundation, and the natures of Śivaliṅga, of the visible Liṅga of Umā and Maheśvara, and of the lord of Gaṇas, or groups, such as Skanda and Nandin, of the rosary used for the muttering of formulas, and the funeral Śrāddhas. This last part appears to contain matters subsidiary to, and explanatory of, the actions enjoined in the second part. The proscribed actions mentioned above are: (1) the eating of the residue of what is offered to another deity; (2) the vilification of (a) Śiva, (b) of the devotees of Śiva, (c) of the system of Śiva, (d) of the practices enjoined in the Śaiva system; (3) the enjoyment of things belonging to God; (4) the killing of animals.

§ 95. The doctrines of the Śaiva school are more moderate and rational than those of the Pāśupata school. This last, as well as the two extreme schools to be mentioned next, are called Atimārgika, or schools that are away from the path or go astray, and are spoken of by Śambhudeva, quoted in the above paragraph, as revealed by Rudra. The Śaiva school he calls the Siddhāntaśāstra, or the true Śāstra

[1]) Śambhudeva's Śaivasiddhāntadīpikā, Sholapur 1909.
[2]) From the same work.

based upon the Mantras, and says that it was revealed by Śiva. The Vāyavīyasaṃhitā also calls it the Siddhānta school. It will have been seen that both this and the Pāśupata school are dualistic or pluralistic and maintain that the supreme and individual souls are distinct entities and the Pradhāna the constituent cause of the material world. In the delivered condition the individual soul shakes off its ignorance and weakness and attains boundless knowledge and power of action according to the Pāśupata doctrine, while the Śaivas hold that he becomes Śiva himself, i. e. attains perfect resemblance with the god Śiva without, however, the power of creation.

The Śaiva school that developed itself in later times and is represented by Śaṃbhudeva, and Śrīkaṇṭhaśivācārya to be noticed hereafter and supported also by texts in the Vāyavīyasaṃhitā holds that Śiva possesses or develops in himself a Śakti, or power, consisting of the rudiments of the individual soul and the material world, and from this power the whole world is developed. This doctrine may, therefore, be called qualified spiritual monism like that of Rāmānuja, in as much as Śiva characterised by the Śakti creates. This last is a tenet of the Liṅgāyat school also.

IX. The Kāpāla and Kālāmukha Sects.

§ 96. Rāmānuja tells us under II, 2, 35 or 36 that the Kāpālikas maintain that a man who knows the essence of the six marks (Mudrikā) and who is skilful in their use, attains the highest bliss by concentrating his mind on the soul seated on the female organ. The six marks are (1) a necklace, (2) an ornament, (3) an ear-ornament, (4) a crest jewel, (5) ashes, and (6) the sacred thread (Yajñopavīta). He whose body bears these marks, is free from transmigration. The Kālāmukhas hold that the following are the means for the attainment of desires concerning this world and the next: — (1) eating food in a skull; (2) besmearing the body with the ashes of a dead body; (3) eating the ashes; (4) holding a club; (5) keeping a pot of wine; and (6) worshipping the god as seated therein. A bracelet of Rudrākṣa, one string of matted hair on the head, a skull, besmearing the body with ashes, and such other things are mentioned in the Śaiva sacred books. They also maintain that people of other castes become Brāhmaṇas and attain to the highest order by the performance of certain rites. For it is said "One becomes a Brāhmaṇa immediately after the process of simple initiation, and a man becomes a holy saint by undertaking the vow of a Kāpāla".

In the Śaṃkaradigvijaya (chap. XV, vv. 1—28) Mādhava brings Śaṃkara into contact with the Kāpālikas at a place which, according to the commentator, was Ujjayinī. The preceptor of the sect came forward to meet Śaṃkara. His body was besmeared with the ashes taken from a burning-ground. He had a skull in his hand and also an iron lance. He said to Śaṃkara: "The ashes on your body are all right [1]).

---

[1]) Lines of ashes are borne on the body by ordinary Śaivas also and Śaṃkara's body was marked with them.

But why dost thou carry an unholy potsherd instead of the holy skull? Why dost thou not worship Kapālin who is Bhairava? How will Bhairava become pleased unless he is worshipped by the skulls red with the blood of men and with wine?" Then ensues a fight between Sudhanvan, the king, who accompanied Śaṃkara in his wanderings and the Kāpālikas. Śaṃkara also pronounced a curse on them, and they were all killed. Then Krakaca, the leader of the Kāpālikas, coming up to Śaṃkara, filled the skull in his hand with wine, drank half of it and left the other half and invoked Bhairava. Bhairava came up and Krakaca prayed to him to destroy his enemy; but as Śaṃkara was his own incarnation, he destroyed Krakaca himself and not Śaṃkara. In Ānandagiri's book the Kāpālikas, whom Śaṃkara meets at Ujjayinī, speak of Bhairava being the great god, who creates, destroys, etc. They profess to have their knowing power sharpened by drinking wine and eating a certain kind of food (probably a disgusting substance) and always being embraced by the power (Śakti) of Kapālin, i. e. Bhairava. Bhavabhūti in his Mālatīmādhava gives Śrīśaila as the principal seat of the Kāpālikas. Miraculous powers of speedy movement attained by the practice of Yoga are attributed to them. The woman Kapālakuṇḍalā wears a garland of human skulls. She carries away Mālatī, the heroine of the play, from the place where she was sleeping in her father's palace in the dead of night and places her before the image of Karālā-Cāmuṇḍā near the cemetery to be killed and sacrificed to the goddess by her preceptor Aghoraghaṇṭa.

It will be seen how horrible and demoniacal this sect was. The fear which some of the phenomena of external nature inspire in the mind of man led to the Vedic conception of Rudra, and this has now culminated into the ideal image of the horrid god Bhairava with his wife Caṇḍikā wearing a garland of human skulls and requiring human sacrifices and offerings of wine for his propitiation. In the account just given there appears to be a confusion between the sects of Kāpālikas and Kālāmukhas. From Rāmānuja's account the Kālāmukhas appear to be the most extreme sect; and they are called Mahāvratadharas in the Śiva-Purāṇa as noticed above. Mahāvrata means the great vow, and the greatness of the vow consists in its extraordinary nature, such as eating food placed in a human skull, besmearing the body with the ashes of human carcasses and others which are attributed to the Kālāmukhas by Rāmānuja. Jagaddhara, the commentator on the Mālatīmādhava, however, explains Kāpālikavrata by Mahāvrata[1]), and this explanation appears to be correct, since the ascetics dwelling in the temple of Kāpāleśvara in the Nāsik district are, as we have seen, called in the grant Mahāvratins, or the observers of the great vow. The account of Kāpālikas given above from other authorities looks like those of the most extreme sect. Ordinarily, therefore, people do not seem to have made a sharp distinction between the Kāpālikas and the Kālāmukhas.

[1]) Act I, p. 33, on l. 127 of my second edition of the play.

X. Kaśmīr Śaivism.

§ 97. It is a relief now to turn away from this ghastly picture of the wild aberrations of the human intellect and spirit to a system of Śaivism more humane and rational. The Kaśmīr Śaivism has two branches, the Spandaśāstra and the Pratyabhijñāśāstra. The authorship of the first is attributed to Vasugupta and his pupil Kallaṭa. The two principal works of the system are the Śivasūtram or Śivasūtrāṇi and the Spandakārikās, which are fifty-one verses only. The first are said to have been revealed to Vasugupta by Śiva himself or by a Siddha, or perfected human being. They were inscribed on a rock on the Mahādeva hill, and Vasugupta was directed to the rock by Śiva. Another account is that they were revealed by the god in a dream, and another account still further confers the credit of the revelation on the perfected human being. These two last occurrences are said to have taken place on the Mahādeva hill. As to the second work, there are also varying traditions, one ascribing the authorship of the verses to Vasugupta and another to Kallaṭa. A third tradition, however, that Kallaṭa obtained the knowledge of the system from Vasugupta and composed the Spandakārikas for the instruction of his pupils seems to contain the truth [1]). What the meaning of the roundabout tradition about the Śivasūtras which do not ascribe their authorship to Vasugupta directly is, it is difficult to say; perhaps the original work was the Spandakārikās and the prose Śivasūtras were composed in later times in the older or more orthodox form, and as Vasugupta was probably too near the time when they were composed and what he did was known to all, a miraculous origin was given to the new Sūtras and Vasugupta was represented to have received them from others and not composed them himself.

§ 98. Kallaṭa lived in the reign of Avantivarman [2]), 854 A. D., wherefore his Guru's literary activity must be referred to the beginning of the ninth century. The followers of this school boldly deny the necessity of God's having a prompting cause, such as Karman, or a material cause, like the Pradhāna, for the creation of the world. Neither do they admit that he is himself the material cause, as the Vedāntasūtras maintain, nor do they think some principle of illusion, such as Māyā, generates appearances which are false. God is according to them independent and creates merely by the force of his will all that comes into existence. He makes the world appear in himself, as if it were distinct from himself, though not so really, as houses or even towns appear in a mirror, and is as unaffected by it as the mirror is by the images reflected in it. Neither does he exist only as realised in the world, which is the conclusion that follows from the doctrine that he is the material cause. In a verse attributed to Vasugupta an obeisance is made to Śūlin, or Śiva, who is represented as por-

[1]) For these various traditions see my Report on the Search for Sanskrit Manuscripts during 1883—84, p. 77 f.

[2]) Bühler, Report of a Tour made in Kaśmīr, p. 78.

traying a picture of the world without a canvass and a collection of materials [1]).

Another illustration that they give of creation without any material or prompting cause is that of a Yogin who creates objects by his mere will without any materials. God himself by his own wonder-working power appears in the form of the many individual souls and by means of another power brings into existence the state of things which goes to form what we call the wakeful and dreamy condition of our life [2]). Thus according to this system the individual soul is identical with the supreme soul. But the former does not perceive this identity on account of his impurity. This impurity, or Mala, is of three kinds. When a soul forgets his own free and universal nature through ignorance and believes himself to be imperfect and regards things, such as the body, which are not himself, to be himself, and thus reduces himself to finiteness or subjects himself to limitations, the impurity is called Āṇava (littleness). Then his remaining in the body, which is prepared by the originator of things, called Māyā, is another species of impurity known as Māyīya, or effected by Māyā. And when under the influence of the internal organ, or the heart, the organs of action are set in motion, the impurity arising from it is called Kārma, or resulting from action, such as that consisting in a man's consciousness of having done a good or evil deed which is to lead to happiness or misery in the end [3]). These several kinds of impurity are brought into action by Nāda, which is the female element constituting a primeval power (Śakti) of Śiva and from which rises speech. Without speech the ideas which render a worldly life possible can not stand or assume a shape or form, and therefore the principle of speech is believed to be the origin of the Mala, or impurity, which leads to a worldly life. This power is associated with others which are personalised as Ambā, Jyeṣṭhā, Raudrī, Vāmā [4]). The impurity vanishes when by means of intense contemplation the vision of the highest being breaks in upon the mind of the devotee and absorbs all finite thought. When this condition becomes stable, the individual soul is free and becomes the supreme soul. The breaking in of the vision is called Bhairava, because it is his and is caused by him [5]).

§ 99. The founder of the Pratyabhijñā school of Kāśmīra Śaivism was Somānanda, the work written by whom is called Śivadṛṣṭi. But the principal treatise of the school was composed by his pupil Udayākara, and contains verses which are called Sūtras. On these Sūtras there are glosses and detailed explanations by Abhinavagupta, the pupil of

---

[1]) See Mādhava's Sarvadarśanasaṃgraha, Pratyabhijñādarśana. This verse is quoted in the Kāvyaprakāśa, chap. IV, and by other writers on Alaṃkāras.

[2]) See the first note on p. 80 of my Report for 1883—84.

[3]) Śivasūtravimarśinī by Kṣemarāja under Sūtras I, 2 and 3, published by the Kāśmīra Government.

[4]) Ibid. Sūtra 4, and Spandapradīpikā, v. 42. These several kinds of Mala and Nāda correspond to Pāśas, or fetters, viz. Mala, Karman, Māyā and Rodhaśakti given by Mādhava in the Śaivadarśana. The word Mala stands here for the Pāśa of that system and Āṇava for its Mala. It is also called Āṇava by Śaṃbhudeva.

[5]) Śivasūtravimarśinī, I. 5.

the pupil of Somānanda [1]). Abhinavagupta wrote between 993 and 1015 A. D. [2]), wherefore Somānanda must be taken to have lived in the first quarter of the tenth century.

The doctrines of the creation of the world and of the relations between the individual and supreme souls set forth by this school are the same as those maintained by the preceding one. But the way of the perception of the identity is recognition according to this system. There is an Upaniṣad text [3]), from which it follows that every thing shines when He shines and everything becomes perceptible by His light, and thus our knowing power is the same as God's and everything outside of us becomes an object of knowledge by his illumining power. Capable of knowledge and action as we are, we partake of the nature of God; but there is no reason to place a limit to this participation, and it must be understood that we are God himself. But the joy and elevation characteristic of God we are unconscious of in our present condition, and that is due to the fact that we do not recognise that we are God, though we are really so. Just as a maiden, stricken with love for a youth whose excellences have been described to her, is not filled with raptures when she is carried to him and looks upon him as an ordinary individual, but is overjoyed and devotes her whole soul to him when she is told that he is the man whose excellences had so fascinated her, so is it with the individual soul. The serene bliss of godly nature he does not feel, though he is himself God, because he is not aware that those high attributes which belong to the divine nature exist in him. But when he is led to believe by his preceptor that he possesses them, i. e. when by his instructions he is enabled to recognise God in himself, then it is that the serene bliss dawns upon him. The Spanda school mentions the dawning of the form or vision of Bhairava, or God, on the mind in the course of meditation and thereby the clearing away of the impurities as the way to the realisation of the identity with God, while this maintains that recognition of oneself as God is the way.

According to Mādhava these two systems do not enjoin restraint of the breath, concentration, and all that course of fantastic external and internal conduct or discipline which the other schools prescribe as essential. These two schools appearently cut themselves off from the old traditional Śaivism, which gradually developed itself into the ghastly Kāpālism or Kālāmukhism, and hence the epithet Pāśupata or Lākula cannot be applied to them in any sense. A fresh revelation, therefore, was claimed for Vasugupta, though some of the doctrines of the more sober Śaiva school were preserved in the Spanda system.

XI. The Vīraśaiva or Liṅgāyat Sect.

§ 100. The foundation of this sect is generally attributed to Basava, who was the son of Mādirāja, a Brāhmaṇa supposed to be of the

---

1) Bühler, Report of a Tour made in Kaśmīr; extract from Nos. 465—66, p. CLX.
2) Ibid. pp. 81—82.
3) KU. 5, 15; ŚU. 6, 14; MU. 2, 2, 10.

Ārādhya sect. His story is given in the Basavapurāṇa [1]) published in 1905, at Poona. From this story it by no means follows that he founded the sect by settling its doctrines and founding what may be called a church. He, however, appears to be a strenuous supporter of the sect. In the beginning of the Basavapurāṇa Nārada is represented to have gone to Śiva and told him that on earth there were devotees of Viṣṇu, followers of the sacrificial religion, Jainas and Buddhists, but there were no devotees of his. He mentions Viśveśvarārādhya, Paṇḍitārādhya, Ekorāma, the great Yogin, and others as having flourished from time to time and established Śivabhakti, but there is none now. Śiva thereupon told his Nandin to become incarnate on earth for the promotion of his religion and the furtherance of the cause of Vīraśaivas. From all this it does not appear that Basava was the originator of the sect. He had predecessors, three of whom have just been named. His was a life of political turmoil. From his native place Bāgevāḍi he went to Kalyāṇa, when Vijjala, or Vijjaṇa, was reigning (1157—1167 A. D.). His maternal uncle Baladeva was the minister of the king, and he himself was raised to the position after his death. Basava's sister, a beautiful woman, was married by the king. He was in charge of the king's treasury and spent large amounts in supporting and entertaining members of Liṅgāyat mendicants, called Jaṅgamas. The matter came to the notice of the king Vijjaṇa, who gradually became completely alienated from him and endeavoured to apprehend him. Basava fled away, and the king sent a few men in pursuit. These were easily defeated by Basava, whereupon the king himself advanced with troops to punish him; but Basava had collected a large number of followers and succeeded in defeating him. The king was reconciled to Basava and brought him back to Kalyāṇa, but there could be no true reconcilement, and after a time Basava caused the king to be assassinated.

§ 101. There is a work entitled Vijjalarāyacarita by a Jaina, which also gives an account of Basava and his relations with Vijjaṇa. It is written from the point of view of an enemy of Basava and mentions Basava's sister as having been given to the king as a mistress, which was perhaps true. But since the Liṅgāyat account and the Jaina account, agree in the main particulars, they may be accepted as historical [2]). Basava thus was a scheming politician and could hardly have been the propounder of a new system of doctrines or the organiser of a new sect. Besides, in the many Liṅgāyat works now available, his name is not mentioned as the name of a teacher of any articles of faith. What he did, therefore, appears to have been that he used his political influence to raise the fortunes of the Vīraśaiva sect, to bring it into prominence, and to disseminate the creed. There is another man who has been brought forward by Dr. Fleet, on the strength

---

1) This book and a good many others appertaining to the Liṅgāyat sect have been published under the patronage of an influential and enlightened member of the sect, the late Mr. Mallappā Vārada of Sholapur.

2) For the Liṅgāyat account see the translation of the Basavapurāṇa, Journ. B. B. R. A. S. Vol. VIII, or the Basavapurāṇa itself, printed at Poona, and for the latter see Wilson's Mackenzie Mss.

of certain inscriptions, as the founder of the Liṅgāyat sect, and that is Ekānta, or Ekāntada, Rāmayya. An account of this person is also given in the second part of the Basavapurāṇa, and this and that in the inscriptions come to this that he was an enemy of the Jainas and wished to destroy their gods and shrines. He laid a wager with them that he would cut off his head and lay it at the feet of Śiva, and if it should be restored to him and replaced on his shoulders as it was before, the Jainas should consent to throw down their idols and profess a belief in Śaivism. According to the inscription, this was first done at Ablūr at the place where it exists, and when Rāmayya compelled the Jainas to destroy their idols, they went to Kalyāṇa and complained to king Vijjaṇa, who thereupon summoned Rāmayya into his presence and required him to explain why he did so. He offered to repeat the feat of cutting off his head and getting it back again in the presence of the king. The Basavapurāṇa represents Basava himself to have been present when Rāmayya laid this wager. So that beyond undermining the Jaina sect there is no evidence of Rāmayya's having built up the Vīraśaiva creed.

§ 102. In connection with Dīkṣās, or initiatory ceremonies, as, for instance, that which one has to go through when one has to choose a Guru, or preceptor, it is necessary to place four metallic vessels full of water at the four cardinal points and one in the middle. This last belongs to the person to be consecrated as Guru, or preceptor, who is supposed to represent an old Ācārya, or teacher, of the name of Viśvārādhya, and the other four to four other priests chosen as having been brought up in the schools of Revaṇasiddha, Marulasiddha, Ekorāma and Paṇḍitārādhya and connected with certain Maṭhas, or establishments [1]. The same list is given in another treatise [2]. These five vessels are consecrated to the five faces or forms of Śiva, Sadyojāta, etc., mentioned in a former section [3]. The Ācāryas, or teachers, named above are believed to have sprung from the five forms of Śiva in this Kali age [4]. Others bearing other names, born in other ages of the world, are also mentioned, but with these we have nothing to do. Of these five teachers three at least are mentioned as having preceded Basava in the passage quoted at the beginning of this section. It will thus appear that the Vīraśaiva, or Liṅgāyat, system came into existence before Basava. It is affiliated to the moderate or sober school of Śaivas known by the name of Śaivadarśana, or Siddhāntadarśana as it is called by its followers; and especially to the later form of it alluded to before [5]. But its technical terms, Sthala, Aṅga, Liṅga, etc., and its ideas are entirely different from those of that school as explained by Mādhava and others. And these terms we do not meet with elsewhere, so that this was a modern school. When it originated, it is difficult to say. But it was clearly in a militant condition in the

---

1) Vivekacintāmaṇi, Pūrvabhāga, Sholapur 1909 A. D., pp. 230 ff.
2) Vīraśaivācārapradīpikā, Poona 1905 A. D., pp. 33—37.
3) P. 124, note 1.
4) Pañcācāryapañcamotpattiprakaraṇa, Bombay 1903 A. D., p. 1.
5) § 95.

time of Basava. It must, therefore, have originated about a hundred years before. The names of two at least of the five teachers as given above end in the word ārādhya, while in other books all the five have that epithet attached to their names[1]). This was the name of a sect allied to the Liṅgāyats.

Of the five Ācāryas represented by the five metallic vessels, Mr. Brown[2]) does not mention the middle one and calls all the other four Ārādhyas, so that all the five preceptors honoured at the time of initiation and other ceremonies belong to the Ārādhya sect, which, according to Mr. Brown, was a sect of the Vīraśaiva creed. There has been a good deal of ill feeling between the Ārādhyas and the ordinary Liṅgāyats, and that appears to be due to the retention by the former of some Brāhmaṇic rites, such as repeating the holy Gāyatrīmantra and wearing the sacred thread. But the very name Ārādhya, which means one to be adored or worshipped, shows that, before the contention between the two sects arose, the Ārādhyas enjoyed very great respect. Taking all these circumstances into consideration, what appears to be the truth is that the Vīraśaiva creed was reduced to a shape by the Ārādhyas, who must have been men of learning and holy living and the subsequent reformers, such as Basava, gave it a decidedly uncompromising and anti-Brāhmaṇical character. And thus these two sects of the Vīraśaiva faith came into existence. We will now give a short account of the doctrines of this school.

§ 103. The One, Highest, Brahman, characterised by existence (Sat), intelligence (Cit), and joy (Ānanda), is the essence of Śiva (Śivatattva) and is called Sthala. Then are given explanations as to why it is called Sthala, two of them based upon an artificial etymology. In the supreme Brahman, or the essence of Śiva, Mahat and other principles exist and are eventually resolved into it. In it first exists the universe, arising from Prakṛti and Puruṣa, and to it it returns at the end; therefore it is called Sthala. (The first part stha signifies sthāna, or standing, and the second part la signifies laya, or resolution.) That name is given to it also because it is the support of the whole moveable and immoveable world and holds all powers, all luminaries, and all souls. It is the resting place of all beings, of all worlds, and of all possessions. It is the highest place to be attained by those who seek the highest happiness, and therefore it is called the One only and non-dualistic Sthala (position). By the agitation of its innate power (Śakti) that Sthala becomes divided into two: (1) Liṅgasthala, (2) Aṅgasthala. Liṅgasthala is Śiva or Rudra and is to be worshipped or adored, while the Aṅgasthala is the individual soul, the worshipper or adorer. In the same manner, the Śakti, or power, divides herself into two by her own will, one of the parts resorting to Śiva and being called Kalā, and the other resorting to the individual soul and being called Bhakti, or devotion. Śakti, or power, has got a certain susceptibility, which leads it to action and entanglement with the world, while Bhakti is free from that susceptibility and turns

[1]) Pañcācāryapañcamotpattiprakaraṇa, p. 35.
[2]) Madras Journal of Literature and Science, Vol. XI.

away from action and from the world and leads to final deliverance. The Śakti, or power, makes one an object of worship, while Bhakti makes one a worshipper; therefore, the former exists in the Liṅga or Śiva, and the latter in the Aṅga or individual soul. Eventually, by this Bhakti, there is a union between the soul and Śiva.

The Liṅga is Śiva himself, and not a mere external emblem of him. The Liṅgasthala is divided into three: (1) Bhāvaliṅga, (2) Prāṇa-linga, and (3) Iṣṭaliṅga. The first is without any parts (Kalā) and is to be perceived by faith. It is simple Sat (existence), not conditioned by space or time, and is higher than the highest. The second is to be apprehended by the mind and has parts and is without parts. The third has parts and is apprehensible by the eye. This confers all desired (iṣṭa) objects and removes afflictions; or it receives its name because it is worshipped (iṣṭa) with care. The Prāṇaliṅga is the intelligence (Cit) of the Supreme Soul, and Iṣṭaliṅga, the joy. The first is the highest principle, the second is the subtle form, and the third, the gross form. These three Liṅgas, corresponding to the soul, the life and the gross form, and being characterised by use (Prayoga), formulas (Mantra) and action (Kriyā), form what are called Kalā, Nāda and Bindu. Each of these three is divided into two; the first into Mahāliṅga and Prasādaliṅga, the second into Caraliṅga and Śivaliṅga, and the third into Guruliṅga and Ācāraliṅga. These six operated on by six kinds of Śakti, or power, give rise to the following six forms. (1) When the Śiva essence is operated on by the power of intelligence (Cit), it forms the Mahāliṅga, the attributes of which are the absence of birth and death, freedom from taint, perfection, unity, subtleness, being higher than the highest, incorruptibility, unfathomableness, capability of being apprehended by faith and love, and idealistic (Caitanyarūpa). (2) When the Śiva essence gets permeated with its highest power (Parāśakti), then is produced a principle called Sādākhya[1]) which is light, eternal, indivisible, imperceptible to the senses, apprehensible by reason, indestructible, and the rudiment that develops; and that principle is called Prasādaliṅga. (3) When the Śiva essence is operated on by its primeval power (Ādiśakti), Caraliṅga is produced, which is infinite and pervades the internal and external world, which is full of light, is a Puruṣa (a person), and is higher than the Pradhāna or Prakṛti, and capable of being contemplated by the mind alone. (4) When permeated by the will power (Icchāśakti), it forms Śivaliṅga, which is a finite principle with a sense of egoism, possessed of knowledge and power (Kalā), having a celestial refulgenee, with one face, and serene. (5) When permeated with the power of knowledge (Jñānaśakti), it forms a Guruliṅga, which possesses agency, presides over every system or science that instructs, is full of light, a boundless ocean of joy, and dwells in human intelligence. (6) When influenced by the

---

[1]) The Sādākhya is the product of the combination of the principle, the Śiva essence, with the two of the five powers, Parā and Ādi. The Sādākhyas are five: (1) Śiva-sādākhya, which develops into Sadāśiva; (2) Amūrta, or not finite, which becomes Īśa; (3) Samūrta, or finite, which results in Brahmeśa; (4) Kartṛ, or agent, which becomes Īśvara; (5) Karman, or action, which develops into Īśāna. The Sādākhya alluded to in the text must be Sadāśiva.

power of action (Kriyāśakti), it is called Ācāraliṅga, which in the shape of action serves as the support for the existence of all things, which is conceivable by the mind, and leads to a life of renunciation.

It will be seen that the original entity becomes divided into God and individual soul by its innate power, and the six forms of the first, that are mentioned, are the various ways of looking at God. The first form is the infinite Being considered independently. The second is the form in which we conceive of him as developing or creating by its highest power. The third is the form in which he is conceived as distinct from the material world. The fourth is a bodily form, the body, however, not being made up of ordinary matter, but celestial like the body attributed to Nārāyaṇa, or Kṛṣṇa, by the Vaiṣṇavas. The fifth is the form in which he instructs mankind. And the sixth involves the idea of his guiding the individual soul in his actions until he is delivered. In this form Śiva is the Redeemer.

Bhakti is the characteristic of the individual souls. It consists in a tendency towards God, and there are three stages in the progress of this tendency and, corresponding to these, there are three divisions of the Aṅgasthala, or the subject of the individual soul. The first or highest division is called Yogāṅga, the second Bhogāṅga, and the third Tyāgāṅga. By the first, a man obtains happiness by his union with Śiva; by the second, he enjoys along with Śiva; and the last involves the abandonment of the world as transient or illusory. The first corresponds to the resolution into the cause and to the condition of sound sleep, the second to the subtle body and to dreamy sleep, and the third to the gross body and to the wakeful condition. Two varieties of each of these are distinguished. Of the first, or Yogāṅga, we have the two, Aikya and Śaraṇa. The first consists in sharing the joys of Śiva after one is convinced of the unreality of the whole world. This is called Samarasā Bhakti, in which God and the soul are united in blissful experience. The second is called Śaraṇabhakti, in which one sees Liṅga, or God, in himself and everything else. It is a condition of joy for oneself. The second is also of two kinds: (1) Prāṇaliṅgin and (2) Prasādin. The first consists in abandoning all regard for life, renunciation of egoism, and concentration of the whole mind upon the Liṅga, or God. The second is realised, when one resigns all the objects of one's enjoyment to the Liṅga, or God, and serenity (Prasāda) is acquired. The divisions of the last are Māheśvara and Bhakta. The first is one who has a firm belief in the existence of God, who goes through the whole discipline consisting in the observance of vows and restraints, which have Śiva for their object, and truth, morality, cleanliness, etc. and a heroically rigid vow based upon a firm belief in the unity of the Liṅga, or God. A Bhakta is one, who, turning his mind away from all objects by which it is attracted and practising devotion and rites, lives a life of indifference to the world [1]).

This represents the progress of the soul from indifference to the world, which is the first step, through the intermediate stages, in a reverse order,

---

[1]) The above is an abstract of the matter contained in the Anubhavasūtra of Māyideva, Sholapur, 1909.

to Sāmarasya, or union in blissful experience with Śiva, which is the highest conditon. The goal thus pointed out does not involve a perfect identity between the supreme and individual souls or the shaking off of individuality and becoming a simple soul unconscious of itself, which is the doctrine of the great non-dualistic school of Śaṃkara. The belief of the Vīraśaiva school that the original essence of Śiva divided itself by its own innate power into Liṅga, or God, and Aṅga, or the individual soul, and under the influence of other powers the essence became the creator of the world, shows that the doctrine of that school is that the rudiment of the creation exists in God himself in the shape of his power, but this power is not unreal. This doctrine, therefore, resembles that of Rāmānuja, but with the latter there is a real rudiment of the soul and of the external world characterising God which afterwards develops, but with the Vīraśaivas there exists a power only in God which leads to creation; so that it is the power that characterises God according to the latter, while the rudiment is his characteristic according to the former. The Liṅgāyat school, therefore, is a school of qualified spiritual monism (Viśiṣṭādvaita). It will also have been seen that the method of redemption taught by this school is that of Bhakti or love of God, and a course of moral and spiritual discipline up to the attainment of Sāmarasya with Śiva. In this respect also it resembles Rāmānuja's system.

Śrīkaṇṭhaśivācārya, whose Bhāṣya on the Vedāntasūtras has long been before the public, holds the same view. Under I, 4, 22, he states that the word Ātman in the sense of the individual soul is used to express the supreme soul in BU. (IV, 5, 6), because the latter is the internal controller of the former and is spoken of as identical with everything in this sense. Under II, 2, 38, he states that Śiva as possessed of powers is the material cause of the world; and in his comment on IV, 4, 3—4 he represents the delivered soul as similar to the Supreme Soul, that is, as having the attributes of the latter. And under IV, 4, 2, he speaks of the delivered soul as Samarasa, or united in blissful experience with the Supreme Soul. Thus Śrīkaṇṭha's view appears to be identical with that of the Vīraśaivas. Therefore unlike the four older schools, Pāśupata and others, which are dualistic, these three Śaiva schools hold a doctrine of qualified spiritual monism.

§ 104. The highest class of Liṅgāyats is composed of those who call themselves Liṅgi-Brāhmaṇas, the other castes or classes who wear the Liṅga being simply their followers. The Liṅgi-Brāhmaṇas consist of two main classes, the Ācāryas and the Pañcamas. The legendary account given of these is as follows. The Ācāryas were originally five in number and sprang from the five faces, Sadyojāta, etc., of Śiva spoken of in a former section. They are the same as those mentioned above as having a metallic vessel placed in their names on the occasion of any holy ceremony. From these five have sprung up all the priestly classes now existing. These five had five Gotras, viz. Vīra, Nandin, Vṛṣabha, Bhṛṅgin, and Skānda, who were originally persons almost as high as Śiva himself. From the Īśāna face of Śiva sprang a Gaṇeśvara (leader of a group), who had five faces. From these five faces sprang five Pañcamas, known by the names of Makhāri, Kālāri, Purāri, Smarāri, and Vedāri, which, the reader will remember, were the names of Śiva himself given to him on account of certain deeds done by him. From these arose others who are called Upapañcamas. Each Pañcama has to connect himself with one of the five Ācāryas as his Guru. The Gotra of the Guru is his Gotra, and there can be no marriage relation between the members of the same Gotra. These Pañcamas have got Gotra, Pravara and Śākhā of their own, and the Liṅgāyats thus seem to have copied the Brāhmaṇic system. The Pañcamas are spoken of as the true devotees of Śiva [1]). According to the ordinary account the true Liṅgāyats are divided into four classes: (1) Jaṅgamas, or priests, (2) Šīlavants, or pious, (3) Banjigs, or traders, and (4) Pañcamsālis. The second and the third classes are based on the occupation or mode of life followed; so that even here, there are only the two classes mentioned in the work referred to above. The members of the first or Ācārya class are popularly called Jaṅgamas. Of these there are some who are called Viraktas (passionless) and who devote themselves to contemplation and other religious exercises and live a life of celebacy and asceticism. They maintain a convent (Maṭha) and are adored by all people. One such convent, which might be called the chief convent, is that which exists at Chitaldrug in the Mysore territory about a hundred miles from Dharwar. The head monk is held in deep reverence and exercises great influence over the followers of the sect. The second division of the class comprises those who follow a priestly occupation and conduct all ceremonies. They are married men and lead the life of householders. They exercise religious control over the Pañcamas and the followers of their sect. These priestly Jaṅgamas are the representatives of one or other of the five principal establishments located in different parts of the country from the Himālaya to the Mysore province. Any knotty question concerning the sect is decided by the final orders issued at one of these establishments. Besides the true Liṅgāyats there is an affiliated class and another composed of half Liṅgāyats. The Liṅgāyats abstain from meat and drink. Their widows are allowed to marry. And women are not considered polluted and untouchable during the days of monthly sickness, as is the case among Brāhmaṇic Hindus.

§ 105. There is a Dīkṣā ceremony among the Vīraśaivas corresponding to Upanayana among the Brāhmaṇas. Instead of the Gāyatrīmantra of the latter, they have the Mantra 'Om namaś Śivāya', and have to wear the Liṅga, or emblem of Śiva, in the place of Yajñopavīta. On the occasion of the Dīkṣā, the Guru holds a Liṅga in his left hand, worships it in the usual sixteen ways, and shows it to the disciple. Then placing it in the left hand of the disciple and enjoining him to look upon it as his own soul and as the highest existing thing and so forth, he ties it round the neck of the disciple with a silken cloth by repeating a Mantra used by the Brāhmaṇas in putting on the Yajñopavīta. This is called the Liṅgasvāyattadīkṣā. This ceremony is performed in the case of girls also, and the women too have to wear the Liṅga like men.

[1]) Pañcācāryapañcamotpattiprakaraṇa.

The Liṅga is generally put into a box made of silver and suspended round the neck. The Vīraśaivas have to go through daily ceremonies similar to the twilight adorations of the Brāhmaṇas, and the Mantra repeated on the occasion is that given above, as also the Śiva-Gāyatrī, the first two lines of which are the same as the Brāhmaṇic Gāyatrī, and the last is 'Tan naḥ Śivaḥ pracodayāt'. In the marriage ceremony the Mantra to be repeated on the occasion of the taking hold of the hand of the bride is the same as among the Brāhmaṇas, and in the ceremony of walking the seven steps together with the bride, the formulas repeated are the same as those used by Ṛgvedin Brāhmaṇas. But in their marriage ceremony, they do not perform the rite of throwing parched rice into the fire as the Brāhmaṇas do. The worship of the Liṅga, called Iṣṭa-Liṅga, worn on the body, is their chief divine worship; and attendance at temples and worship of the Liṅga therein are by no means necessary for them. They do not concern themselves directly with the public temples of Śiva.

§ 106. There is a traditional legend among the Liṅgāyats that, when Śiva brought Brahmadeva into existence, he told him to create the world. But Brahmadeva said that he did not know how to do it. Whereupon Śiva created it himself in order that it might serve him as a model. And the Ācāryas and Pañcamas, as detailed above with their Gotras and Śākhās, are that creation of Śiva. The true import of this legend is that the Liṅgāyats set up a system for themselves as a rival to the Brāhmaṇic system and the close resemblance between the two confirms this view. But a mere copy was not their object, and they introduced several reforms, especially in the condition of women, as will have been seen from the above notice. In this respect, this system differs from all other schools, Vaiṣṇava or Śaiva or even Buddhist or Jaina, who did not set up for themselves a special system of social relations and domestic rites, though, as shown above, that framed by the Liṅgāyats for themselves is a copy of that of the Brāhmaṇas, which, however, is a reformed copy.

The impression that this whole account creates in one is that Liṅgāyatism owes its origin to a spirit of jealousy of the power exercised by Brāhmaṇism and of rivalry with the system. Such a spirit of jealousy and rivalry cannot be expected to have arisen in thoroughly depressed minds. The system therefore must have come into existence among the spirited members of the upper classes of non-Brāhmaṇic Hindus under the leadership of a body of men composed of Brāhmaṇas known by the name of Ārādhyas. Some of the members of this body did not go far enough in the desired reform, as mentioned before, and formed a distinct sect [1]). It will thus be seen that all the

[1]) An Ārādhya sect is mentioned by Anantānandagiri as having come into conflict with Śaṃkarācārya (See Śaṅkaravijaya, Bibl. Ind., p. 37.). In the corresponding portion of Dhanapati's Ḍiṇḍima which accompanies Mādhava's Śaṃkaravijaya the name of the sect does not occur; so that it is questionable whether the Ārādhya sect came into existence before Śaṃkara even if we suppose that the sect mentioned by Anantānandagiri was the same as the one we have noticed as affiliated to the Liṅgāyats. Or, on the evidence of Anantānandagiri the Ārādhya sect may be considered to have come into existence about the time of Śaṃkarācārya, that is, before the ninth century A. D., and the

Liṅgāyats have not sprung up from the Śūdra caste, but there is a mixture of the three higher orders among them. The claim that the two main classes of the sect put forward of their being Liṅgi-Brāhmaṇas, i. e., Brāhmaṇas wearing the Liṅga, seems to be founded on truth. The Ācārya or Jaṅgama class is said to have sprung from the five holy persons, adored on the occasion of a religious ceremony, whose names end in the suffix ārādhya significative of their being Brāhmaṇas. We might therefore safely take them to be of a Brāhmaṇic descent [1]). As to the Pañcamas, they probably represent the Vaiśya order of the Brāhmaṇic system which followed the occupation of traders and cultivators, and as the Vaiśyas belong to the class of the twice-born, so also do the Pañcamas and hence they are included in the Liṅgi-Brāhmaṇa group.

XII. Śaivism in the Draviḍa Country

§ 107. Śaivism prevails in the Draviḍa or Tamil country, and possesses an extensive literature of its own. It consists of eleven collections. The first three contain the hymns composed by a saint held in great reverence, of the name Tiruñānasambandha. They are three hundred and eighty-four in number, each being called a Padigam which consists of ten stanzas with an eleventh containing the author's name usually added. The next three were composed by Appar who was an older contemporary of Sambandha, who had renounced Buddhism or rather Jainism, and become a Śaiva. The seventh collection belongs to Sundara who was a Brāhmaṇa devotee of a later generation. These seven books are called Devāram and are compared to the Brāhmaṇic Veda. In certain processions, while on the one side the hymns of the Brāhmaṇic Veda are repeated, on the other are sung those contained in the Devāram which are addressed to the deity. The Tiruvāśagam forms the eighth book, and it resembles the Upaniṣads. The author of this book is Māṇikkavāśagar. The ninth group is made up of hymns composed in imitation of the Devāram hymns. One of the writers is Kandarāditya, a Cola king, from whom Rājarāja Cola, who came to the throne in 984-85 A. D., was fifth in descent. The tenth contains mystic songs of a Yogin called Tirumūlar. The eleventh collection is composed of miscellaneous pieces, the last ten of which were written by Nambi Āndār Nambi. The third of these ten forms the basis of

theory advanced that the Liṅgāyat reform was carried out within its limits and a portion of the Ārādhya sect adopted the new creed and developed it, while another remained orthodox and staunch to some of the Brāhmaṇic practices. To this portion is to be traced the Ārādhya sect of the present day.

[1]) There are Jaṅgamas who know Sanskrit, and I have been in communication with one such of the name of Mallikārjunaśāstrin, who directed me to some of the books of the sect wich I have followed in this section, and also gave oral information on some points. He claims to be a Brāhmaṇa authorised to study the Vedas, his own Veda being the White Yajurveda. The head monk of the Chitaldrug convent alluded to above was on a visitation to Poona about two months ago with all the state of a spiritual potentate, having four elephants with him and a number of followers. He was a good, courteous and kindly person, had studied Sanskrit grammar and was able to converse fluently in pure Sanskrit. Some of the books of the sect are written in Sanskrit.

the Tamil Purāṇa called Periyapurāṇa. These eleven collections together with the Periyapurāṇa, which are all written in the Tamil language, form the sacred literature of the Tamil Śaivas. Besides these there are the works of what are called Santāna-Ācāryas, which are fourteen in number and called Siddhāntaśāstras. Their contents are of a philosophical nature. The most highly honoured of all these writers is Tiruñānasambandha. He was a Brāhmaṇa by birth, and the poetic faculty was developed in him very early in life. His hymns are full of the purest devotional feeling and are melodious. The tunes in which they were originally sung were Dravidian, but in later times northern melodies with northern names came to be used. Sambandha's image is set up for worship in every Śaiva temple, and he is adored by Tamil poets and philosophers in the beginning of their works. He was a great enemy of Buddhists and Jainas; and every tenth stanza of his Padigams, or hymns, contains an imprecation against them. On one occasion, he was invited by the queen of Kuni Pāṇḍya of Madhurā, where he held a disputation with the Buddhists or Jainas, which ended in the conversion of the king to the Śaiva faith [1]).

In an inscription in the Rājarājeśvara temple at Tanjore the king Rājarājadeva, after whom the temple was named, makes a daily allowance for the support of the reciters or singers of the Tiruppadiyam or the Padigams of Tiruñānasambandha, before the twenty-ninth year of his reign [2]). The date of Rājarāja's accession to the throne has been determined by the mention of a lunar eclipse in one of his inscriptions to be 984-5 A. D. [3]) This is consistent with the fact mentioned in another inscription [4]) that he conquered Satyāśraya, who was the immediate successor of Tailapa, the founder of the later Cālukya dynasty of Mahārāṣṭra, and died in Śaka 930, or 1008 A. D. Thus before the twenty-ninth year of Rājarāja, i. e. before 1013 A. D., the Padigams of Sambandha had come to be looked upon as so sacred that the recitation or singing of them was considered an act of religious merit like the repetition of the Śatarudriya by the followers of the Brāhmaṇic Veda. This character the hymns of Sambandha could not have acquired unless they had come into existence about four hundred years before the beginning of the eleventh century. This is consistent with the conclusion arrived at by Mr. Pillai that Sambandha flourished in the seventh century.

The inscriptions in the temples at Kāñcipura contain evidence of Śaivism being in a flourishing condition in the sixth century. The Pallava king Rājasiṃha constructed a temple, and the god inside was named after him Rājasiṃheśvara. Rājasiṃha appears from some of the inscriptions to have been a contemporary of the early Cālukya prince Pulakeśin I. [5]), who may be referred to about the year 550 A. D.,

[1]) The above account is mostly taken from the able paper of P. Sundaram Pillai published in the Ind. Ant. Vol. XXV, pp. 113 ff. It is to be regretted that Mr. Pillai does not give us precise information as to whether it was the Buddhists against whom Sambandha directs his attacks or the Jainas.

[2]) South-Indian Inscriptions ed. by E. Hultzsch, Vol. II, p. 252, No. 65.

[3]) Ind. Ant. Vol. XXIII, p. 297.

[4]) South-Ind. Inscrs., Vol. II, p. 2.

[5]) South-Ind. Inscrs., Vol. I, p. 11.

as his son Kīrtivarman I came to the throne about the year 567 A. D.[1])

The Śaivism that prevailed in the Tamil country seems to have been generally of the ordinary kind, since the hymns in the Devāram sing the praises of Śiva and exhibit fervent devotional feeling, but there must have been some Darśana or system of philosophy also, since in an inscription in the Rājasiṃheśvara temple at Kāñci Atyantakāma, which was another name of Rājasiṃha, is represented as proficient in the system of the Śaivasiddhāntas. And the last species of the Śaiva literature detailed above is, it will have been seen, called Siddhāntaśāstra composed by Santāna-Ācāryas. These must be philosophical works on Śaivism. And the system therein taught appears in all likelihood to be the same or similar to the Śaivadarśana, which has already been explained. But what exactly the system taught by the Siddhāntas was, we have not the means of finding out, as none of the works is available for examination. The Periyapurāṇa gives an account of sixty-three Bhaktas or devotees of Śiva, and these correspond to the Āḷvārs of the Vaiṣṇavas. The enemies that both these classes of devotees had to contend with were Jainas, and it appears to me that both Śaivism and Vaiṣṇavism penetrated to the extreme south of India after the revival of Brāhmaṇism in the north during the fourth and fifth centuries. Buddhism and Jainism had been introduced earlier and were in possession of the field when the two later systems of theistic belief were introduced into the southern country. Hence arose the necessity of controversies and contests which these systems carried on with their earlier predecessors. Whether Śaivism extended itself to the Tamil country before the revival, we have not the means of determining.

XIII. The Śāktas or Śakti Worshippers.

§ 108. In the Vedic literature down to the Gṛhyasūtras which we have examined for tracing the development of the idea of Rudra-Śiva, no female devotee of predominant power is mentioned. We have such names as Rudrāṇī and Bhavānī, which are simply derivatives and do not show a belief in the existence of an independent powerful goddess. Umā, too, is the wife of a god and does not overshadow her male consort. In the MBh. (Bhīṣmaparvan, chap. 23), however, there is a hymn addressed to Durgā by Arjuna under the advice of Kṛṣṇa in which she is prayed to for granting victory in the forthcoming battle. This hymn itself shows that at the time when it was composed and inserted in the poem, Durgā had already acquired such an importance that she was adored by men as a powerful goddess, able to fulfil their desires. Among the names by which she is addressed occur the following: Kumārī (maiden), Kālī (black or female time as destroyer), Kāpālī (wearer of skulls), Mahākālī (the great destroyer), Caṇḍī (angry), Kātyāyanī (of the Kātya family), Karālā (frightful), Vijayā (Victory), Kauśikī (of the Kuśika family), Umā, Kāntāravāsinī (dwel-

[1]) Early History of the Dekkan, Second Ed., p. 61.

ling in the forest). There is another hymn in the Virāṭaparvan (chap. 6) sung by Yudhiṣṭhira. It does not exist in the principal southern Mss., and is probably an interpolation, as it contains almost the same matter as in a similar passage in the Harivaṁśa. The points and epithets in this hymn which deserve notice are these. She is called Mahiṣāsuranāśinī (or the destroyer of the demon in the shape of a buffalo, and she is fond of wine, flesh and beasts. She was born to Yaśodā and dashed against a stone, whereupon she went to heaven. She is called the most beloved of Nārāyaṇa and the sister of Vāsudeva. She resides permanently on the Vindhya mountain. It is related in the Harivaṁśa (vv. 3236 ff.) that Viṣṇu descended into the Pātāla, and asked sleep in the form of destroying time (Nidrā Kālarūpiṇī) to become the daughter of Yaśodā. She is told that she would become Kauśikī and would have a permanent residence on the Vindhya mountain. There she was told that she would kill Śumbha and Niśumbha and would be worshipped by animal sacrifices. There is given a hymn to Āpyā (Durgā) in which she is represented as the goddess of Śabaras, Pulindas, Barbaras and other wild tribes, and as fond of wine and flesh. The goddess that killed the buffalo-demon, was, according to the Mārkaṇḍeya-Purāṇa (ch. 82) made up of the fierce radiance of Śiva, Viṣṇu and Brahmadeva, and all the other gods contributed to the formation of her limbs as well as her ornaments. She is called Caṇḍī and Ambikā. The formation of the goddess that killed Śumbha and Niśumbha, according to the account which follows, is thus explained. The gods being oppressed by the demons Śumbha and Niśumbha went to the Himālayas and praised the goddess, whereupon Pārvatī came out to bathe in the Ganges. Then Śivā, also called Ambikā, came out of the body of Pārvatī, and said that it was she whom the gods were praising to induce her to kill Śumbha and Niśumbha. She was called Kauśikī, because she sprang out from Kośa or frame of Pārvatī's body. When Ambikā came out of her body, Pārvatī's complexion became dark, and hence she rceived the name of Kalika (dark one). In the course of the fight, when Śumbha and Niśumbha pounced upon her, her forehead became dark with anger, and from it came Kālī with a frightful face wearing a garland of skulls and a tiger-skin and with an infernal weapon (Khaṭvāṅga) in her hand. She killed the demons Caṇḍa and Muṇḍa, and went back to Ambikā, who thereupon, since she had killed those demons, gave her the name Cāmuṇḍā. The seven Śaktis, Brāhmī, Māheśvarī, Kaumārī, Vaiṣṇavī, Vārāhī, Nārasiṃhī and Aindrī, which are the powers or spirits of the gods from whom their names are derived, are called her excellent forms (Vibhūtis). At the end, the goddess says that she would, in the Vaivasvata Manu, destroy Śumbha and Niśumbha again by assuming the form of the goddess residing on the Vindhya mountain, and proceeds to give the other forms that she would assume on other occasions such as the daughter of Nanda, Śākambharī, Bhīmā,. Bhrāmarī, etc.

§ 109. In the account here given, it will be seen that there is one goddess with a number of different names. But the critical eye will see that they are not merely names, but indicate different goddesses who owed their conception to different historical conditions, but who were afterwards identified with the one goddess by the usual mental habit of the Hindus. First we have Umā, the protectress, the consort of Śiva. Then we have Haimavatī and Pārvatī, which are the epithets of Umā, since Śiva, her consort, was Giriśa, or dweller on the mountain, and she was a woman born on the mountain. Then there are goddesses, dwelling in forests and on the Vindhya mountain, to whom animals and even human beings were sacrificed and oblations of wine were given and who were also the goddesses worshipped by the wild tribes, such as Pulindas, Śabaras and Barbaras. These were fierce goddesses and have the names of Karālā, Kālī, Caṇḍī, Cāmuṇḍā, and others. It must be admitted, however, that the first two names came into use when in an early age Rudra was identified with Agni, whose flames, which were considered his tongues, have those two names and five others. Probably the ferocity of the later goddesses of those names was due to this identification and not to their being the objects of worship to the ferocious barbarous tribes. In all likelihood, however, both the elements contributed to give that character to Kālī, Karālā and Cāmuṇḍā. That an aboriginal element should have contributed to the formation of Rudra's consort in later times as it did in earlier times towards the formation of Rudra himself as he is represented in the Śatarudriya, is a matter that might be expected. A third and powerful element in the conception of these goddesses is that of Śakti, or power. The powers of willing, acting, creating, illuding, etc. were conceived of as goddesses as the noun Śakti is of the feminine gender. The seven goddesses named above, Brāhmī, Māheśvarī, etc. owe their origin to this conception of Śakti and the powers of the seven gods. In later times some of the Brāhmaṇic families came to have tutelary goddesses, and thus we have Kātyāyanī, or the goddess of the Kātyas, and Kauśikī, the goddess of the Kauśikas. A further development went on especially under the influence of the idea of Śakti, or power, and thus we have three forms in which the goddess was worshipped. First we have the ordinary bland form, in which the goddess is worshipped. Then we have the fierce form, in which she is associated with the schools of Kāpālikas and Kālāmukhas, and animals and human beings are sacrificed. And the third is the sensual form, in which she is the object of worship with the school of the Śāktas, who are so called because they are worshippers of Śakti.

§ 110. The Tantras inculcating the worship of the goddess in these various forms, constitute a considerable body of literature. We will here notice the formation, doctrines and practices of a school based on one of these forms, that which we have called sensual. The goddess here is called Ānandabhairavī, Tripurasundarī, and Lalitā. Her dwelling is thus described. There is an ocean of nectar, in which there are five celestial trees. Then there is a row or enclosure of Nīpa or Kadamba trees, in the midst of which is a pavilion made of jewel stones. In that pavilion is situated a palace made of the wish-giving stone, where lies the great Īśānī, the great Tripurasundarī, on a couch, which is Śiva, with Maheśāna for its coverlet and Sadāśiva for its pillow. The legs of the couch are Brahmadeva, Hari, Rudra and Īśvara. These are spirits discharging certain functions contained in the essence of Maheśvara [1]). This is a mythological explanation of certain figures in the mystic cirles and of technical terms. The goddess is thus elevated to the highest position. Ānandabhairava or Mahābhairava, which is the name given to Śiva, is the soul of, or is composed of, the nine collections of things of which the world is made up, such as time and its various forms (Kālavyūha), existing things like the blue substance (Kulavyūha), names (Nāmavyūha), perception (Jñānavyūha), the five faculties, viz. consciousness, heart, will, intelligence, and mind (Cittavyūha). Mahābhairava is the soul of the goddess; therefore she also is the soul of, or composed of, the nine collections. Both, therefore, constitute one entity. When there is Sāmarasya, or community of joy or intense love between them, creation follows. The female element, or Mahābhairavī, however, is predominant in the process of creation and the male element, or Mahābhairava, in the work of destruction [2]).

The metaphysical doctrines of what is called Śāṃbhavadarśana, on which the usual practices and rites of the Śāktas profess to be based, are these [3]). Śiva and Śakti are the primordial substances. Śiva in the form of Prakāśa (light) enters into Śakti in the form of Vimarśa or Sphūrti (feeling or appearance), and assumes the form of a Bindu (drop); and Śakti similarly enters into Śiva, whereupon the Bindu develops, and there arises out of it the female element called Nāda (sound). These two, the Bindu and the Nāda, becoming united, form one compound Bindu, and that substance represents the intense affinity between the female and male energies and is called Kāma (love). Again, there are two drops, one of which is white and represents the male element, and the other, red, which represents the female element. These form the Kalā; these three again, the compound Bindu, and the white and red drops form one substance called Kāmakalā. Thus there are four powers united here: (1) the original Bindu representing the material of which the world is made; (2) Nāda, or sound, upon which depends the naming of the substances, arising from the development of the Bindu. Between these two there is intense love, but no creation follows simply from it. They only contain the materials of things and speech. Therefore a productive energy is associated with them by (3) the white male drop which, however, by itself cannot produce, and by (4) the female red drop which is fecundated by the male drop. When all these four principles unite into one substance, Kāmakalā, the whole creation of words and the things expressed by them (Vāgarthau), proceeds. Another substance called the Hārdhakalā is also developed, according to some, along with the Nāda, when the female element first enters into the simple Bindu. In a certain text the highest deity, or Kāmakalā, is spoken of as having the sun (compound Bindu) for her face, fire and moon (the red and white Bindus) for her breasts, and the Hārdhakalā for her organ of

---

[1]) Saundaryalaharī with Lakṣmīdhara's commentary, Maisur Ed., comment. on vv. 8 and 92.

[2]) Ibid. v. 34.

[3]) The following contains in a recast form the matter given in pp. 89—91 of my Report on the Search for Sanskrit Manuscripts during 1883—84.

generation. This view provides a womb from which creation springs out. The creative agent, therefore, is a goddess thus constituted, and she is the highest deity and is called Parā, Lalitā, Bhaṭṭārikā and Tripurasundarī. Śiva is symbolically identified with the letter *a* and Śakti with *h*, the last letter of the Sanskrit alphabet. This *h* is called Ardhakalā, or half part, and hence the female element, or womb, mentioned above is called the half part in the shape of the letter *h*. This *h*, or the half part, together with *a* which stands for Śiva is a symbolic representation of Kāmakalā or Tripurasundarī, who is the result of the combination of Śiva and Śakti. She is thus called Aham, the ego, and is invested with egoism or individuality, and hence it is that all her developments (i. e. the whole creation) have egoism or individuality; and all souls are but forms of Tripurasundarī and become Tripurasundarī when they study and practise the Kāmakalāvidyā with its series of Devīcakras, or mystic circles. *A* and *h*, being the first and last letters of the alphabet, contain between them all letters and through them all words, i. e. the whole speech; and just as all things are produced from Tripurasundarī, so are all words which express the things. She is thus called Parā, the first of the four kinds of speech. Creation is Pariṇāma, or development, and not Vivarta, or the generation of false appearances. This is the philosophy of the Śāṃbhavadarśana, and it will be seen that, though it admits a male element in the beginning, still it is thoroughly subdued by the female element which becomes predominant; and the highest deity is a goddess, viz. Tripurasundarī. The ambition of every pious follower of the system is to become identical with Tripurasundarī, and one of his religious exercises is to habituate himself to think that he is a woman. Thus the followers of the Śakti school justify their appellation by the belief that God is a woman and it ought to be the aim of all to become a woman.

Tripurasundarī is propitiated and eventually attained by assuming the vow (Dīkṣā) of a devoted worship of her. This vow is of three kinds. The first consists in fully concentrating the mind on the Devī as sitting on the lap of Śiva in the Mahāpadmavana (a garden of lotuses), as possessed of a body which is pure joy and is the original cause of all, and as identical with one's own self. The second is the Cakrapūjā, the worship by means of the mystic circles, which is a Bāhyayāga, or material worship; and the third consists in studying and knowing the true doctrine. The second is the proper Śakti ceremonial. It consists in the worship of a picture of the female organ drawn in the centre of another consisting of a representation of nine such organs, the whole of which forms the Śrīcakra. The pictures are drawn on a Bhūrja leaf or a piece of silken cloth or on a gold leaf[1]). With reference to this worship it must be observed that there are two classes of Śāktas: (1) Kaulika and (2) Samayin. The former worship the gross material object, while the latter have a recourse to imagery. The worship of the pictures just mentioned is resorted to by ancient (Pūrva) Kaulas, while the modern

[1]) Saundaryalaharī v. 41, commentary.

(Uttara) Kaulas worship the organ of a living beautiful woman. The Kaulas worship their goddess by offering to her, and themselves using, wine, flesh, honey (Madhu), fish and such other things. The Samayins, of course, abstain from such practices. There are even Brāhmaṇas, who secretly profess the doctrines of the Śākta school and worship the goddess Tripurasundarī in accordance with the Pūrva-Kaula or Uttara-Kaula way. There are no distinctions of caste when the worship of the Bhairavīcakra is going on. Men of all castes become Brāhmaṇas, but they resume their own castes when the worship is over [1]. There are several more innocent and decorous modes of worshipping the goddess under the names of Lalitā and Upāṅgalalitā mentioned in the ordinary religious books. The worship of the latter comes off on the fifth lunar day of Āśvina and of the former for the first ten days. The latter, when so worshipped by women, wards off widowhood [2].

XIV. The Sect of Gāṇapatyas.

§ 111. Rudra had his hosts of Maruts, who were called his Gaṇas, and the leader of these Gaṇas was Gaṇapati. The name Rudra, as we have seen, was generalised and signified a number of spirits partaking of the character of the original Rudra; and so was the name Gaṇapati generalised and meant many leaders of the Gaṇas, or groups. Another name, Vināyaka, denoting a spirit also came into use. In the AU. Rudra is identified with many gods or spirits, and among these there is one called Vināyaka. In the MBh. (Anuśāsanaparvan 151, v. 26) Gaṇeśvaras and Vināyakas are mentioned amongst the gods, who observe the actions of men and are present everywhere; and again (57) Vināyakas are said to remove all evil from men when praised. Gaṇeśvaras, or Gaṇapatis, and Vināyakas are here represented, as the former are in the Śatarudriya, many in number and present everywhere. In the Mānavagṛhyasūtra (2, 14) is given an account of Vināyakas. They are four in number. And their names are (1) Śālakaṭaṅkaṭa, (2) Kūṣmāṇḍarājaputra, (3) Usmita, and (4) Devayajana. When possessed by these a person pounds sods of earth, cuts grass, and writes on his body, and sees in dreams waters, men with shaved heads, camels, pigs, asses, etc., and feels he is moving in the air, and when walking, sees somebody pursuing him from behind. Again, when possessed by these, Princes Royal do not obtain the kingdom, though qualified to govern. Girls do not obtain bridegrooms, though possessed of the necessary qualities. Women do not get children, even if otherwise qualified. The children of other women die. A learned teacher qualified to teach does not obtain pupils, and there are many interruptions and breaks in the course of a student. Trade and agriculture are unsuccessful. A person, who shows such signs of being possessed by Vināyaka, is made to go through the ceremony of bathing in waters brought from four places and with a little earth from four different quarters thrown into them. After bathing oblations of mustard oil

1) Aufrecht's Oxf. Cat. p. 92, n.
2) See Hemādri, Vratakhaṇḍa.

extracted afresh should be offered to the four Vināyakas in a ladle made of the wood of the Udumbara tree and poured over the head of the individual. Then food of many sorts, rice, husked and unhusked, flesh, and fish, cooked as well as raw, pulse of various kinds, etc. should be put into a basket and the basket placed on the ground where four roads meet, the ground first being covered with Kuśa grass. Then certain deities including evil spirits are invoked, and a wish expressed that they may be satisfied, and, becoming so, satisfy the worshipper, etc. This is the ceremony which frees the persons haunted by the Vināyakas.

Yājñavalkya in his Smṛti (I, 271 ff.) gives the same ceremony and frequently in the same words. But the ceremony appears in a somewhat more developed or complicated form. He begins by stating that Rudra and Brahmadeva appointed Vināyaka to the leadership of the Gaṇas, (i. e. made him Gaṇapati) and assigned to him the functions of raising difficulties and obstructions in the actions of men. In the Smṛti one Vināyaka is only addressed, but instead of the four names occurring in the Sūtra six are given, viz. (1) Mita, (2) Sammita, (3) Śāla, (4) Kaṭaṅkaṭa, (5) Kūṣmāṇḍa, and (6) Rājaputra, and these are said to be six different names of the one Vināyaka. After the basket with various kinds of food has been prepared, directions are given to make an obeisance to Ambikā, the mother of Vināyaka.

The form of the ceremony contained in the Sūtra is unquestionably more ancient than that contained in the other work. But the difference between the two shows that during the period that had elapsed between the composition of the Sūtra and that of the Smṛti, the four Vināyakas had become one Gaṇapati-Vināyaka, having Ambikā for his mother. It will thus be seen that, in his own nature, this last god is an unfriendly or malignant spirit, but capable of being made friendly and benignant by propitiatory rites. In this respect, he resembles Rudra himself. That the Vināyakas had come to be objects of faith before the Christian era, may be taken to follow from the occurrence of the ceremony mentioned above in a Gṛhyasūtra. But the one Gaṇapati-Vināyaka, the son of Ambikā, was introduced into the Hindu pantheon much later. None of the Gupta inscriptions which I subjected to an examination on a former occasion [1]) contains any mention of his name or announces any gift or benefaction in his honour. But in two of the caves at Ellorā, there are groups of images of Kāla, Kālī, the Seven Mothers or Śaktis, and Gaṇapati [2]). These caves are to be referred to the latter part of the eighth century. So that between the end of the fifth and the end of the eighth century the Gaṇapati cult must have come into practice, and the Smṛti of Yājñavalkya must have been written not earlier than the sixth century. Another inscription and an old relic which indicate the prevalence of the worship of Gaṇapati are found at a place called Ghaṭiyālā, 22 miles north-west of Jodhpur. There is a column there, on the top of which there are four images of Gaṇapati facing the four quarters. In the opening sentence of the inscription

[1]) See my 'Peep into the Early History of India'; Journ. Bo. Br. Roy. As. Soc. Vol. XX, pp. 356 ff.

[2]) In Rāvaṇa-ki-khāī, in the circumambulatory passage and Rāmeśvara temples See Cave-Temples by Fergusson and Burgess.

engraved on it an obeisance is made to Vināyaka. The date of the inscription is Vikrama-Saṃvat 918 = A. D. 862 [1]).

When and how the god came to have the elephant's head, it is difficult to determine. The images in the cave-temples at Ellorā have that head, and Bhavabhūti also in the beginning of the eighth century describes him, in the opening stanza of the Mālatīmādhava, as possessed of such a head. Rudra-Śiva and the gods allied with him were connected closely with forests and wild places, in which elephants also were found. The hide worn by Rudra and by his consort also in one of her forms was the hide of an elephant, and it perhaps suited the fancy of some men to place the head of that animal over the body of a god originally mischievous. Gaṇapati's reputation for wisdom is, I believe, to be attributed to the confusion between him and Bṛhaspati, who in RV. II, 23, 1 is called Gaṇapati. Bṛhaspati, of course, is the Vedic god of wisdom, and is called the sage of sages.

§ 112. Six varieties of the Gāṇapatya sect are mentioned by Ānandagiri, or Anantānandagiri as he is sometimes called, in his Śaṃkaradigvijaya as well as by Dhanapati in his commentary on the corresponding work of Mādhava. The first consists of those who adore Mahāgaṇapati. Mahāgaṇapati is, according to them, the creator, and he alone remains when Brahmadeva and others have been destroyed at the time of the dissolution. He should be meditated upon as possessed of his peculiar face with one tooth and as embraced by the Śakti. By his own wonderful power, he creates Brahmadeva and others. One, who repeats the original Mantra and meditates on this Gaṇapati, attains supreme bliss. The name of the person who expounds these doctrines to the Ācārya is given as Girijāsuta.

Another interlocutor follows. His name is Gaṇapatikumāra, and he adores Haridrāgaṇapati. He takes his stand on RV. II, 23, 1, and makes out this text to mean "We meditate on thee who art the leader of the group of Rudra, Viṣṇu, Brahman, Indra and others, and art the instructor of sages, Bhṛgu, Guru, Śeṣa and others, the highest of all who know the sciences, the greatest lord of the Brahmans engaged in the creation of the world, i. e. adored by Brahman and others in the work of creation and others". He should be worshipped and meditated on as being dressed in a yellow silken garment, bearing a yellow sacred thread, having four arms, three eyes and his face suffused over by turmeric ointment, and holding a noose and an elephant-goad and a staff in his hand. He who worships the god in this form, obtains emancipation. Gaṇapati is the cause of the whole world, and Brahmā and others are his parts. The worshipper of this Gaṇapati should bear, on both of his arms, the marks of Gaṇapati's face and one tooth impressed upon them by a heated iron stamp.

Then came Herambasuta, who was the worshipper of Ucchiṣṭagaṇapati. The followers of this variety resort to the left handed path (Vāmamārga), which probably was set up in imitation of the Kaula worship of Śakti. The form of Gaṇapati meditated on is very obscene. There is no distinction of caste among the followers of this sect.

[1]) Ep. Ind., Vol. IX, pp. 277 ff.

No restriction is to be observed, such as marriage imposes, and promiscuous intercourse is allowed and also the use of wine. The follower should have a red mark on his forehead. All the ordinary ceremonies, such as twilight adorations (Saṃdhyāvandana), are left to a man's own will.

The followers of the other three Gaṇapatis, Navanīta, Svarṇa, and Saṃtāna, worship their god, they say, according to the Śruti. But since Gaṇapati is adored in the beginning of every religious act, he is the chief god and all the other gods are parts of him and should be worshipped as such. They regard the whole world as Gaṇapati and adore him as such.

Since the god Gaṇapati-Vināyaka was introduced about the sixth century, it is questionable whether these several sects existed at the time of Śaṃkarācārya. The imprinting of the face and the tooth of the God on the arms was a custom common to them with the Mādhva Vaiṣṇavas, though it is hardly indicative of the period in which the sect arose. But the worship of Gaṇapati without reference to any particular sect is practised by nearly all Hindus at the beginning of any religious ceremony and on special occasions. His image made of clay is worshipped with great pomp in the Marāṭha country on the fourth lunar day of the month of Bhādrapada (September), and at Chinchwaḍ near Poona there is a special establishment for the exclusive worship of that god.

XV. Skanda or Kārttikeya.

§ 113. Another god whose worship was extensively practised in ancient times, but is now rare, is Skanda or Kārttikeya. The general belief is that he was the son of Śiva and Pārvatī. But in the Rāmāyaṇa he is represented as the son of the god of fire and Gaṅgā (I, chap. 37). The foetus was thrown by Gaṅgā on the Himavat mountain, and it was nourished by the six stars constituting the constellation of Kṛttikā (Pleiades) and was thus called the son of the Kṛttikās or Kārttikeya. In the MBh. (Vanaparvan, chap. 229) also he is represented as the son of Fire, but the mother was Agni's true wife Svāhā, who had assumed the forms of the wives of six Ṛṣis, whom Agni loved. But here he is called the son of Śiva also, as Agni is a form of that god. There are other stories connecting him with Śiva and Pārvatī as his parents. But whatever the legend may have been, there is no question that he was connected with Śiva, and was the leader of one of his Gaṇas. There is a Liṅgāyat tradition reported in the section on that sect that he was a founder of a Gotra, and was a form of Śiva himself. His having the peacock for his vehicle is also consistent with his connection with Śiva, as peacocks are found in forests of which Rudra and his attendants were gods . His being the leader of the army of the gods was an idea probably suggested by his being the leader of a Gaṇa of Rudra. And in historical times he has been associated with Śiva. Under P. V, 3, 99, Patañjali mentions the images of Śiva, Skanda and Viśākha as being worshipped in his time. On the reverse of the coins of the Kuṣana prince Kaniṣka, there are figures with their names in Greek letters of Skando, Mahaseno, Komaro and Bizago [1]. The first is Skanda, and because he was the commander of the army of the gods, he was also called Mahāsena, which is the second name on the coin. The third is Kumāra, which is also a name of Skanda, and the fourth is the Skr. Viśākha. If the first three were the names of one deity only, there was no necessity for giving three names and three figures. These, therefore, must have been regarded as three different gods as Viśākha undoubtedly was from his being mentioned separately from Skanda by Patañjali. In the story in the MBh. referred to above Viśākha is mentioned as having arisen from the right side of Skanda when it was struck by Indra's thunderbolt. This is indicative of the tendency to make the two as one person; and they appear to have been so made in later times. Or, looking to the fact that there are two names of Buddha on the coins, the above three may have been the names of one single deity. There are also other indications of the prevalence of the worship of Skanda or Mahāsena in the early centuries. In the year 414 A. D. was built a Pratolī, or gallery, in the temple of Svāmi-Mahāsena by one Dhruvaśarman at Bilsāḍ [2]. Several holy observances and vows in the name of Kumāra and Kārttikeya are mentioned in Hemādri's Vratakhaṇḍa, and the worship of that god has not become obsolete even at the present day.

XVI. The Sect of Sauras and the Northern Sun-Worship.

§ 114. Sūrya, or the sun as the orb that is seen in the sky and not as an imaginary god of light, was a Vedic deity. It is but reasonable to expect that the worship of such a deity should not become obsolete in later times, since the orb of the sun is daily seen in the sky. In two passages in RV. (VII, 60,1; 62, 2) the singer wishes the rising sun to declare him sinless to Mitra, Varuṇa, and other gods. This idea probably arose from the fact that the rising sun by his bright light discloses everything that has been done in the darkness of the previous night, and thence it developed into a belief that the sun destroys sins. Kauṣītaki is represented to have adored the sun in the morning, at midday, and in the evening, and having made offerings of water with flowers, sandal, etc. or without (Arghya), prayed for the removal of his sins (KBU. II, 7). And this is what we do or are expected to do in our twilight and midday adorations. Water is sipped by repeating a formula expressive of a wish that the Sun, Manyu and Manyupati may protect the adorer from sins (ĀG. Pariśiṣṭa I, 3 and TĀ. X, 25, 1). After that three offerings of water with or without the other ingredients are made to the sun after repeating the Gāyatrī, and then the water is whirled round his head by the adorer by repeating the Mantra "That Āditya is Brahman" [3]. Āśvalāyana directs that, while adoring the morning twilight, one facing the east should repeat the Gāyatrī-Mantra till the whole disc of the sun has risen, and in the evening with his face towards the west till the whole

[1]) See Journ. Bo. Br. Roy. As. Soc. Vol. XX, p. 385.
[2]) Ib. p. 393.
[3]) Asāv āditGyo Brahma.

has gone down and the stars have begun to appear (ĀG. III, 7, 4—6). In the Upanayana ceremony, when the boy is invested with the sacred thread and other badges of a student's life, he is made to look at the orb of the sun, when the preceptor, addressing that deity, prays "Oh god Savitar, this is thy student, protect him. May he not die" (ĀG. I, 20, 6). Khādira prescribes the adoration of the sun for the enjoyment of riches and for the attainment of fame (Khādiragṛhyasūtra IV, 1, 14 and 23). The hymn addressed by Yudhiṣṭhira to the sun after he entered his forest-residence, and his having obtained a vessel from him for the production of all the food wanted by him, his family and followers, are well-known. In the seventh century Mayūra, who lived at the court of Harṣavardhana, composed a hundred stanzas to obtain relief from the white leprosy from which he suffered About the beginning of the eighth century Bhavabhūti makes the Sūtradhāra, or the manager, of the Mālatīmādhava offer prayers to the rising sun to remove all his sins and bestow holy blessings on him. Thus the sun has been adored since the Vedic times for the removal of sins, and the bestowal of riches, food, fame, health, and other blessings. At the present day twelve prostrations are made to Sūrya by repeating twelve of his names, all of which have a Sanskrit etymology, and there is no foreign look about them. There is also a more elaborate set of such prostrations.

§ 115. It cannot but be expected, therefore, that a school should come into existence for the exclusive worship of the sun. And such a school is that of the Sauras. Ānandagiri brings Śaṃkara into contact with the followers of this sect at a place in the south called Subrahmaṇya situated at the distance of fourteen days' journey from Anantaśayana or Trivendram. The name of their leader was Divākara, and they wore a circular spot of red sandal on the forehead and bore red flowers. The substance of the account of this school given by Divākara is as follows. The Supreme Soul, the Sun, is the author of the world. He is the tutelary deity of the Sauras and is adored by them. The Śrutis themselves speak of him as the cause of the world, such as "The sun is the soul of moveable and immoveable things" (RV. I, 115, 1) and "That Āditya is Brahman". Brahman with which the the sun has thus been identified is the cause of the whole world, according to the text, from which all these beings originate, etc. (TU. III, 1, 1). There is also a Smṛti text in favour of this doctrine. There are six classes of devotees of the sun all bearing a mark made by red sandal, wearing a garland of red flowers, and repeating the formula of eight syllables. Some worship the orb of the sun who has just risen as Brahmadeva, the creator, others, the sun on the meridian as Īśvara, the destroyer. He is also regarded as the originator. Some regard the setting sun as Viṣṇu, the protector, and, considering him as the cause of the creation and destruction also and as the highest entity, worship him. There are some who resort to all the three suns as a triple form. Others, observing the vow of regularly seeing the orb, adore the Supreme Soul as existing in it with golden whiskers and golden hair. One section of this class is devoted simply to the vow of the observation of the disc, and they see the orb, worship it in the sixteen ways, dedicate all their actions to the god, and do not eat without seeing the orb. The devotees of the sixth class imprint the orb on their forehead, arms and bosom with a heated iron piece and meditate on the god in their minds continuously. All these six classes have to repeat the same Mantra, or formula, of eight syllables. The followers of this creed like other sectarians interpret various Vedic texts as setting forth the greatness and the supremacy of their own god. The Puruṣasūkta (RV. X, 90) and the Śatarudriya are so expounded, and the conclusion is that all who desire emancipation should adore the sun, should bear his marks on the body, and mutter the Mantra.

§ 116. So far there is no trace of foreign influence in the development of the Saura system. But such an influence undoubtedly contributed to the growth of the sun-worship prevalent in Northern India from the early centuries of the Christian era. Varāhamihira in the stanza twice quoted before (Bṛhatsaṃhitā, chap. 60, 19) tells us that the installation and consecration of the images and temples of the sun should be caused to be made by the Magas, and generally those who worship a certain deity according to their special ritual should be made to perform the ceremony concerning that deity. This shows that the Magas were, according to Varāhamihira, the special priests of the sun-god. There is a legend concerning this matter in the Bhaviṣyapurāṇa (chap. 139). Sāmba, the son of Kṛṣṇa by Jāmbavatī, constructed a temple of the sun on the banks of the Candrabhāgā, the modern Chenāb in the Panjāb, and no local Brāhmaṇa would accept the office of a regular priest of the temple. He thereupon asked Gauramukha, the priest of Ugrasena. He told him to get Magas, who were special sun-worshippers, from Śākadvīpa. Then is given the history of the Magas. Sujihva was a Brāhmaṇa of the Mihira Gotra. He had a daughter of the name of Nikṣubhā, with whom the sun fell in love. The son of these two was called Jaraśabda or Jaraśasta, and from him sprang all Magas. They wore a girdle round their waist, which was called Avyaṅga. Thereupon Sāmba went on the back of Garuḍa, his father's vehicle, to Śākadvīpa, brought some Magas from it and installed them into the office of priests of the temple he had constructed. The Magas have long been known in the literary history of India. There is an inscription at Govindapur in the Gayā District dated Śaka 1059, corresponding to 1137-38 A. D., in the opening stanza of which the Magas, who sprang from the sun, are represented to have been brought into the country by Sāmba. Six great poets, the works of some of whom are extant, are also mentioned. There are traces of the Magas elsewhere, and there are Brāhmaṇas of that name in Rājputāna and some other provinces of Northern India. Now these Magas are the Magi of ancient Persia, and the name Jaraśasta mentioned above as occurring in the Bhaviṣyapurāṇa connects them with the Avesta prophet Zarathushtra. The Avyaṅga, which according to the Purāṇa they wore round their waist, was the same as the Aivyāonghen of the Avesta language, which last signifies the Kusti worn by the Parsees at the present day. Alberūnī, speaking of the Persian priests Magians, says that they existed in India and were called Magas [1]). The idea of locating them on a continent called Śaka-dvīpa must have arisen from the fact that they were foreigners like the Śakas with whom the Indians had been familiar since the second or third century before the Christian era. Evidently then the worship of the sun or Mihira-worship was brought into India by the old Persian priests Magi, but at whose instance and under what circumstances they came it is difficult to say. The legendary tradition of their having been brought by Sāmba was current in the first half of the twelfth century, as we have seen from the inscription. The temple on the Candrabhāgā referred to above was that which existed at Multān and a glowing description of which is given by the Chinese traveller Hiuen Tsiang. Four centuries later it was seen by Alberūnī [2]). It existed till the seventeenth century, when it was finally destroyed by Aurangzeb. Multān is the same as the Sanskrit Mūlasthāna, and this name may have been given to the place, because the new worship of the sun was first organised there and it was its original seat. On the coins of Kaniṣka there occurs a figure with the name Miiro = Mihira by its side. Mihira is the Sanskritised form of the Persian Mihr, which is a corruption of Mithra, the Avestic form of the Vedic Mitra. The cult of Mihr had originated in Persia, and it extended itself up to Asia Minor and even Rome, and the proselytising energy which characterised its first adherents must have led to its extension towards the east also, and of this extension the figure of Mihira on Kaniṣka's coin is an evidence. The cult, therefore, must have penetrated to India about the time of that Kuṣana prince, and the Multān temple, which was its original seat, must have been constructed about the same time.

An inscription at Mandasaur records the construction of a temple to the sun in the year 437 A. D. by a guild of weavers, and its repair in the year 473 A. D. Another on a copperplate found at Indor in the Bulandshahar District in the United Provinces mentions an endowment of Devaviṣṇu in 464 A. D. for lighting a lamp in a temple of the sun. And in a third is recorded a grant in 511 A. D. to a temple of Āditya, or the sun. A great many more sun temples have been discovered especially in Western India from Multān down to Cutch and northern Gujarāt [3]). The ruins of one exist at Moḍherā, eighteen miles to the south of Pāṭaṇ in the last-named province, and they contain the date Vikrama 1083 corresponding to 1027 A. D. There was another at Gwalior constructed in the time of Mihirakula, the Hūṇa Prince, in the beginning of the sixth century.

The form of the idol of the sun worshipped in such temples is described by Varāhamihira (Bṛhatsaṃhitā, chap. 58), but the features mentioned by him which have a significance for our present purpose are that his feet and legs should be enclosed or covered up to the knees and he should be dressed in the fashion prevalent in the north (v. 46), and that he should be encircled by an Avyaṅga (v. 47). Accordingly the images of the sun that are found in the temples mentioned above have boots reaching up to the knees and a girdle round the waist

[1]) Sachau's Translation, Vol. I, p. 21.
[2]) Ibid. vol. I, p. 116.
[3]) Burgess, Architectural Antiquities of Northern Gujrat, London 1903.

with one end hanging downwards[1]). This last is a Persian feature, as we have already seen, and the other also must have the same or similar origin. It certainly is not Indian. The features of the idol of the sun and the fact of Magas, who were descended from the Persian Magi, being its priests point unmistakably to the conclusion that the cult was introduced into India from Persia, and I believe that the construction of so many temples was also due to the foreign influence. For, in the account of the Saura systems we have given above, there is not the remotest allusion to a temple of the sun. According to all appearances, therefore, the cult prevalent in Northern India was entirely distinct from those systems. It does not appear to have allied itself with any one of these latter. But it was accepted by the mass of the Hindus as a general worship of the sun, and the feelings which it evoked could not have been different from those which the indigenous worship gave rise to. And the manner in which devotion to the sun is expressed in the inscriptions which we find in some of the temples, has nothing special or foreign in it. The Magas themselves, the priests of the new cult, were gradually thoroughly Hinduised until they became undistinguishable from the other Hindus and formed only a separate caste. In the copper-plate grant of Harṣavardhana, who lived in the middle of the seventh century, his father Prabhākarvardhana, his grandfather Ādityavardhana and his great-grandfather Rajyavardhana are all styled great devotees of the sun (Paramādityabhakta)[2]). This is an evidence to show that the sun cult, probably made up of a mixture of the indigenous and foreign forms, prevailed in the beginning of the sixth century and was professed by great princes.

XVII. Résumé.

§ 117. The fearful and destructive phenomena of nature led to the conception of, and belief in, the god Rudra, the terrible howler, accompanied by his groups, or Gaṇas, called sometimes Rudras or Rudriyas, who were minor howlers. This god, when propitiated, became the auspicious Śiva, the beneficent Śaṃkara and the benignant Śambhu. The conception gradually developed further, until Rudra became the god of wild and awful scenes, such as cemeteries, mountains and forests. Of the beasts and savages that dwelt in these last and of the thieves and outcasts that resorted to them, he became the lord. Subsequently he developed into the god who pervades the universe, dwells in fire and water, in all beings and in herbs and trees and was the supreme ruler of all. When he rose to this position, he became the subject of Upaniṣad speculation, by meditating on whom and seeing whom everywhere in the universe a man attained blissful serenity.

But the awful and wild side of his nature was not effaced, but went on developing; and when religious schools such as that of the Pāñcarātras came to be established, one with Rudra or Paśupati as the god to be adored was set up some time after. Its founder was a human

[1]) Ibid. Plate LVI.
[2]) Epigraphia Indica, Vol. I, pp. 72—73.

being, who came to be known as Lakuṭin or Lakulin, the holder of a club, and Lakulīśa or Nakulīśa, the lord, the holder of the club. Pañcārtha was the title of the work attributed to him, and his system came to be known by the name of Pāśupata. Two extreme schools were developed out of this, and also one which was more moderate known by the name of the Śaiva. Traces of these schools have been found from about the second century of the Christian era to about the twelfth. But the repulsive nature of the two extreme schools and the wild and fantastic character of the other two led to a reaction, and in the beginning of the ninth century we have the first Kaśmīr school; and about a hundred years afterwards was founded another. These are very sober in their doctrines and practices, and may be considered to have been influenced by the school of Śaṃkara, though an escape from his severe spiritual monism has been provided for, so as to allow of an individual existence to the delivered soul. A further reform was effected about the middle of the eleventh century by the Liṅgāyat school. The philosophical doctrines of this school amount to this: that God is infinite intelligence and joy, is the creator of the world and the instructor and redeemer of mankind, and that the individual soul attains to a unity of blissful experience with him by gradually estranging himself from the world, pursuing a course of devotional worship, abandoning himself to God and seeing him in everything. This philosophy seems to have been influenced by the tenets of the school of Rāmānuja. The spirit of the Liṅgāyats was, however, combative, and they set up for themselves a community distinct from that which owes its origin to the Brāhmaṇic system. All the while, however, during the existence of these schools the general worship of Rudra-Śiva has prevailed among ordinary people regardless of the doctrines of these schools.

Śiva was associated with his consort Pārvatī or Umā. She too had a beneficent and majestic character as alluded to in the KnU. But just as an aboriginal element contributed to the formation of the character of Rudra-Siva, so an aboriginal element of a more distinct nature came to be combined with his consort, and she became a terrible goddess that had to be appeased by animal and even human sacrifices. But since the lustful nature of man is very strong in him, that goddess under the name of Tripurasundarī (the beauty of the three cities) or Lalitā (sportively graceful) became the creator of the world, and was also worshipped with debasing and sensual rites; and thus came in the school of the Śāktas, who looked forward to an identity with Tripurasundarī as the goal of their existence. Gaṇapati as the leader of a host was, of course, connected with Rudra-Śiva. That idea became mingled with the idea of Vināyaka, an evil spirit that possessed men, and thus the combined god Gaṇapati-Vināyaka became an object of worship on the principle that an obstructive and evil spirit should be first propitiated before beginning an action. Thereafter he became the special god of six minor sects, one of these, holding doctrines as debasing as those of the Śākta cult. Skanda was more closely connected with Śiva as the lord of one of his Gaṇas or groups; and afterwards came to be believed to be his son; and his worship prevailed for several centuries from the time of Patañjali downwards and has not become obsolete even at the present day. The sun was a god worshipped in early times and his cult did not disappear, as his orb was daily visible. But he became the object of sectarian worship some time later. About the third century, however, of the Christian era, another cult of the sun was introduced from Persia. It took root on Indian soil and prevailed for a long time in North-Western India, a good many splendid temples having been erected from time to time for his worship. A special caste of priests of the name of Magas was associated with the cult, and the masses of the Hindu population adopted it as if it had been indigenous to the country.

XVIII. Hindu Theism and Pantheism.

§ 118. As the theoretic or philosophic portion of the doctrines taught by the founders of most of the various systems we have examined are based on certain fundamental ideas contained in the Upaniṣads and the Bhagavadgītā, I deem it necessary to devote this last section to a consideration of the question as to what those ideas definitely are and to what extent they have been adopted or modified by the promulgators of those systems to suit their specific purposes.

In discussing these ideas some scholars make a broad distinction between Vedāntism, which they identify with Pantheism, and Theism. If they find any passage expressive of the immanence of God in the world in a work whose main aim is theistic, they consider such a passage to be interpolated. I have already alluded to this mental attitude in the beginning of the present work, but it is necessary to say something more on the subject. If they mean by Theism the Deism of the eighteenth century according to which the world is a machine constructed and set in motion by God who remains apart from it, with perhaps the additional doctrine that he enters into relations with men who worship him and appeal to him, they are probably right. But this is not Hindu Theism. The immanence of God in the external world and in the heart of man is its essential doctrine. But that is perfectly consistent with the belief in God's transcendency, that is, his being distinct from the world and man and above them, influencing them, controlling them, protecting them, and listening to prayers. That the ideas of immanence and transcendency are not incompatible or inconsistent with each other is admitted even by European thinkers. The Theism of the Bhagavadgītā is a Theism of this nature, and consequently the passages expressive of immanence are by no means to be regarded as interpolated. Theism of this nature is contained in the Upaniṣads also, though there are pantheistic doctrines of varied sorts. Pantheism as formulated by Spinoza is thus stated: — "God, though undetermined *ab extra*, is capable of infinite self-determination. Thus God, the *causa sui* manifests himself in an infinite multiplicity of particular modes. Spinoza is, therefore, both pantheist and pancosmist: God exists only as realised in the cosmos: the cosmos exists only as a manifestation of God[1])." The

[1]) Encycl. Brit. Eleventh Edition, Vol. XX, p. 683a, under Pantheism.

Upaniṣads contain pantheistic doctrines corresponding to what is stated in the first two sentences of this quotation. There are affirmations that when one thing is known, everything becomes known, as in the case of a ball of earth, on knowing the true nature of which one knows the true nature of all that is made of earth, etc. (ChU. VI, 1, 4); that when the soul is seen, heard and known, all this becomes known, and the Brahman, the Kṣatra, these worlds, these gods, these Vedas, these elements, — all this is the soul (BU. IV, 4, 6). Then again there are such statements as that Sat alone existed in the beginning, one without a second. That reflected "I may be many and multiply". It created light. This statement is to the effect that everything existing is a form or modification of God. There are many such passages in the Upaniṣads and several of these are quoted in Śaṃkarācārya's Bhāṣya on the Brahmasūtras I, 4, 23—27. But it is by no means to be inferred that the Upaniṣad Pantheism is of the nature set forth in the last sentence of the quotation from Spinoza, that is: Brahman is not exhausted in the world, but it exists separately also. But the objection to this view is that Brahman being of the nature of spirit is not like the body divisible into parts, so that one may become developed into the world and another remain outside; and this is affirmed in a text of the ŚU. (VI, 19). This inconsistency is removed by Bādarāyaṇa in Brahmasūtras II, 1, 26—27. The argument is that though the Upaniṣads state that the constituent cause of the world is Brahman, they at the same time affirm the existence of Brahman separately from the world (ChU. III, 12, 6; and VI, 3, 2.). The two are inconsistent on the theory that Brahman is a spirit and not discerptible into parts. Though they are thus inconsistent, they must both be accepted on the authority of the sacred texts, since the true nature of Brahman and the world is beyond the reach of human intellect. This solution of the difficulty is inadmissible to non-believers in the sacred texts, but it shows that Bādarāyaṇa does not agree with the latter part of Spinoza's definition of Pantheism, i. e. according to him the sacred texts do not affirm that "God exists only as realised in the cosmos: the cosmos exists only as a manifestation of God". The inconsistency pointed out by him is based on the impossible conception of Brahman's being divisible into parts. But it will not arise if, instead of bringing in this conception, we suppose that in one aspect Brahman is the material or constituent cause of the world or realised in the world and from another point of view it remains pure and becomes the object of contemplation and devotion. Whatever it may be, Bādarāyaṇa's view appears to me to be correct, and the Pantheism of the Upaniṣads is not exactly the same as that formulated by Spinoza.

But even this partial Pantheism is only one of the doctrines set forth in the Upaniṣads. As mentioned in the beginning, they contain the rudiments not only of one system of religious philosophy, but of a good many and even of Buddhism. When Brahman or the Supreme Soul is affirmed to be distinct from the world and thus there is a denial of the partial Pantheism I have spoken of, that soul is represented as dwelling in the external world and in the soul of man; that is to say,

Theism is taught with the immanency of God in the world and in man. For instance in the BU. III, 7, 7—30 [1]) we have first "He who dwelling in the earth is distinct from it, whom the earth does not know, whose body the earth is, and who, being in the inside, controls the earth, is the indestructible controlling soul". In the following passages up to 30 we have precisely the same statement about water, fire, the sky, wind, the sun, the moon and stars, the quarters, the lightning, thunderbolt, all the worlds, all the Vedas, all sacrifices, all beings, the vital breath, speech, the eye, the ear, the mind, the skin, light, darkness, the seminal fluid, and the (individual) soul. Here the inward controlling soul is mentioned as distinct from the earth and all the rest, up to the individual soul, and still as dwelling in them, controlling them from the inside, and having these for his body. The whole section winds up with the affirmation that this controlling soul is not seen, but is the seer; is not heard, but hears; is not apprehended by thought, but apprehends by thought; is not known, but knows; there is no other seer, no other hearer, no other apprehender, and there is no other knower. Herein are brought out the peculiar points of Hindu Theism: God is the only seer, the only hearer, and the only knower, that is, he is all-seeing, all-hearing, and all-knowing; and nobody can see him, hear him, or know him. He is distinct from all objects, but dwells in them and controlls them. Texts expressive of such an immanency are to be found in many places in the Upaniṣads. God being thus distinct from the world, though immanent, can be the object of devoted meditation and can be attained by means of truth, knowledge and purity. Mere immanency of this nature does not at all constitute the Pantheism formulated by Spinoza. There is therefore no ground whatever for regarding as an interpolation the occurrence of texts expressive of it in such a theistic work as the Bhagavadgītā.

We have noticed above the manner in which Bādarāyaṇa removes the inconsistency between God's developing himself into the world, while at the same time he is transcendent, and his being a simple spirit without parts. Śaṃkarācārya fairly explains, I think, Bādarāyaṇa's view. But raising a further objection he brings in his own doctrine eventually, that the so-called development of Brahman into the world is fancied by ignorance and is not true, that is, the world is an illusion. There are two doctrines indicative of the relation of God to the world, the so-called Pariṇāmavāda and the Vivartavāda. The former implies real development and the latter, an illusive development. This last is the doctrine of Śaṃkarācārya, wherefore his system should be called Singularism rather than spiritual monism; while the first is that clearly held by the author of the Sūtras. This is evident from his very definition of Brahman as that from which everything originates, in which everything lives, and into which everything resolves itself in the end, and from the manner in which in the first Pāda of the second chapter he answers the objections based upon the theory that an intelligent being cannot develop

[1]) Mādhyaṃdina recension.

into non-intelligent or insensate matter; and Śaṃkarācārya himself acknowledges at the end of his comment on II, 1, 14 that the author of the Sūtras follows the Pariṇāma doctrine, though to save his theory he imagines without any grounds that Bādarāyaṇa has in view the ordinary or illusory condition of things in doing so. Śaṃkarācārya's Vivartavāda it was which the later schools of Vaiṣṇavism and Śaivism contended against; for even according to him it leaves no scope for the relation of the ruler and the ruled, i. e. God and the devotee in the condition of reality when all illusion is dispelled and one spirit alone exists (II, 1, 14). Most of them adopted Bādarāyaṇa's Pariṇāmavāda, but the distinctness of God, man and the world, which was necessary for the validity of their doctrines of worship and devotion, they secured by qualifying the mode of development. By this qualification they also steered clear of the inconsistency pointed out by Bādarāyaṇa in II, 1, 26, so that his mode of satisfaction was not necessary for them. Rāmānuja lays down that the rudiments of the individual souls and of the insensate world exist in God himself as his characteristics or body, and with these he develops into the world, thus giving rise to the three distinct substances, the material world, the individual soul, and God as the controller. Nimbārka maintains that the other two substances do not characterise God or form his body, but are dependent upon him for their existence, and in a subtle form constitute his power or capacity, which develops into the animate and inanimate world. Viṣṇusvāmin, and therefore Vallabha, hold that the highest God, or Parabrahman, manifests himself as the material world, the individual soul, and the supreme controller, but in the course of development his attributes of intelligence and joy are concealed by his mysterious power, and thus is produced the material world, while, his joy alone being concealed, individual souls come into existence, and when the three are manifest or unconcealed, he becomes the supreme controller. Vallabha adds two other forms of Parabrahman or Puruṣottama, as mentioned in the section on his system. Madhva rejects the doctrine of God being the constituent cause of the world and consequently that of his development, and lays down the five eternal distinctions between God, man, and the world and between different individuals and objects involved in the last two. Of the older Śaiva schools, the Pāśupata brings in the Pradhāna of the Sāṃkhyas with its developments as the material cause of the world with Paśupati as the efficient cause. Śrīkaṇṭha Śivācārya in his comment on Br. S. II, 2, 38 states that according to his predecessors a certain branch of the philosophy based on the sacred texts revealed by Śiva (Āgamas) held Śiva to be only the efficient cause of the world. This must be a reference to the Śaiva school which, as we have already stated, was a dualistic or pluralistic school. The Vāyavīyasaṃhitā according to him states that Śakti, or power, first originates from Śiva, thence Māyā, thence Avyakta (I, 7, 3). By Māyā is to be understood the wonderful creative power of Śiva, as is evident from the following verse 4; and Avyakta means the Pradhāna, as appears from that verse as well as verse 7. He gives another verse which sets forth that everything from the Śakti to the earth is produced from the essence of

Śiva, so that Śiva through the Śakti is both the efficient and the constituent cause of the world. This Śakti is brought in by those who hold creation to be the development of Śiva, while it is not wanted for those Śaiva philosophers who would keep the creative principle Māyā or Pradhāna as distinct from Śiva and undergoing independent development. Śrīkaṇṭha explains the expression 'Śiva alone existed' occurring in ŚU. IV, 18, under I, 4, 27, by 'Śiva, with whom the Śakti (the power) in the form of the animate and the inanimate world was united, alone existed so as to form one entity', so that he here understands Śiva as possessed of the Śakti to be the constituent cause. In this respect his doctrine is similar to that of Nimbārka. But immediately afterwards he speaks of the Cit and the Acit forming the body of Śiva and thus puts forth the same theory as that of Rāmānuja. Practically he makes no distinction between the two. The theory of the Liṅgāyats is the same as the first form of the theory set forth by Śrīkaṇṭha Śivācārya. Śiva as qualified by the Śakti is the creator, that is, is the efficient and the constituent cause of the world. The Kaśmīr Śaivism attributes the production of the world to the will of God without any material cause or affirms that God makes the world appear in himself.

Thus most of these schools avoid the Pantheism of Spinoza and the incompatibility between God's development into the world and his transcendency by holding that the rudiments of the material and the spiritual world associated with God as his characteristics or as his body or as his power only undergo development, he himself remaining pure. Viṣṇusvāmin and Vallabha, admitting, as they do, the development of Puruṣottama into the world and at the same time his trancendency, follow Bādarāyaṇa. The mysterious power which causes the differences by rendering certain qualities imperceptible, may be compared to the self-determining power of God involved in Spinoza's statement. The Kaśmīr Śaivas do not bring in the idea of God as a constituent cause undergoing development and seem to admit the doctrine of creation out of nothing.

List of Abbreviations.

AB. = Aitareya-Brāhmaṇa.
ĀG. = Āśvalāyana-Gṛhyasūtra.
AU. = Atharvaśiras-Upaniṣad.
AV. = Atharva-Veda.
BhG. = Bhagavad-Gītā.
Bibl. Ind. = Bibliotheca Indica.
Br.S. = Brahma-Sūtra.
Bṛ.S. = Bṛhat-Saṃhitā.
BU. = Bṛhadāraṇyaka-Upaniṣad.
Chowkh. = Chowkhamba Sanskrit Series.
ChU. = Chāndogya-Upaniṣad.
HG. = Hiraṇyakeśi-Gṛhyasūtra.
KB. = Kauṣītaki-Brāhmaṇa.
KBU. = Kauṣītaki-Brāhmaṇa-Upaniṣad.
KnU. = Kena-Upaniṣad.
KU. = Kaṭha-Upaniṣad.
MaiU. = Maitri-Upaniṣad.
MBh. = Mahābhārata.
MU. = Muṇḍaka-Upaniṣad.
P. = Pāṇini.
PG. = Pāraskara-Gṛhyasūtra.
RV. = Ṛg-Veda.
RVS = Ṛg-Veda-Saṃhitā.
ŚB. = Śatapatha-Brāhmaṇa.
ŚU. = Śvetāśvatara-Upaniṣad.
TA. = Taittirīya-Āraṇyaka.
TS. = Taittirīya-Saṃhitā.
TU. = Taittirīya-Upaniṣad.
VS. = Vājasaneyi-Saṃhitā.
YV. = Yajur-Veda.

I. INDEX OF SANSKRIT WORDS AND PROPER NAMES.

[The Indexes have been compiled by V. Sukthankar, M. A. Throughout the references are to pages.]

II. GENERAL INDEX.

III. LIST OF SECTARIAN WORKS CONSULTED.

Table of Contents.

Part I.

Vaiṣṇavism.

Part II.

Śaivism and Minor Religious Systems.